Colin Duck and Martin Thomas are two senior Melbourne journalists. Duck is editor of the *Sunday Press* and Thomas is editor of *Australasian Post*. Both have worked extensively in Australia and on Fleet Street.

WHOSE BABY?

COLIN DUCK AND MARTIN THOMAS

FONTANA/COLLINS

Authors' Acknowledgment

More than one hundred people assisted the authors in their research and preparation of *Whose Baby?* We wish to thank them all for their time and trouble.

The authors also owe their gratitude to Noel and Jessie Jenkins, Arnold Jenkins, the late William Henry Morrison, Blair and Colleen Morrison and the two girls — Lee and Nola.

We offer particular thanks to the following people without whom we could not have completed the story: George Alcorn, the late Graham Bolton, Brian Birrell, Columb Brennan, Lloyd Brown, Dr David Burke, Col Dawson, Jim Edwards, Bill Gray, Gary Hughes, Bryan Kelly, Martin King, Ken Lake, Brian Ledwidge, Percy Melbon, Peter Norris, John Royle, Christine Smith, Bernie Teague, Dr Gerald Ungar and Carol Veitch.

The *Herald and Weekly times*, the *Age* and Henk Rem Photographics gave permission for a number of their photographs to be used.

Modern pictures in this book were taken by Bruce Postle, winner of the 1984 Australian Press Photograph of the Year and numerous other awards.

Cover photograph: Angela Punch McGregor (Gwen Morrison) with Lauren Dell (Lee Morrison). Courtesy of Crawford Productions.

© Colin Duck and Martin Thomas, 1984
First published in 1984 by William Collins Pty Ltd, Sydney
This edition published in 1986 by Fontana, Sydney
Printed and bound by the Dominion Press-Hedges & Bell, Maryborough, Victoria

The National Library of Australia Cataloguing-in-publication data:
  Duck, Colin, 1943–
    Whose baby?
    ISBN 0 00 636908 1 (pbk.)
    1. Jenkins, Nola, 1945– . 2. Morrison, Alberta Gwen.
    3. Morrison, William Henry. 4. Custody of children–
    Victoria. I. Thomas, Martin, 1943– . II. Title.
346.945018

All rights reserved. No part of this publication may be reproduced, stored in a retrieval system, or transmitted in any form, or by any means, electronic, mechanical, photocopying, recording or otherwise, without the prior permission of the publisher.

This book is sold subject to the conditions that it shall not, by way of trade or otherwise, be lent, re-sold, hired out or otherwise circulated without the publisher's prior consent in any form of binding or cover other than that in which it is published and without a similar condition including this condition being imposed on the subsequent purchaser.

CONTENTS

Prologue
1. The births   **1**
2. Angry words in the street   **9**
3. The *Truth* bombshell   **25**
4. The battle begins   **34**
5. 'Springtime' turns sour   **45**
6. Tears in court   **54**
7. The nurse who cannot remember   **73**
8. The doctor departs   **88**
9. A nurse breaks down   **101**
10. Two little girls in court   **115**
11. Judgement   **136**
12. The lioness and her cub   **160**
13. A breathtaking verdict   **173**
14. A knock on the door   **193**
15. Nola decides   **215**
16. The crash   **223**
17. Fight for life   **235**
18. The long road back   **247**
19. Who was right?   **264**

Appendix   **280**

THE JENKINS FAMILY

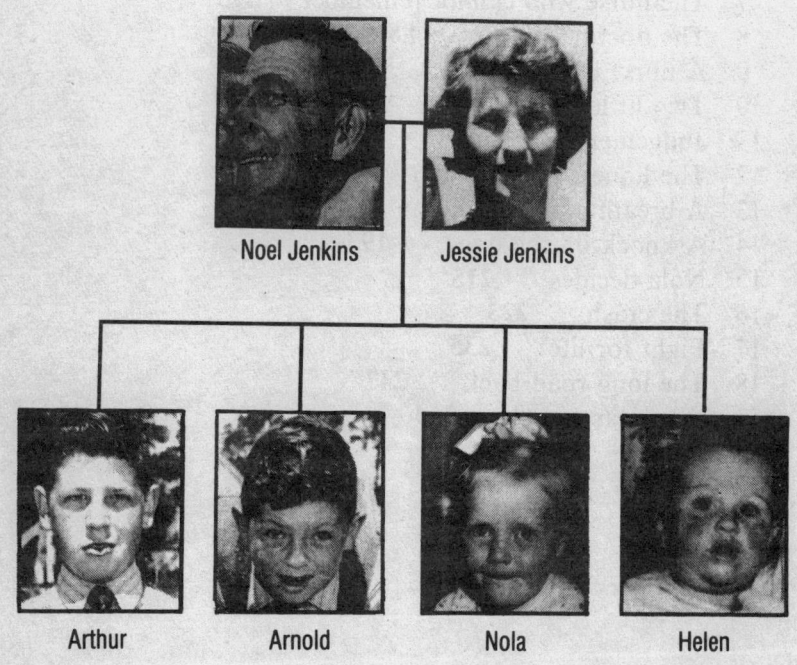

Lawyers:
E.H. "Ted" Hudson, K.C.
Henry Winneke
Bernard Nolan (solicitor)

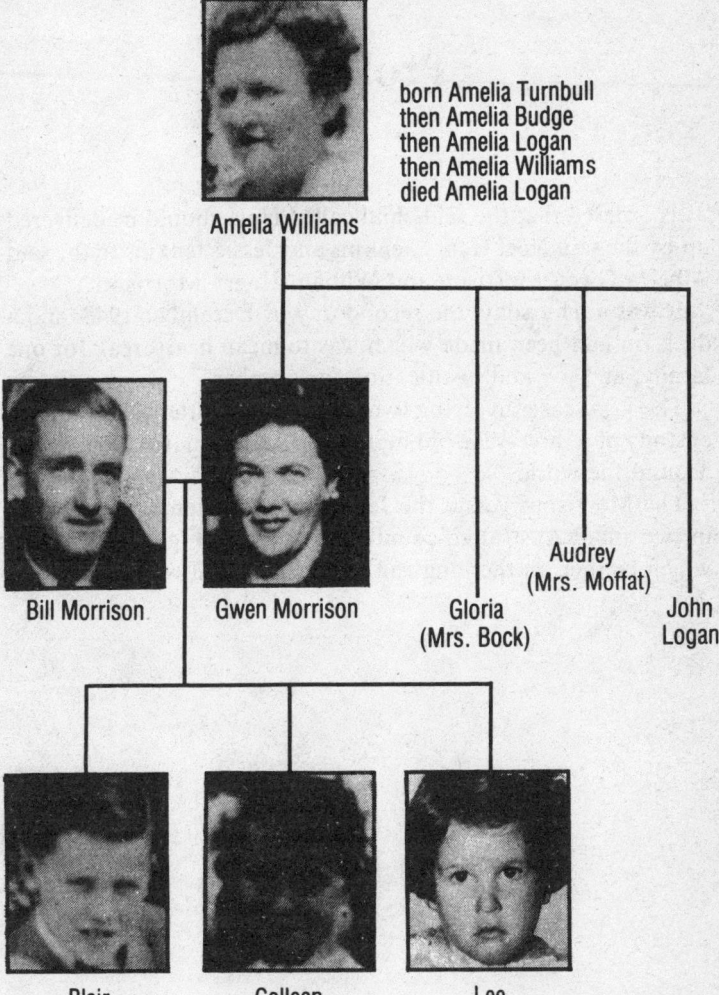

Prologue

'It is ordered that the said child called Nola should be delivered up by the said Noel Henry Jenkins and Jessie Jenkins to the said Alberta Gwen Morrison and William Henry Morrison...'

It was a Thursday, the second day of December 1948, and a decision had been made which was to mean heartbreak for one family, and joy and justification for another.

The legal case involving two families in a bitter battle for the custody of a three-year-old blonde girl had been front-page news around the world.

The Morrisons versus the Jenkins. Two insignificant families in two small Australian country towns had fought a contest in which neither, in the long run, could be a real winner.

1 THE BIRTHS

On a cold winter's morning of 22 June 1945, in the Victorian town of Kyneton, Mrs Jessie Jenkins shook her husband awake: 'Noel, I think the baby's coming.'

A few streets away, another young housewife, Gwen Morrison, was getting her mother out of bed with the same mission in mind. Her husband Bill was in an army camp, so she was relying on her mother, Mrs Amelia Williams, to take her to the old bluestone hospital on a hill overlooking the town where she was to have her third child.

Jessie Jenkins, too, was expecting her third child. After two sons she was praying for a daughter and her thirty-five-year-old builder husband Noel had confided to one or two close friends that a little girl was what he wanted most in the world.

Noel Jenkins, always a cool man, hard to fluster in most circumstances, had trouble getting the car started on that cold, drizzly morning.

Mrs Williams was first to the hospital, ushering her daughter up the stairs to the maternity section. Both were familiar with the surroundings and with the nurses. Gwen Morrison had been in a couple of weeks earlier with labour pains but had had to return home sheepishly when they came to nothing. As they walked along the corridor towards the labour ward, Sister Olive Cass stepped out to greet them.

'It's me again,' said Gwen Morrison, taking a wet scarf from her head. 'I trust it's the real thing this time.'

Gwen Morrison, always independent, waved aside Sister Cass when she offered to help, undressed herself and climbed into the only bed in the labour ward. She had no baby clothes to hand over to Sister Cass because she had left them behind on her brief previous visit. It may have been just after three o'clock in the morning but the motherly Olive Cass treated Gwen Morrison's arrival as just another routine admission to the labour ward. Later, she might have to ring the doctor, when the baby showed signs of arriving, but she would take care of that when the time came. For the moment, that time was obviously some way off.

Sister Cass walked the full length of the long corridor to the medical and surgical ward to tell the only other sister on duty on that floor that she might need some assistance. Sister Annie Teresa ('Tessie') Atkinson followed her back to the labour ward and walked across to Gwen Morrison's bed. The cheerful young Tessie helped to relax the expectant mother with a few words of idle chatter.

By now, Noel Jenkins was turning into the hospital's gravel drive with a second patient for the labour ward. On the back seat inside Jessie Jenkins' packed suitcase were a dozen or so garments for her baby, all clearly marked 'Jenkins'. Mrs Jenkins had urged her husband to get a move on as she felt her baby could arrive at any time. It was 4 a.m.

For Olive Cass the sight of Jessie Jenkins, obviously suffering advanced labour pains, was cause enough for her to decide rapidly that she and Tessie Atkinson would need more help. She turned to Sister Atkinson and instructed her to get a message across to the nurses' home to get a third sister, Elizabeth Lockhart, out of bed. Then she went to the phone and called the doctor, telling him it was urgent — not one, but two babies were on the way.

The scene was now set for something that had never happened in the ninety years the small Kyneton hospital had been in existence; two births about to occur at the same time.

To handle this emergency, were three nurses of varying stages of experience and vastly differing personalities. The natural leader, Olive Cass, was a sturdy woman who at twenty-seven years of age had attended scores of births and prided herself on her efficiency and professional competence. Quite a contrast, was dark, attractive Tessie Atkinson. Not for her the utter dedication

THE BIRTHS

of Olive Cass, although she regarded herself as swift and neat in her work. Tessie hated the horrible hours that went with her job, but she adored the off-duty camaraderie and gay social life of the wartime country nurse. That left Elizabeth Lockhart, a quiet, shy girl, who had grown up near the hamlet of Wood Wood, a speck on the map near the Murray River, about 320 kilometres to the north of Kyneton.

The nurses did have three things in common: all were trained at Melbourne hospitals; all had been assigned to Kyneton under wartime regulations; all were newcomers, having been there for less than six months.

There was one important difference however, Cass and Lockhart were trained midwifery sisters, whereas Tessie Atkinson was not, and may have never even seen a woman give birth to a baby. Now they were all waiting for the doctor.

As she lay in bed, Gwen Morrison heard the nurses rushing about, wheeling in a second bed for Mrs Jenkins and generally preparing for the births. A screen went up between the two beds and after that she could see only the shadowy figures of the nurses moving about on the other side. Suddenly she heard the cries of another woman outside the labour ward, interrupted by one of the nurses saying, 'You'll have to keep quiet.'

Jessie Jenkins was in a great deal of pain and welcomed the anaesthetic she was given before she was wheeled in.

Sister Cass came up to Gwen Morrison's bed and said cheerily, 'If you hurry up we'll get you both finished by seven o'clock', (when the night nurses' shift was due to end).

On the surface, Olive Cass appeared in command of the situation but beneath that air of confidence she was a worried woman. Both patients were well advanced in their labour and Doctor Loughran was still not there.

By now, the two expectant mothers were crying out with pain and their contractions were coming more and more quickly. More alarmingly, they were almost simultaneous. Just then, the door into the labour ward swung open and in strode Gerald Loughran as if he had all the time in the world.

'So I've got two on the way, have I?' he laughed. 'What's all the fuss about?'

WHOSE BABY?

Gerald Loughran appeared not at all concerned about the prospect of delivering two of his patients at the same time. At twenty-nine, he was not long out of university although one would not think it from his manner — that of a young man exuding confidence. Loughran might still have been in uniform had not his father's death forced him out of the Army to return to Kyneton and take over the family's practice. He was popular in the town which was not surprising because his father, also Gerald, had given Kyneton almost thirty years of dedicated, caring service. Young Gerald was friendly enough, although the nurses did find him a bit aloof at times.

He approached the impending double birth in a relaxed fashion. Why not? He had delivered dozens of the citizens of Kyneton without mishap and here in front of him were two mothers whose births were proceeding without any apparent complications.

Loughran walked over to each of the two beds, separated by their thin partition of cloth, quickly establishing that Jessie Jenkins was further advanced in her labour than the woman beside her. The doctor and Sister Cass concentrated on delivering Mrs Jenkins while Sister Lockhart tended Mrs Morrison.

Gwen Morrison, battling severe labour pains herself, was still able to grasp what was happening in the bed next door. She could clearly see the silhouette of Dr Loughran holding up a baby by the feet, tapping it on the back and telling the half-concious but delighted Jessie Jenkins: 'You've got a girl.'

Moments later, Loughran came around the screen to be with Sister Lockhart just as Gwen Morrison's baby was born. It was an easy, quick birth. Another girl. By now it was 6.45 a.m. and she heard two of the sisters discussing the births and one saying: 'Let's make it five minutes apart for the records.'

As for the record, what happened next was to become a matter of great conflict. But to Gwen Morrison it was perfectly clear. In her own words:

'After Dr Loughran had finished attending to me, either Sister Cass or Sister Lockhart took the two babies, one in either arm, out of the room. Each child was wrapped in a blanket or some covering cloth. As the sister was carrying the babies out of the ward, Dr Loughran, who was standing by my bed, turned to her and said: "Are you sure you have those babies tagged?"

... Shortly after the babies were taken out, a sister brought one baby back to me and said: "This is your baby, Mrs Morrison." I remember the baby was not dressed properly but only had a napkin or blanket around her and it was a dark-skinned and dark-haired baby. From my experience I know it to be very unusual for the baby to be brought back to the mother in the labour ward undressed. I distinctly remember that the baby which was brought back to me had no tag or identifying disc. On various occasions afterwards when I had the baby in my presence I noticed that it had no identifying disc or tab on it.'

Although Gwen Morrison swore it was either Olive Cass or Elizabeth Lockhart who carried the babies out, she could not be really sure if it was one of them or some other nurse. Later she was to admit that she never saw the face of the person carrying the babies.

For Jessie Jenkins, the birth of her treasured 9 lb 1 oz girl had been much like those of her two sons Arthur and Arnold, both hefty boys. 'They were all big. I never got below 8 lb.'

There had been a fair amount of pain for Jessie, relieved slightly towards the end by the anaesthetic which clouds her memory of the birth itself. However, she does remember this:

'After my baby was delivered, I was taken to my room and given a cup of tea. Soon after this, Sister Lockhart brought in my baby, dressed in the garments supplied by me. I was at once struck by her resemblance to my other two children when they were born. The three children were fair and their features were similar. They had eyes set wide apart, a broad bridge to the nose, small noses, faces wider than long and the hairline was similar. Each of them at birth was practically without hair.'

Although they had been within a few feet of each other as their babies were coming into the world, Jessie Jenkins says she had no idea that Gwen Morrison was the woman on the other side of the thin screen. 'I didn't know who was there. I knew that somebody else was in the ward but I didn't know who.'

By nine o'clock that morning, both women were asleep. Jessie Jenkins, thirty-three, had a private room but Gwen Morrison, three years her junior, had to settle for the public ward. In tiny cots nearby in the hospital nursery were their baby girls, both in perfect health. With them in that nursery were two other baby girls, born a couple of days earlier. It had been a big week for girls in Kyneton.

Soon after the births, at about 7 a.m., Sisters Cass and Atkinson trooped wearily off to their beds while Sister Lockhart worked on. Most of the participants in the drama were sound asleep by mid-morning.

Noel Jenkins was feeling mighty pleased with himself as he sat down to lunch that day. The news of his baby daughter's arrival was far more palatable than the grim wartime headlines he was glancing at over his meal. The big news of the day was a massive American raid on Japanese targets and the taking of a record number of Japanese prisoners after the Battle of Okinawa. Arguments were still raging over the fate of Adolf Hitler. Two new versions of what happened to the Fuhrer and his newlywed wife Eva Braun came from a chauffeur and a German policeman. One said the couple shot themselves, the other that they took poison. A lighter item referred to a consignment of choice Australian oysters sent as a gift to British Prime Minister Winston Churchill. They turned up in London (a previous batch disappeared around Karachi) but all six dozen were bad.

Noel Jenkins turned to the entertainment section, a favourite with the man who produced, directed and starred in plays and musicals in his own home town. Noel Coward's *The Happy Breed* was showing at the Athenaeum in Melbourne and King's Cinema was advertising 'definitely last days' for *Casablanca* with Humphrey Bogart and Ingrid Bergman.

Word that he had a daughter was a bit slow coming through to Gunner Bill Morrison at his army camp, about fifty-six

THE BIRTHS

kilometres from Kyneton. When he did hear the good news, he jumped on his old motorbike and rode through pouring rain to get to Kyneton. By the time he arrived he was soaked through and it was already evening, so instead of going to see his wife he decided to stay the night with his mother-in-law. He would see his baby girl the next day.

Even before Bill Morrison got away from camp, the mothers had already breastfed their babies for the first time and received their first visitors. Noel Jenkins had a grin from ear to ear as he gleefully inspected his new daughter, the girl he and his wife had agreed to call Nola.

In Bill Morrison's place at his wife's bedside was a rather remarkable woman, Amelia Williams — stout, dark-haired, strong-willed, determined to the point of being domineering; but, for all that, a free-wheeling cheerful personality who was fond of her drink and smoked like a chimney. She was in her fiftieth year at the time but had crammed a lot of living into every single one of those years; married three times, widowed twice and separated once. No one who met Amelia Williams ever forgot her. She was a woman who sometimes seemed out of place in the more sedate and restrained country communities in which she had spent much of her life.

Her first call was to see her daughter, then on to the nursery to take a look at her new granddaughter. The person who showed the tiny youngster to her was the nurse who had helped bring her into the world, Elizabeth Lockhart.

According to Amelia Williams, the baby shown to her was 'fair-skinned' and resembled her daughter's other two children. Fair-skinned? The baby that had been given to Gwen Morrison a few minutes after the birth was dark. There was another thing that the observant Mrs Williams noted: '... the baby did not have any identification disc or tab visible on it.'

The following day, Bill Morrison visited his wife in hospital and was shown his daughter for the first time. It might have been his second little girl but she was immediately something special. On that day they formed a bond that was to last a lifetime.

Ten days passed uneventfully before Noel Jenkins made his final visit to the hospital to pick up his wife and chubby new daughter. He had two excited youngsters in the car beside him. His sons, Arthur, then almost eight, and Arnold, three, were having their first glimpse of the first girl in the family and they were thrilled that Mum was coming home at last. There was much joy in the Jenkins home that night.

Gwen Morrison spent twelve days in hospital before she, too, returned home with her daughter tucked up tightly against the winter cold in her bassinet. Like the Jenkins boys, the two older Morrison children, Blair, aged seven, and Colleen, two, were delighted to be welcoming the baby home. Amelia Williams was stalking impatiently about the house as the car pulled up with her daughter and granddaughter inside. She had not been to see mother or child since the day of the birth.

Amelia Williams dashed out and took the baby from her daughter, eager to nurse the infant and to rush her inside out of the biting cold of the Kyneton winter. They sat by the fire, the doting grandmother and the proud mother, with the two youngsters hovering around, anxious for their turn to cuddle the baby.

Mrs Williams carefully removed the layers of blankets from her grandchild, one by one, until the baby girl was pink and naked before the flames of the fire. There was a moment or two of hesitation, then the grandmother's brow furrowed. She held the baby up to the light, carefully scrutinizing every feature.

Then, in a calm voice, devoid of doubt, she declared: 'Gwen, this is not the baby I saw in hospital. You've got the wrong baby!'

2 ANGRY WORDS IN THE STREET

Amelia Williams was the kind of woman who imposed her opinions on others, particularly her own family. She was used to having her own way, even with her strong-willed daughter, Gwen. Her instant decision that the baby that came home from the hospital was not of her blood was to prey on her mind day after day until it became an obsession. That obsession was taken up by her daughter, then her son-in-law and eventually the entire family was overwhelmed by it. A tragedy for two families was in the making.

At first, however, it was just the meandering of a grandmother who paid too much attention to family similarities.

'This child is nothing like the others,' her mother harped, drawing Gwen Morrison's attention to the facial features of the two older children, Blair and Colleen.

'When she fills out she'll be better,' replied Gwen, trying to explain the apparent differences. But, she too began to have nagging doubts.

The eyes were the trouble. The Morrisons all had blue eyes, this infant's were brown. Even that she tried to explain away, saying the eyes would change colour as the baby grew older. When she was a month old, the little girl was christened Johanne Lee but everyone called her by her second name, Lee.

Noel Jenkins was absolutely delighted with his daughter. She was a blonde, blue-eyed creature, very affectionate and idolized by her two older brothers. Jessie Jenkins could see the likeness, a striking likeness, between the baby girl and brother Arnold. As planned, they christened her Nola.

Whose Baby?

As Nola grew into a plump tot, Jessie Jenkins was reminded of her own grandfather, Robert King, a man of vivid blue eyes and fair skin. That explained why Nola was blue-eyed when she and her husband and the two boys had brown eyes. Jessie Jenkins had spent much of her early life in the King home in Kyneton. Born Jessie Bull, in the little country township of Tatura, she was only eighteen months old when her mother returned to the family home after an unhappy marriage which ended in divorce.

A strikingly attractive young girl, Jessie was blessed with a quick mind and a lovely soprano voice. When she left school she got a job as book-keeper with the leading grocer in Kyneton. Her spare time was spent mainly in the local theatre group where she teamed up with her baritone, the young builder Noel Jenkins.

He was a local lad, son of another builder who had been born in Kyneton when the town was a thriving community with twenty-nine hotels to cope with thirsty goldminers passing through on their way to the rich diggings of Ballarat and Bendigo. Noel's grandfather had been a seaman from Northern Ireland who jumped ship in Melbourne and hiked more than ninety-six kilometres to Kyneton to be reunited with his sweetheart, who had migrated some time before.

Noel Jenkins showed early signs of the solid country-town citizen that he is today. At the age of sixteen he was the talk of Kyneton when he was picked among a handful of Victorian scouts to go to Canberra for the opening of Australia's first parliament. As a young man he grew into a tall, lean, outdoors type, affable, kind and generous, seldom without a smile on his weatherbeaten face. At the outset of war he volunteered for service but was rejected on medical grounds, a surprise for a man who looked so fit and healthy and was used to hard work.

Unlike Noel and Jessie Jenkins, the Morrisons were outsiders, relative newcomers to the town of Kyneton. Bill Morrison was a wanderer who had come from Western Australia, his wife and her mother had spent some time in the West but had lived most of their lives in Melbourne or country Victoria. Bill had been quick to sign up for the Army when war broke out. He enlisted as an infantryman and was dismayed when the Army dispensed with his services because his feet weren't made for marching. After mulling over his predicament for some time, he volunteered a second time and was accepted into the artillery.

His wife was less than happy when he was posted to a camp in New South Wales, hundreds of miles from where they had been living in the Melbourne suburb of Coburg. It was 1943 and Amelia Williams had sold a farmlet she owned outside Kyneton and had moved into the town itself. She proposed that Gwen, her favourite daughter, move from Melbourne and stay with her until Bill was discharged. Gwen had two youngsters to cope with: Blair, aged five, and Colleen, just a few months old. Her mother's offer was too good to refuse. Fate had brought the Morrisons to the Jenkins' home town.

In early October 1944, Bill Morrison was able to arrange a move back to Victoria, a move that saw him stationed at Darley Camp, just outside the quaintly named town of Bacchus Marsh. It was a splendid arrangement, Kyneton was only a short drive away and he could spend all of his free time with Gwen and the children.

Six weeks after Lee was born, Gwen Morrison decided to move into a flat in Bacchus Marsh so they could spend even more time together. Bill Morrison was oblivious to the debate over the new baby that had raged inside his mother-in-law's home in Kyneton, but he was soon to become embroiled.

Like any soldier penned up in an army camp, Bill Morrison was looking forward to being with his family more often, strengthening his ties with the two youngsters, Blair and Colleen, and playing the father's role with the new baby. If he had hoped for it to be a happy homecoming, he was to be bitterly disappointed. Gwen Morrison, like her mother, now wanted to talk about just one subject. That baby.

'She's not like either of ours,' she told her husband. 'I don't know where she gets those brown eyes.'

Bill tried to get her off the subject, shrugging off his persistent wife. 'Don't be bloody silly,' he admonished her, 'you're imagining things.'

He knew just who was behind this obsession and was grateful that his wife would be apart from her mother while he talked some sense into her.

WHOSE BABY?

Meanwhile, back in Kyneton, the lively grandmother Amelia Williams, was still having her say. She was fond of a drink — 'She drank her spirits fairly short of water or soda,' as one family friend recalls — and the town soon began to learn of the family row and the grandmother's theory on the 'mixed babies'. Rumours began.

Bill Morrison took a lot of convincing that there was anything amiss with the little brown-eyed baby girl. She was an instant hit with her father and, as he was to confess in tears many years later, he could never have parted with her.

Although Amelia Williams had lived in Kyneton for a couple of years and her daughter had been with her for much of that time, Jessie Jenkins scarcely knew either woman. Their first meeting, by ironic coincidence, was in a ward of Kyneton Hospital. Forty years later, Jessie can still recall that chance encounter.

'A couple of years before Nola was born, it must have been. I had a miscarriage after the bushfires, I lost the child. When I was in hospital with infections, they needed my room, so they shifted me in with Mrs Morrison's sister. She was a very nice lady. Mrs Morrison and her mother came to visit her one day and I think the sum total of our conversation was, "Good afternoon, how are you?" I think she had her tonsils out. She wasn't there long and then she went home. That's the only time I've really spoken to them.'

Jessie Jenkins doggedly insists that those few words were the only ones she has ever exchanged with the Morrison family, except for a formal 'Hullo' when they passed in the streets of Kyneton. Gwen Morrison's recollections are far different. One weekend after she had been living in Bacchus Marsh for about five months she returned to Kyneton to visit her mother and have a day at the races. She recalled:

'Whilst walking in Piper Street, Kyneton, I saw Mrs Jenkins ahead of me wheeling a pram. I caught up to her and asked her if I could have a look at her baby as I was then anxious to see what her baby's appearances were like as the appearances of Johanne Lee in no way resembled my family. I noticed that the child which she had in her pram was about the same age as Johanne Lee and was a blue-eyed, fair-skinned and fair-haired baby. I then noticed that Mrs Jenkins' eyes were brown.'

According to Gwen Morrison, she then tackled Jessie Jenkins about the possibility of there having been a mix-up.

'I have blue eyes and I said: "You have the blue-eyed baby and I have the brown-eyed baby. I think they must have got them mixed up." She replied: "Oh, no."'

Amelia Williams had not seen her granddaughter for about five months and the visit that weekend convinced her more than ever that Lee was no Morrison: 'I noticed then that the child was not like my daughter's other two children,' she was to swear later.

Gwen Morrison returned to her husband and told him of the meeting in the street, of the evidence of her own two eyes and of her determination to have blood tests carried out to settle the matter. By now she was adamant and he was beginning at last to believe that his precious Lee may have been someone else's child. It was an agonizing situation for them both and a desperate dilemma. What could, or should they do?

Gwen Morrison had no doubts. She was convinced that Jessie Jenkins was nursing her baby and there must be some way to get her back. The rumours were now rife in Kyneton and the names Jenkins and Morrison were household words. The gossip had even reached the nurses' home.

No one dared broach the subject directly with Noel or Jessie Jenkins — they would be the last to know — but there was plenty of chatter around the Kyneton Hospital and there is little doubt that Dr Gerald Loughran, the man who delivered the babies, had heard it. Into this small town full of rumour and counter-rumour Gwen Morrison returned with her three children, in March 1946, to await her husband's release from the Army.

Less than a month later, Jessie Jenkins had another confrontation in the street, but this time it was with the far more formidable personage of the doughty grandmother, Amelia Williams.

Whose Baby?

It was a Saturday morning, in Mollison Street, Kyneton, and both women had been shopping. Amelia Williams puts her side of the terse conversation which followed:

'She had her eldest son with her. I was immediately struck by the likeness between him and Johanne Lee. I said to Mrs Jenkins: "I think you have our baby and we have yours." She said: "Don't be silly." I said: "It's strange that we have the brown-eyed baby and you have the blue-eyed baby." She replied: "Don't be silly."'

Not satisfied with this preliminary skirmish, the bulldog Amelia Williams went back into action less than a month later. The date was 13 May and Mrs Williams had Lee in the pusher with her, again in Mollison Street. She marched straight up to Jessie Jenkins and said: 'You have our baby!'

According to Amelia Williams she received unexpected support from another quarter. 'A woman came up and said to Mrs Jenkins, indicating Johanne Lee, "Oh, Jessie, hasn't your baby grown." Mrs Jenkins said: "That's my baby," pointing to the baby she had in her pram.'

Jessie Jenkins tells a different version of her brushes with the Morrison grandmother.

'About nine months after the birth of Nola I was wheeling her in a pram when Mrs Williams came up. She looked at Nola and said: "Oh, she has blue eyes." She then asked me what colour eyes my husband and my boys had.'

So much for the first meeting.

'About a month later she met me in the street and said: "Our baby should have blue eyes and yours should have brown." I laughed and said: "Nola was a real throwback," meaning that she had taken after my grandfather who had very blue eyes and very fair skin. From this conversation I did not gather from Mrs Williams' remarks that she considered that a mistake had been made.'

And as for the other woman pointing to the wrong child, Jessie Jenkins swears that didn't ever happen.

By now the Morrisons may have become obsessive about the two little girls but the Jenkinses, in turn, soon became increasingly defensive and protective of Nola. Real or imagined stares in the street became worse day by day and Jessie Jenkins' way of dealing with them was to stare straight back.

Nola and Lee were ten months old when the Morrison family finally became reunited in Kyneton after Bill Morrison was discharged from the Army. He decided to settle in the town. Gwen liked being near her mother, although he had reservations about that, and he could see good prospects ahead for a panel-beater and spray painter in a community where cars were becoming more and more common.

One day while he was spray painting a car, as usual without a protective mask because he shunned such 'sissy' devices, Bill Morrison saw a young boy watching him. 'I was struck by the resemblance between him and Johanne Lee,' he recalled later, 'and on inquiry I found the boy was Arthur Jenkins, a son of Mr and Mrs Jenkins...'

Gwen Morrison was counting the days until Lee's first birthday. She had been told by someone who claimed to have some knowledge of such matters that an infant could not have satisfactory blood tests until it was at least a year old. She was loath to consult Dr Gerald Loughran, who had delivered Lee, because he was the Jenkins' family doctor. In fact, for some time now she and the rest of the family had been attending a rival practice run by Dr Jim Downing.

Downing was an elderly man and he had been delighted when in January 1946, a young Army medico visited Kyneton and expressed interest in joining a practice. The army man was Dr John Connell, then aged thirty-three, and a veteran of war service in England, the Middle East, New Guinea and Borneo. One of his superiors had suggested he might try the thriving town of Kyneton when it came his turn to return to civvy street.

Connell still remembers clearly that hot January day when a young woman driver was assigned to take him up to the town for a look around.

'When we got to the town she said, "Where to?" I said, "We'll drive, we'll drive and count the pubs. And we'll count the banks." That's the way a doctor always looks at a township, you know. If there are good pubs and good banking chambers, that's a very solid town. Well there were six banks in Kyneton and about four pubs and they all seemed to be doing very well. I said: "This is the place for me."'

He started the following week.

Connell felt at home right away, particularly as he already knew Dr Gerald Loughran, from their days together at Melbourne University. For the first six months his work was merely the routine coughs and sneezes that come the way of the country GP, a pleasant change after his years of war service. Then in August 1946, Connell encountered a problem that had never been dealt with in any of his textbooks or lectures at university. He was confronted by a nervous woman in his surgery posing the strangest of questions. Could he tell her if she was the mother of her own daughter?

Gwen Morrison explained the circumstances of the birth and the great family dilemma.

'They thought the child wasn't theirs, there could have been a mix-up at the hospital,' Connell recalled. 'I didn't know anything about it. I'd never met her or her family as I'd just arrived in the town. I said, "I will get some advice."'

Connell decided that the best course of action was to carry out blood tests on Gwen and Bill Morrison and Lee, who was now fourteen months old. However, it was a difficult and complex problem for a young doctor to face so he telephoned a friend in Melbourne, a bio-chemist.

A couple of days later the Morrisons walked into his surgery with Lee in the arms of her father. Connell took small samples of blood from all three, carefully labelled them, and told the couple he would contact them when he had some definite results. He sent the blood samples to Melbourne for analysis while the Morrisons spent ten troubled days, wondering whether their suspicions, or really convictions, of the past year would prove correct.

Eventually, Gwen Morrison could stand the waiting no longer.

While her husband was at work she went alone to Dr Connell's surgery and sat her turn in the waiting room. Her face was glum, as if she already knew what the result would be and what tragic consequences it would have for her family's future life.

Connell invited her in and immediately asked her to sit down. The pathologist's finding had just arrived. Further tests would be necessary, he explained, but the evidence appeared beyond doubt. Lee could not be their child.

These were the words that Gwen Morrison had expected to hear, had known she would hear, but she was still dumbstruck. Here at last was physical proof of what her heart and her eyes had been saying for many months. She walked out of the surgery in a trance, trudging slowly home through the streets of Kyneton. Her mind was in a daze, her thoughts racing, her emotions jumbled and confused.

A calmer counsel was provided that night by her mother. 'Tomorrow,' she told her daughter and her son-in-law, 'we are going back to see Dr Connell. I want to hear it for myself.' There was a note of triumph in her voice. Amelia Williams had been proven right after all and she was determined to press on with her all-consuming quest to have the right granddaughter returned to her.

Bill and Gwen Morrison, and Amelia Williams all trooped into Connell's surgery the following morning and heard again the fateful report. Morrison felt physically sick at the thought of what lay ahead. He couldn't conceive of life without that little brown-eyed girl. Beneath the surface he was far different from the cocky character he displayed to outsiders. He was later to confess publicly that he was not persuaded by the vehement attitude of his mother-in-law that the children should be exchanged at all costs. 'I had my own ideas about it,' he admitted, 'but I was not anxious to go on with the matter. We had had the child a long while.'

It must be remembered that he was the one person in the clan who had formed a special attachment for young Lee. However, by now he was being swept along by the currents of emotion pouring from Gwen Morrison and Amelia Williams, and he was dispatched, forthwith, to have it out with Noel Jenkins.

WHOSE BABY?

Early that evening the good-natured young builder was up the ladder working on his new home in Mitchell Street, Kyneton, when he was summoned into the street by Bill Morrison, a man he knew only vaguely. There was little authority in Morrison's voice; he was still feeling the after-effects of the shock he had received and his air of confidence was notably absent. Even Noel Jenkins at a distance noticed that the man standing in the street calling out to him 'was a bit on the shy side'.

Noel took his time about walking across, sensing that something was badly amiss. His first impression of Bill Morrison was to prove correct. 'He wasn't full of confidence or anything like that. He was a little bit embarrassed about how to approach things.' The two men had never spoken before but each knew who the other was.

Haltingly, Bill Morrison broached the subject. 'You know the girls are quite certain there's been a mistake made. I think we should get together and prove there's been a mistake made.'

Morrison explained that he and his wife and Lee had had blood tests which proved Lee was not their child. She must be a Jenkins.

Noel Jenkins was stunned, almost unable to reply, but he is anything but an emotional man, at least in front of strangers, and was not going to let this virtual stranger become aware of his inner anguish. 'He asked me to have blood tests made and said that if such tests proved a mistake had been made he would make someone pay.' Noel was left with the distinct impression that the Morrisons wanted him to join them in legal action against the hospital.

Noel Jenkins' mind was racing and he wasn't even aware of the two other faces in the street, watching him intently. Gwen Morrison and Amelia Williams were sitting anonymously in a small black car, out of sight, the windows wound down so they could catch every word. They heard the builder's voice raised, saying firmly: 'There's been no mistake made, Bill.' However, as the two men were about to part, the women heard Noel Jenkins finally say grudgingly: 'I'll see my wife and talk the matter over.'

He wasn't giving much away, but he returned home in some haste, 'shaking like a leaf', to his wife for the most critical discussion of their married life. Neither of them believed for a moment that Nola was a Morrison but the seeds of doubt had been sown. Noel and Jessie Jenkins, a couple who would not shy away from their problems, did not take long to reach a decision. Noel drove straight to Gerald Loughran's surgery and put the allegations to him. Could the babies have been mixed? And if not, what could they do to prove it?

Gerald Loughran's professional reputation was on the line but he did not show the concern he must have felt. He scoffed at the suggestion. Ridiculous, he said. However, he did make one concession, he would carry out blood tests and swiftly set their minds at rest. If Loughran was so unconcerned, he acted with remarkable speed. That night he called at the Jenkins' home and took samples of blood from Noel, Jessie and Nola. He was just as smart in getting the results back to them. Two nights later he called again, reassuring them that they had 'nothing to worry about' as the tests showed Nola could be their child. He deliberately used that word 'could' but that was good enough for Noel and Jessie. They had their first good night's sleep since Bill Morrison's startling visit to the site of their new home.

The following morning, Noel Jenkins confidently sought out Bill Morrison. He put it bluntly: as far as he and his wife were concerned no mistake had been made and they intended to do nothing further. There would be no shared blood test. Nothing. What's more, they wanted the whole thing laid to rest, forever. Nola was their child and that was that.

Strangely, Noel Jenkins did not tell Bill Morrison of the blood tests carried out by Dr Loughran. Asked about it years later, Noel could never really explain why. It was a curious omission and certainly did nothing to allay the Morrisons' concerns. If he had convinced the Morrisons that Nola's blood conformed with that of his wife and himself, would they have looked elsewhere for the solution to their dilemma, or simply dropped the whole subject? It was possible, of course, but a quick look back through the history of the Morrison family suggests otherwise.

Bill Morrison grew up almost 5,000 kilometres from Kyneton, in Western Australia. The son of an electrician, he was born on 9 July 1909, in the gold rush town of Boulder, perched on the

Whose Baby?

July 1909, in the gold rush town of Boulder, perched on the famous Golden Mile, one of the richest strips of gold-bearing dirt in the world. When he was about twelve or so, the family moved further west, settling in the suburb of Victoria Park in Perth, Western Australia's fast-growing young capital. Times were tough when Bill Morrison, eldest of the four children, left school and attempted to join the workforce. Strong, willing, determined to succeed, he was still hard-pressed to find a job. The Great Depression was beginning to sweep Australia.

Undeterred, the self-assured, blond teenager travelled about the State picking up work wherever he could find it. His brother, Ray, says Bill was an eager worker who would chase everywhere for a job and was unafraid to tackle anything. He had a succession of jobs, never staying too long in one place. Already the patterns of his life were forming. Whether or not it was the Depression which set those patterns, Bill Morrison later found it difficult to shake off the wanderlust and impossible to curb his tongue if he didn't see eye to eye with the boss.

He was inclined to be a bit of a romantic and, like many a father, tended to glamorize his past and exaggerate his achievements when recounting them to his children years later. Blair Morrison grew up believing his father lost the tips of the fingers on his right hand in a crash while racing motorcycles, whereas the truth lay in a more mundane plasterworks mishap.

One weekend Bill Morrison returned from the bush to find new neighbours had moved in next door to the Morrison home in Perth. The Logan family had come across from Victoria: farmer William Edward Logan, his plump, personable wife Amelia, their three daughters, Gwen, Gloria and Audrey, and a son, John Allan. It did not take long for Bill to strike up a friendship with Gwen, the eldest girl, a friendship that flourished even under the stern gaze of Amelia Logan, who was not about to lose one of her girls to the first man who came along.

When the Logans elected to return to Victoria, Bill Morrison made up his mind to follow. As soon as he could raise sufficient funds he set off in pursuit, driving on the unmade road across the treeless, parched Nullarbor Desert in his tiny Whippet car. They were reunited, Bill and Gwen, on a sheeprun called 'Linwood', where William Logan had settled his family and Amelia Logan was in the uncharacteristic role of farmer's wife.

The property ran close to the banks of the Murray River, near Mildura, in north-west Victoria, and to the whole family it seemed the perfect place to settle down. And so it was until their dream was shattered midway through 1936. One day in August that year the handsome William Logan complained of a terrible headache. He rested in bed but the headache grew worse, he rapidly developed a fever, then lapsed into a coma. The doctors diagnosed meningitis, inflammation of the lining of the brain, but he could well have been suffering from the related but more serious disease encephalitis, frequently spread by mosquitoes in the Murray Valley area. Whatever the illness, William Logan was dead within a few days at the age of forty-seven and Amelia Logan, now in her early forties, found herself a widow for the second time in an eventful life.

She had been born Amelia Elizabeth Turnbull in September 1895, in the Wimmera wheat and wool town of Horsham, and grew up in the smaller town of Donald, not far away. At the age of seventeen she married a railwayman, Herbert Gordon Budge, and they set up home in Melbourne. Within half a dozen years she had given birth to three girls and had been tragically widowed. The youngest daughter, Audrey, cannot remember her real father but she does remember her mother's happiest period when she met and married William Logan. 'She loved Dad Logan, she loved him very much. He died a very tragic death. Poor Mum had a lot of tragedy.'

Audrey says her mother, all five foot nothing of her, never knew how to take a backward step. She met everything head on and brought the children up the same way, with her motto ringing in their ears: 'Never give up, never let anything get you down.'

Audrey, like the rest of the family, speaks of her mother with awe: 'I'm extremely proud of my Mum. She was left with three children at a very, very young age and she battled on and we three girls went through college and were very well educated. She was always, as my brother used to say, "The Boss". She was a tough lady. No one could put it over her.'

The three girls adopted the name Logan, an obvious step as

they had scarcely known Herbert Budge. In 1926 Amelia enrolled her three daughters, Gwen, eleven, Gloria, ten, and Audrey, seven, as boarders at the Academy of Mary Immaculate, a Catholic convent school in the Melbourne suburb of Fitzroy. Later that year the three girls were baptized in St Patrick's Cathedral, embracing the Catholic faith of their new father.

All three of Amelia's girls had inherited some of their mother's fire, although in Gwen's case, particularly, it lingered fairly deep beneath the surface. Gwen was a pretty girl with pleasant, rounded rather than classical features, and a tendency to put on weight. Unlike her mother, the extrovert, Gwen preferred to listen and absorb rather than run the conversation.

On 23 January 1937, William Henry Morrison married his sweetheart, Alberta Gwen Logan, then twenty-two, at St Margaret's Church, in Mildura. Although Gwen had been given a Catholic education, her mother owed no allegiance to any church, she had not even been baptized, so the ceremony was held in the local Church of England.

The Logans were certainly no celebrities in the district but the ceremony rated a substantial report in the *Sunraysia Daily* newspaper. Obviously the widow Amelia Logan had spared no expense and the newspaper recorded:

> 'On the arm of Major Chanter (Trentham Cliffs station) Miss Alberta Gwen Logan made a dainty picture... for her marriage to William Henry Morrison. Her gown of pearl-tinted satin and linen lace was shown to perfection against the soft shade of lemon worn by her bridesmaid. Cut on softening lines, the bridal gown had long sleeves ending in a point at each wrist. The square neckline suited the bride and the moulded skirt was cut to flow into a long train behind her. A plaited halo of pearl-tinted tulle caught a long billowy tulle veil to her head, and she carried a trail of water lilies on her right arm.'

Bill Morrison looked nothing like the raw, young jack-of-all-trades from outback Western Australia. He had attired himself splendidly in a hired dinner suit with black bow tie and winged collar. His fair hair was brilliantined and slicked down so that the parting looked as if it had been traced with a set square.

Gwen's sister Gloria was the lone bridesmaid and a Mr Ted Mayall was best man. Bill Morrison's mother, also a widow, had made the trip from Perth to see her eldest boy wed. According to the *Sunraysia Daily*, Amelia Logan was done up to the nines herself, 'in a very smart tailored frock of a cocoa brown shade with matching accessories and carried a posy of autumn-tinted flowers'.

After the ceremony and a reception at a private home in Mildura, the happy couple was cheered by the guests as they set off on a motor honeymoon to Melbourne and Adelaide. Just short of a year later a birth notice appeared: 'Morrison (née Gwen Logan). On 6 January at Miss Harvey's Private Hospital, to Mr and Mrs W. H. Morrison — a son (William Edward Blair). Both well.'

Gwen's sister Gloria married in the same church, taking as her husband a strapping young sportsman named George Spencer Bock. Meanwhile Amelia Logan had been trying to run her late husband's farm 'Linwood' with her own two hands. She tackled all the farming chores with willingness and determination, shocking some of the local people by even shearing and crutching her own sheep, alien tasks for any woman, let alone one approaching middle age. Twice married, twice widowed, she decided to take the plunge again and wed Thomas Williams, a local man who seemed a likely type to take over the running of the farm.

It was a disastrous decision. Amelia and her groom fell out almost immediately and whatever feeling she may have originally held for Thomas Williams soon turned to an intense dislike. They parted after the briefest of unions and she never saw him again. The name was rarely mentioned and late in her life Amelia Williams, not knowing or caring if her husband was alive or dead, changed her name back to Logan by deed poll.

By the time her third daughter Audrey married journalist Frank Moffat, just after the war, Thomas Williams was already a name banished from the household. Says Moffat, 'He was never within sight.' And, in obvious understatement: 'There was no great love between them at all.' Audrey dismisses her mother's third marriage coldly: 'A catastrophe. An unfortunate episode.'

Having parted from Williams, the family matriarch sold the farm and moved on from Mildura to a succession of homes in various parts of Victoria, staying only briefly in each but always leaving behind the impression of a jolly, fun-loving character, although not a person to be trifled with.

Bill Morrison had picked up the trade of spray painter and panelbeater but he was an ambitious man and decided he could do better as a salesman, working for a Mildura radio firm. His spell as a salesman did not prove to be as successful as he had hoped so he moved on, too, eventually taking up residence in the Melbourne suburb of Coburg. Then the war intervened, thrusting the wandering Morrisons into the path of the Jenkinses of Kyneton. Two families on the same path, going in opposite directions. They had to collide.

3 THE *TRUTH* BOMBSHELL

If the Jenkinses had hoped their lives would return to normal after the showdown with Bill Morrison, they were to be sadly disappointed. There were to be no more first-hand contacts between the two families but the whispering campaign and the stares in the street grew worse and worse. There was no mistaking the looks directed at Jessie Jenkins whenever she took her little blonde girl for a walk to the shops, and if the two boys were with them, the citizens of Kyneton looked all the harder. She knew that all the time they were making comparisons.

Meanwhile the Morrisons had gone further with their blood testing. On Dr Connell's advice they visited two experts in the field, Dr Douglas Thomas and Dr Lucy Bryce, who both had rooms in Melbourne's Collins St, home for eminent specialists in every field of medicine. Both gave the same opinion: Johanne Lee Morrison could be the child of Gwen Morrison but she definitely could not have been fathered by William Morrison.

Gwen Morrison now found herself with an enormous burden. Firstly she had to convince someone, somewhere, that Jessie Jenkins had her daughter. Added to that, she knew that if she fought her case in the public arena she must endure the wagging tongues of sceptics who would simply say that she had not been a faithful wife to her husband Bill. Nevertheless, she did not waver in her resolve and when her fidelity did come into question she swore: 'As I have never had sexual intercourse with any man, other than my husband, Johanne Lee cannot be my daughter.'

Bill Morrison was still very much in love with his wife but he, too, had some moments of doubt about her baby and the prospect of another man being the father. As the discussions and arguments flared, on one occasion he let his doubts spill out. He wanted to know straight out: had she ever been with another man? After all, he had been in an army camp and she was a young and attractive woman.

Gwen Morrison's sister Audrey was one of the few people who ever heard of this incident. Gwen blurted out to her: 'Bill thinks I was out with another man.' That was not really so; he had spoken in the heat of the moment and was to regret what he had said. Nevertheless it was something Gwen Morrison could never erase, unless she proved once and for all that it was a terrible mistake, that she had been given the wrong baby.

Armed with the concrete evidence of the blood specialists, the Morrisons travelled to Melbourne to see a prominent solicitor. He listened patiently but told them their position was hopeless. They could never succeed. He could see no way of getting the matter heard, short of kidnapping Nola Jenkins. It was almost as if he did not believe them and who could blame him? It all sounded pretty farfetched and there were lots of odd babies as a result of husbands going off to war.

Dispirited, they returned to Kyneton. As Bill Morrison was to explain later, they did not want to let the matter slide. They wanted to stage a legal fight for Nola but simply could not afford it.

On 22 June 1947, there were two birthday parties a few streets apart in Kyneton. Nola Jenkins and Lee Morrison had turned two.

Later that year a member of the Morrison family devised a way of getting their case before the public gaze — and it would not cost them a penny. The inspiration came from Frank Moffat, the journalist who had married Gwen's sister Audrey. He was now working for *Truth*, a newspaper that thrived on the sensational.

Out of all the family, Audrey and Frank Moffat were the easiest to convince that there had been a mix-up of babies. The first moment Audrey saw Lee in her sister's arms she said tactlessly: 'Gwen, that's not your child.'

Frank Moffat was sure his wife's judgement was right: 'I think I probably thought it more than anybody. Lee was darker-haired

The *Truth* BOMBSHELL

and darker-skinned and she looked quite different.' They talked it over every time they met the Morrisons and Moffat found himself feeling a great compassion for his sister-in-law. 'She was getting depressed about the whole thing. It got her down a fair bit.'

He decided that what was needed was less talk and more action.

Early in the new year, 1948, a curious thing happened which caused Jessie Jenkins more than a little concern. She had always been very protective of her children, allowing them to visit only a select group of friends. This day the two boys, Arthur, ten, and Arnold, who was nearly six, defied her ruling and slipped away to a friend's house.

The two youngsters were more than eager to pose when a visitor to the home produced a camera. Arnold remembers: 'When we got there we all got our photos taken. It turned out they were friends of the Morrisons. Mum and Dad were really wild.'

Jessie Jenkins was even more angry about what happened a couple of days later. Nola had been playing on a vacant block of land next to their new home in Mitchell Street. Mrs Jenkins recalls:

'Nola just walked over across the paddock and the chappie evidently called her over to the gate and took her photo. I went outside and saw the man there and called her back. And that was it. I didn't know who he was, I had no idea. He came down and took that photo without our knowledge. We didn't even know he was in town.'

Even today Jessie Jenkins speaks emotionally of that incident.

'It was sneaky. I'd cheerfully slit his throat if I could have caught up with him for doing a thing like he did, taking advantage of a little child. The Morrisons could have been with him. She just happened to be walking in the block next door and he called her over.'

Up until now the Morrisons and the Jenkinses had admitted no real animosity towards each other, but things were changing fast. For the Jenkinses, the last straw was about to arrive on their doorstep. *Truth* was not the sort of newspaper that found its way into the Jenkins household. However, the issue of 31 January 1948 was something out of the ordinary. That evening the family was having dinner when a friend banged loudly on the front door and thrust a copy into Noel Jenkins' hands. 'This has just come in,' he told the astonished couple. 'You're all over page one. Photos and all.'

Indeed, *Truth* had done full justice to a story which was very soon to make world headlines. Its own headline read: MOTHER CLAIMS TWO BABIES WERE SWITCHED.

Taking up the entire front page and half of page two, it was illustrated by eight pictures, each carefully captioned. They showed Nola Jenkins and Lee Morrison, Nola's two brothers Arthur and Arnold, Lee's sister and brother, Colleen and Blair, Bill and Gwen Morrison and Kyneton Hospital manager John Cuddihy. The article had obviously originated from the Morrison household and presented the situation almost entirely from their point of view. It read:

> One of the most poignant and continuing human problems in Australia's history has developed around two little Kyneton kiddies — Lee Morrison and Noella Jenkins [this misspelling first appeared in *Truth* but was to crop up continually in various newspapers and even in court transcripts] — who were born within a few minutes of each other on June 22, 1945.
>
> For almost two years the Morrisons have been tormented by fears and doubts that the child they nursed and nurtured, and naturally grew to love intensely, is not their own child at all!
>
> The blue-eyed Morrison couple is convinced that a terrible mistake was made at Kyneton Hospital soon after the birth of the two babies in adjoining beds, and that the infants were switched to the wrong mothers.
>
> Blue-eyed William Henry Morrison and his wife Gwen think the world of brown-eyed Lee, who has become part of their life, but they want blue-eyed Noella who lives with the brown-eyed Noel Jenkins couple and their two brown-eyed sons.

The Morrisons claim that Noella is their child 'without a doubt'. Blood tests made some time ago confirmed their earlier suspicions that the child they took away from the hospital was not their own, they told *Truth*.

They say doctors have established they could not possibly be the parents of Lee.

Yet doctors and hospital authorities claim that a mix-up of babies could not happen at a hospital: that these things only happen in Hollywood films.

It has happened in Australia before today, however — in Queensland some years ago, for instance.

And there are fairly substantial grounds for fears that it has happened again, for according to the Morrisons, the doctor who told them their suggestion was like something from Hollywood, said after receiving the result of the blood tests: 'I MUST APOLOGISE TO YOU; IT LOOKS LIKE IT HAS HAPPENED HERE.'

Since completion of the original blood tests, the results of which were borne out by check tests, the Morrisons have striven unavailingly to have what they considered a grievous wrong put right.

They told *Truth* they invited the Jenkins family to co-operate in blood tests with a view to establishing the parentage of the children.

But the Jenkins family is content to accept the position as it stands today. 'We have suffered enough over this and it is no use,' Mr Jenkins told *Truth*, and added with firmness, 'I am not interested in blood tests.'

Nevertheless all Kyneton, except the hospital authorities, appears to be interested in and anxious to talk about the strange case of these two-year-old kiddies...

Even the tradesmen comment upon the case. 'That's not your baby,' the Italian greengrocer told Mrs Morrison one day. 'Your baby round in Mitchell Street.'

The Jenkins family lives in Mitchell Street. And whenever Mrs Morrison goes to Mitchell Street and sees little Noella she cannot restrain her emotions.

Noella was standing at the Jenkins gate when *Truth* visited the home and on seeing her, Mrs Morrison collapsed into tears.

'That's my baby,' she said, 'and I want my baby back.'

Mrs Morrison also told the president of the hospital (Mr Thomas Willis) that she wanted her baby back. That was many months ago but nothing has been done about an official inquiry to determine whether or not the hospital blundered over the babies.

Truth was told by Mr Jack Cuddihy, manager of the hospital, who was in the armed forces when the babies were born, that the committee had never discussed the case; that he had never heard of it.

It struck *Truth* that the official hospital view of this strange case was that the least said about it the better.

'THE PARENTAGE OF CHILDREN IS KNOWN ONLY TO GOD', WAS THE STRIKING RESPONSE HE MADE WHEN *TRUTH* INDICATED WHAT THE BLOOD TESTS REVEALED.

He declined to make a statement when asked what the hospital was going to do about the case.

While the hospital does not appear anxious to do anything, Mr Morrison is eager to do everything possible to get back the child he is convinced rightfully belongs to him.

'I am very hostile about this matter,' he said to *Truth*. 'My home life has been wrecked since it happened. My wife has not been the same. She's not happy and contented. How could she be when she knows her child is with someone else?'

Mr Morrison has consulted legal advisers on the case and says he has been told that the only way to force matters to a decision is to kidnap little Noella and fight the case to the bitter end.

If this advice was given, *Truth* is not in accord. A writ of *habeas corpus* seems to be the appropriate remedy to determine the issue.

Suspicions of the Morrisons and of Mrs Morrison's mother were aroused as soon as the baby was taken home. No move was made then, however.

It was not until persistent references by outsiders to the resemblance of the baby to the Jenkins children fanned the suspicions of the Morrisons that it was decided to have blood tests taken. Now, nothing would make the Morrisons believe that they have their own child.

Apart from the colour of the eyes, other characteristics of the two groups of children provide some evidence for claims that the babies might have been switched. Mrs Morrison's other girl, Colleen, now four, still has her first teeth. Those in the bottom jaw are widely spaced; so are little Noella's.

Yet the teeth of little Lee are close together, like those of the Jenkins boys. And like them Lee is a very exuberant, high-spirited child, not at all shy. On the other hand, Noella appears to be shy and restrained like Colleen Morrison.

The important question is: Could the children have been mistaken, one for the other, during the first hours of their life and thus handed to the wrong mothers?

Mrs Morrison says that when she was about to have her baby at 6.45 a.m. on June 22, 1945, Mrs Noel Jenkins was brought to the labour ward and placed in the next bed to her.

A screen was placed between them and through the silhouette on the screen she observed the birth of Mrs Jenkins' baby. Three minutes later her own baby was born. The same doctor (Dr Loughran, of Kyneton) and the same staff nurses attended at both confinements.

As one of the nurses took the two babies from the ward, she heard the doctor ask: 'Are you sure you have the babies tabbed (or tagged)?' The nurse replied: 'Yes, doctor.'

When her mother visited the hospital that afternoon to see her grandchild, she was shown a fair-haired baby, Mrs Morrison said, but next day her husband was shown a baby with dark brown hair. It was the baby with the dark brown hair that she took home from hospital several days later.

Shortly after leaving hospital, Mrs Morrison went to live at Bacchus Marsh. Owing to her mother's belief and her own growing suspicions at seeing the Jenkins baby at nine months old, it was decided to have blood tests made. They went to see Dr Connell at Kyneton. Ten days after the blood samples were taken, Mrs Morrison went on, the doctor told her something that confirmed her doubts.

WHOSE BABY?

That day they approached Mr Jenkins, who is a carpenter at Kyneton and highly respected, seeking his co-operation in blood tests of himself, Mrs Jenkins, and little Noella.

Some days later, so Mrs Morrison said, Mr Jenkins saw Mr Morrison and said he would have nothing to do with it. It was decided to have check blood tests made, and Dr Connell suggested that the Morrisons should see Dr Douglas Thomas, of Collins Street, Melbourne.

Several days elapsed and they were advised to have still another test made. This time they were sent to Dr Lucy Bryce, a leading pathologist.

In other statements made to *Truth*, Mrs Morrison said that when she saw Dr Thomas after the check tests were made, she was told that Lee could be her child but not her husband's. And she said the doctor added: 'I think the best thing you can do is to ask your husband to go with you to some other town.'

When she asked him why, she said his reply was: 'Mother love is very overpowering. You would not want to do anything to harm your little daughter. There is a million to one chance that your son would grow up and want to marry his own sister.'

Truth could not interview Mrs Jenkins and get her views on this extraordinary case. She was not at home when we called.

'Thank God she's not,' said Mr Jenkins. 'We have copped enough over this already. We don't want any investigations. We accept the facts as they stand.'

And there the story ends, except that when Mrs Morrison puts little Lee to bed each night she weeps and yearns for little Noella who is sleeping more than a mile away.

Frank Moffat had done his job well. Although he had not written the story himself, for obvious ethical reasons, he had certainly set it in motion and was well pleased with the final results. In Kyneton the newspaper sold out in a couple of hours.

No one looked closer at the *Truth* article and the set of pictures of all the children than Jessie Jenkins. She scrutinized every last feature of Colleen and Blair Morrison, her own sons Arthur and Arnold, but, most of all, the two little girls, Lee Morrison and Nola Jenkins. 'Nola and the other kids were very much alike when they were born,' she explains. 'They were all, strange as it may seem, blonde and curly-haired, with fair complexions, when they were little.'

If the Morrisons thought the pictures were compelling evidence that the babies had been switched, Jessie Jenkins thought the opposite. She was more than ever convinced that Nola was a Jenkins.

4 THE BATTLE BEGINS

The *Truth* article was too much, even for the mild-mannered Noel Jenkins. Spurred on by his wife, he decided to travel to Melbourne the next day to see a solicitor. It was an angry man who paced into the offices of one of the city's most prosperous and capable solicitors, Bernard ('Rookie') Nolan.

Nolan was a big, strong man, tough both physically and mentally. He was just the type to have on your side for a prolonged encounter in the courts. As a younger man he had captained Melbourne Football Club, one of the country's most famous Australian Rules teams and he still maintained a keen interest in sports, including boxing and shooting. Saturday nights would find him driving the notorious promoter, gambler and business czar John Wren to the Wren-owned stadium for an evening of pugilism. Sundays were often spent on a farming property near Kyneton and it was here that he and Noel Jenkins became shooting partners and later friends. Now, however, the partnership was to be professional.

Nolan tried to soothe his friend, reassuring him there was little to worry about, saying, 'It's a lot of hot air that will soon blow over.' The eminent solicitor was soon to learn that there was a fire burning behind that hot air and that it would soon be out of control.

Visiting Melbourne that same day was William Henry Morrison, en route to his role in Australian legal history. Morrison was armed with the address of another top solicitor, John William Galbally, better known as Jack. *Truth* newspaper had pointed Bill Morrison in that direction. Galbally, like Nolan, had been a top-class footballer, but he had played with the opposition working-class team of Collingwood. He was at the peak of his career, one of Melbourne's great criminal lawyers, with a massive practice. Again, like Nolan, Galbally was a man of tremendous physical strength, described by one of his colleagues as 'a brave trier, no style, but terrific determination'.

Galbally was no instant convert to the Morrison cause. He was too worldly wise to believe the story that Bill Morrison told him. Something about it though, had a ring of truth. It sounded utterly implausible, laughable perhaps, but he could not just dismiss it.

In the end he compromised. He told Bill Morrison: 'Bring your wife down and I'll have a chat with her.'

Their meeting, face-to-face, was momentous. They quickly forged an unlikely bond, the urbane city lawyer and the honest, straightforward country housewife. When she left Galbally's offices Gwen Morrison was carrying a promise of unstinted legal support.

Galbally, a devout Catholic, was unable to resist the challenge to right what he saw as a terrible wrong. No worthy mother, he reasoned, should be deprived of her own flesh and blood. Gwen Morrison, too, was a Catholic, but her faith was not the motivating force in her desire to win Nola from the Jenkinses. True, they were Protestants, but that did not concern her greatly. Like Galbally, she believed passionately in a mother's right to her own child and could not imagine why Jessie Jenkins would not 'see reason'.

The memory of that early meeting with Gwen Morrison and her husband has never left Jack Galbally:

'These people came to me and I thought it was my professional obligation, wasn't it? Particularly where children were concerned, who couldn't speak for themselves. I thought, well, the matter had to be sifted and cleared if possible. I thought they were understanding people. No histrionics about it. But they were anxious that the truth should prevail.'

Despite the ages of the two children — they were now nearly three and strongly attached to their families — Galbally is certain to this day that the Morrisons did the right thing in deciding to pursue their case in the courts since the belief that the child was not theirs, would have tainted the rest of their lives.

The Morrisons were frank with their solicitor. They told him they wanted to fight a case but where could they raise the money? Galbally told them he would take up their cause, even if he had to do it for nothing.

So, with Nolan representing the Jenkinses and Galbally taking on the Morrisons' case, both sides had chosen excellent captains for the legal struggle that was to follow.

Galbally acted promptly with a letter dated 6 February 1948, addressed to Mr and Mrs N. Jenkins. It read:

Dear Sir and Madam,

I have been consulted by Mr and Mrs Morrison of Kyneton with reference to what they claim to be the mistaken identity of their child Johanne Lee and of your child Nola.

At the outset, let me convey to you that I regard this as being a matter of a delicate nature and in acting herein I am most anxious to avoid causing any distress to either yourselves or my clients.

The matter is to me something more than a mere matter of litigation and as children of a tender age are concerned I am desirous of settling this matter in a lawful and amicable manner.

Mrs Morrison advises me that as a result of certain observations made at the time of the birth of the said children and as a result of subsequent medical tests, she is now in possession of information which proves that you have the custody of the child born to her on or about the 22nd day of June 1945 and that she has the custody of the child born to you on or about the 22nd day of June 1945.

Mr and Mrs Morrison have great love and affection for Johanne Lee and would be loath to part with her. No doubt your feelings are the same in regard to Nola. Nevertheless my clients are most anxious that the mistake be immediately rectified so as to avoid as much upset to the children as possible.

With a view to settling this matter with the minimum of distress, I would be pleased if you both would make an appointment to see me at your earliest convenience and, if you feel so inclined, to bring with you your local clergyman or other trusted confidante.

Yours faithfully,
John W. Galbally

On 10 February Bernard Nolan replied:

Dear Sir,
Re Jenkins and Morrison
Yours of the 6th instant to Mr and Mrs N. Jenkins of Kyneton has been handed to me with instructions to reply thereto.

My clients are satisfied that there has been no mistake about the children and that they have their own child.

They are, therefore, not prepared to do anything further and resent the publicity being given to the matter which can serve no useful purpose.

Yours faithfully,
Bernard Nolan

Just three days later Galbally wrote again, this time direct to Nolan:

Dear Sir,
Re Morrison and Jenkins
I have your letter of the 10th instant.

My clients are very anxious to have this matter determined without recourse to litigation and the consequent sorrow and anguish which must occur to all parties concerned.

In an effort then to adjust this matter amicably I suggest that two prominent and highly qualified doctors be appointed, one to be selected by either party, who would carry out blood tests on both the children concerned and their parents.

Whose Baby?

My clients had a blood test by a leading Collins St specialist on the 9th September, 1946. The finding of the doctor may be inspected by you at my office.

Blood tests are well known at law and are a scientific formula which do not permit of any mistake. In this regard I would refer you to articles in the *Australian Law Journal*, Volume 6, Page 113, Volume 9, Pages 53 and 131, Volume 12, Pages 413 and 416, and Volume 13, Page 479.

The reluctance on the part of your clients to submit to a blood test can hardly be said to do their cause any good and I would strongly urge them to reconsider their earlier attitude.

No harm, I suggest, can possibly result from the taking of a blood test and, as I say, it may be the means of having this matter determined with a minimum of distress.

Would you please be good enough to take this matter up with your clients in the spirit which it is intended and I trust the matter may then be determined speedily and with as little inconvenience as possible.

Yours faithfully,
John W. Galbally

Nolan did not reply.

By now the Morrisons realized that they could no longer remain in Kyneton, so close to the family they were preparing to fight. Thirty-five years later Bill Morrison could still remember those harrowing last days in Kyneton with the tongues wagging. 'Too much speech and conversation about the baby case and it didn't appeal to me.' But where could they go? They talked of returning to Bill Morrison's home State, Western Australia, and they also considered a move back to the Murray River town of Mildura. Ultimately though, they settled for a most unlikely place, the dry, dusty little wheat township of Woomelang in Victoria's Mallee district.

Few people in Victoria know where Woomelang is but to the Morrisons it offered a kind of haven, a place where they could live anonymously. Even more, it promised them the comfort and support of close relations, Gwen Morrison's sister Gloria and her policeman husband George Bock, who had made their home in Woomelang. Constable Bock was the right man to help you in a crisis. He was close to being the number one citizen of Woomelang, a tall, broad-shouldered man who had coached the local football team, was an excellent tennis player, loved shooting and fishing and, on top of all that, maintained what law and order was needed in the peaceful little town.

Woomelang was not a very exciting place in which to live. Just a hundred or so houses, one main street, one pub, a few shops and a hall. Early this century it had enjoyed remarkable prosperity as a major railway junction, but gradually declined. The surrounding countryside is flat and featureless and used to be covered with clumps of scrub-like, stunted eucalypts, known as mallee scrub, the only vegetation able to survive the sparse rainfall which averages only 250 mm a year. When the farmers moved in and cleared thousands upon thousands of acres to plant wheat and raise sheep they created an imbalance in nature which still affects Woomelang in bad years.

The absence of the mallee scrub makes the fine, red topsoil turn into vast, thick, choking dust storms when the strong summer winds blow. Woomelang can just disappear beneath a carpet of red dust which easily penetrates closed windows and doors.

There's another odd natural phenomenon in that little Mallee town. Every few years the mice come. Mice by the billion. A plague of mice that cannot be stopped, that eat their way through doors and walls and drive people from their homes. The stench is unbelievable, the droppings everywhere, and that army of tiny rodents become so numerous that the cats of Woomelang and other Mallee towns have long become indifferent to them.

The townspeople use every means at their disposal to kill them, even elaborate traps involving complex mazes and pits. Some have even adopted a siege mentality and surrounded their homes with medieval style concrete ramparts or moats.

When they gather up the corpses it's not by the bucket, or by the bag but by the truckload. Tonnes of dead mice go on to a giant pile, petrol is tipped over them and the blaze can be seen for miles.

Whose Baby?

When the Morrisons arrived in Woomelang, religion still ruled the town. Drinking and Sunday sport were taboo. Longtime resident Dorothy ('Dot') Dettmann, George Bock's doubles partner on the tennis court, recalls the arrival of the Morrisons and how they joined a small rebel group of which she was a leading member. These were the ones who did not frequent the Methodist Church, enjoyed a few beers and played sport whenever they felt like it, Sundays included.

'There was a group of us that would go to the hotel and have a drink. The Morrisons joined that group,' she remembers. Dot's husband George, prosperous proprietor of the general store, donated some land to the town to be used for a lawn bowling club. He had been there since 1912 and had more than a little influence among the populace. However, even though he was the donor of the land, he could not prevent the 'wowsers' from writing into the constitution of the bowling club that strong liquor would never be permitted on its premises. That rule still applies.

Only George Bock and his wife Gloria knew the real reason for the Morrison family's arrival in the town. Eventually, however, the gossip started to spread.

For Bill Morrison, the move to Woomelang meant more than escaping from the gossip-mongers of Kyneton. It presented him with the opportunity of going into business on his own, something that had been a lifetime dream. He was always a bit of a dreamer and the business at Woomelang, like so many other ventures in his life, was doomed to failure. The idea seemed sound and he was depending on George Bock to open a few doors for him. Ultimately the town was too small to support his business and he had to abandon his grand ideas and take a job working for an established panelbeater in the town.

Bill Morrison was not a sportsman but he mixed freely with his brother-in-law George Bock and others who gathered for a few beers in the local pub most evenings after work. Gwen Morrison, made rare visits to the pub, preferring to be at home with her family or passing the time of day with her sister, Gloria Bock, or close friends Marge McIntosh, Vera Hatcher and Dot Dettmann.

The sisters Gwen and Gloria were both 'home bodies', quiet,

reserved women who took some time to loosen up and make new friends. What a contrast it was when their mother, Amelia Williams, freewheeled her way into Woomelang for an occasional visit. Everybody got to know her in a hurry. As word got around about the alleged mix-up of babies, everybody also started to take notice of the youngest Morrison, the brown-eyed, dark-haired Johanne Lee.

Vera Hatcher remembers Lee well as 'the sweetest little kid'. And she remembers the Morrisons' obvious, outward affection for the girl — 'They were just devoted to Lee.' In fact, as Mrs Hatcher explains, the whole town took Lee to their hearts: 'I don't think there was a person in Woomelang who didn't love that kid.'

However, like every other mother in the town, Vera Hatcher unwillingly found herself comparing Lee with the two other Morrison children, Blair and Colleen. 'With her dark looks she was just like a fish out of water in the Morrison family,' she recalls.

There was one thing the three Morrison children *did* have in common: they were all groomed and dressed impeccably, by a mother who had little money but made all their clothes and would not let them set foot outside unless they were spotlessly clean and tidy. Dot Dettmann recalls: 'Gwen used to have them looking beautiful. She was a good mother.'

While the Morrisons were settling in to life in Woomelang the Jenkins family had tried to put behind them the traumatic story in *Truth* and the exchange of letters which followed. Their lawyer had assured them the Morrisons were only bluffing and with the departure of the Morrison family, Noel and Jessie Jenkins began to believe him.

Far from bluffing, the Morrisons were now embarked on a legal campaign to win custody of Nola. Galbally decided that the best manoeuvre was for them to take civil action against the Jenkinses in the Supreme Court. He assigned his younger brother, Francis Eugene Joseph Galbally, to start digging into the facts surrounding the birth. On 19 March Sister Elizabeth Lockhart was in her sickbed at St Andrew's Hospital where she had been working. There was a firm knock on the door and in strode an impressive-looking young man she had never set eyes on before. He introduced himself as Frank Galbally and, using his undoubted charms, asked her to assist him in a 'very important matter'. But when he explained what this 'important matter' was, Elizabeth Lockhart was very wary indeed. Soon the younger Galbally was finding the going tough.

He asked her whether she remembered an occasion about June 1945, when two children were born within a few minutes of each other at Kyneton. Sister Lockhart shook her head. She didn't remember that at all.

According to Galbally's notes, this is the conversation that followed:

Galbally: Well, their names were Morrison and Jenkins.
Elizabeth Lockhart: No, I don't remember that.
Galbally: You may have heard of a controversy about the circumstances of their births?
Lockhart: Oh yes, I do remember now.
Galbally: Do you remember any of the details about the circumstances of their birth?
Lockhart: No, not a thing.
Galbally: Well, Mrs Morrison says that she got the wrong baby on that occasion.
Lockhart: No, that would not be possible.
Galbally: Why not?
Lockhart: Because I dressed Mrs Morrison's baby before Mrs Jenkins' baby was dressed.
Galbally: Who took the babies out of the labour ward?
Lockhart: I don't know.
Galbally: Did you?
Lockhart: I took one of them out of the labour ward and another Sister took another one.

Galbally's manner was warm and friendly but his questioning was beginning to border on a courtroom cross-examination of a difficult witness. He tried another tack.

Galbally: Mrs Morrison says that on this occasion Dr

Loughran said to you, 'Be careful not to get those two babies mixed up and see that they are tagged.'
Lockhart: Oh, Dr Loughran was just being facetious.
Galbally: I thought you told me you didn't remember anything about the details of this occasion?
Lockhart: Oh well, some things stick out in my mind.
Galbally: Were the babies tagged?
Lockhart: Of course they would be.
Galbally: Well, I have been informed that the babies were not tagged at the hospital at that time?
Lockhart: Oh well, I would not know. I don't know that.

Sister Lockhart had had enough. She told the young lawyer she wanted no further part in any arguments about the babies. As he left that afternoon Frank Galbally realized there were going to be tough times ahead getting any assistance from the nurses to support his case. After all, if they were to admit that any slip might have occurred they could be seen to have been negligent themselves.

He reported back to the master tactician, brother Jack, who already had reached the same conclusion. Jack Galbally knew his best weapons for the fight ahead lay with the Morrisons themselves, particularly Gwen, the woman willing to risk her reputation to win back the child she considered hers. He sent instructions for Gwen and Bill Morrison and Amelia Williams to swear affidavits giving their side of the story.

Gwen Morrison outlined her recollections of the night of the birth, in detail from the moment she arrived at the hospital. A key section of her sworn statement referred to the babies being taken out of the labour ward:

> 'After Dr Loughran had finished attending to me either Sister Cass or Sister Lockhart took the two babies, one in either arm, out of the room. Each child was wrapped in a blanket or some covering cloth.'

This claim was to be hotly disputed and, even today, two of the nurses involved in the birth say that no trained person would ever carry two babies, one under each arm, as described by Gwen Morrison.

The affidavit also referred to Lee Morrison's appearance:

'As the baby grew older it was obvious that she was not like my other children or my husband or myself... I respectfully ask that the court order that the child Nola be returned to my husband and me.'

5 'SPRINGTIME' TURNS SOUR

The teenagers Noel Jenkins and Jessie Bull were drawn together by their love for music and the theatre and it was almost a foregone conclusion among their friends that they would eventually marry. Jessie had been singing from her early childhood, 'from the time I was old enough to remember the lines'. Although they had no ambitions to venture on to the stage in the big cities, they proudly trod the boards in Kyneton and little bush halls around the countryside. With groups of their friends they would pack into a few cars, drive out at night to some tiny hamlet and put on a musical for the gathered farmers and their wives, raising a few pounds for some local charity. They literally sang for their supper, taking no money for their services but enjoying a giant, country-style buffet after the curtain fell. It would be the early hours of the morning when they drove wearily home to Kyneton.

Jessie's birthday was 16 September and in 1936 they decided to make it a double celebration. A wedding and a birthday on the same day. She turned twenty-five that day and Noel was just two years older. Their theatrical flings were briefly interrupted in August 1937, when their first child, a boy they named Arthur, arrived. Again, in February 1942, Jessie was off centre stage for a time for the birth of another son, Arnold, and, of course, there was Nola's arrival in June 1945. Now it was August 1948, and Jessie was expecting their fourth child in a matter of a few weeks. For this reason she had again declined a leading role in one of her favourite shows, the hit musical 'Springtime'.

Baritone Noel was also on the sidelines because someone had

to look after the kids if Jessie was rushed off to hospital. Usually he either produced or starred in the Kyneton Musical Comedy Company productions and, even on this occasion, he couldn't keep himself out of the action entirely. He took the unlikely role of usher for the opening night while Jessie rested at home. The date was 10 August 1948, a bitterly cold winter's night, but the shire hall was packed with close to 850 people. These were the days when movies were infrequent, television was unheard of and locally staged theatre was just about the biggest entertainment available for country people.

There are many things in the past that Noel Jenkins cannot remember but he remembers with remarkable clarity the conversation that took place in the darkened theatre that night. 'On the night of the show I ushered a friend, Tom Quinn, to his seat and he said, "It was bad luck for you on the news tonight, Noel."

I said, "Oh yes, Tom, that's probably right."

I went away and it never registered. I didn't know what he was talking about. However, it played on my mind so I went back to him.'

In the darkened theatre he leant across from the aisle and whispered: 'Tom, you said something about me being on the news tonight. What do you mean?'

Quinn was obviously embarrassed and tried to brush it off, realizing he'd made a mistake. 'Forget it, forget about it,' he said, trying to reassure Noel Jenkins.

But Noel persisted, his voice rising, 'No, Tom. You've got to tell me.'

Reluctantly, Tom Quinn repeated: 'Didn't you hear the news tonight?'

'No, I was flat out getting up here and getting things ready.'

'Oh, you had an injunction brought down tonight, it was on the news. Nola is not your daughter.'

'You'd be joking?'

'No, it was on the news at seven o'clock.'

Noel didn't wait to hear any more. He rushed to the back of the hall, tossed his torch to someone else and muttered: 'You'll have to get another usher.'

As he raced out the doors of the hall there was one thought uppermost in his mind: to get home and break the news to Jessie before someone else beat him to it. The news was devastating enough to him, he hated to think what effect it would have on his pregnant wife. However, he was too late. Two reporters were standing on the doorstep of his home talking to Jessie as Noel turned into the drive. One was a local, a young man from Kyneton who was now working for the *Sun* newspaper in Melbourne.

Jessie Jenkins had been startled to hear the hammering on the door a few minutes earlier. She knew the young reporter from Kyneton but what he had to tell her was indeed shocking news, and she was too taken aback to invite them inside. So they began their interview in the cold and the dark. Noel had more presence of mind and suggested they all go inside and sit down by the fire. The two reporters were able to explain exactly what had happened.

The Morrisons had issued a writ demanding that the now three-year-old Nola Jenkins be handed over to them as their rightful child. Supreme Court Judge, Mr Justice Barry, ordered that Noel and Jessie Jenkins should appear on 20 August to show cause why Nola should not be taken from them. Australia's most famous legal case was about to begin. But, that night the reporters just wanted to know the Jenkins' side of the story. Up to that time, apart from a few scant remarks in the *Truth* article, there was nothing on the public record to dispute the Morrisons' claim.

Noel and Jessie Jenkins were polite but strictly formal with the newsmen. Any comment would have to come after they had consulted their solicitor. They maintained a stiff upper lip in front of the two journalists and it was not until the two men had left for the drive back to Melbourne that the Jenkins were able to let their emotions tumble out. In the past they had both been angry with the Morrisons. Now they were furious. More than that, they vowed that Nola would never be taken from them. Regardless of cost. Regardless of sacrifice.

Noel Jenkins was also perturbed that his good friend, solicitor Bernard Nolan, had somehow let him down. 'I still couldn't work out why somewhere along the line we weren't told that this was happening. It seems rather strange that the first we should know of it was that way. Out of the blue.'

Bernard Nolan had not, in fact, let him down. The news of the Morrison move was a bombshell to him, too. As he was to explain later, the first he heard of it was when he read it in the *Herald* newspaper.

Noel Jenkins had a troubled sleep that night so he was ready and eager to get up the following morning to catch the first train to Melbourne to see his solicitor. He and his wife had decided that they would instruct Nolan to take whatever action he felt necessary to end this whole heartbreaking affair once and for all.

Bernard Nolan had just finished reading the formal letter from the Morrisons' solicitor, Jack Galbally, notifying him of the legal move of the previous day, when Noel Jenkins was ushered into his office. Nolan was a little ill at ease explaining to Jenkins that he had been mistaken in his advice that the Morrisons were merely bluffing with their letters in February that year. Now they had a real fight on their hands.

Nolan agreed with his friend that only the best would do when it came to getting a barrister to represent them in what was going to be a case without precedent in Australian legal history. They would need a King's Counsel and junior and the two names he mentioned were already prominent among the country's legal fraternity.

Mr Edward Herbert ('Ted') Hudson, KC, was a big man in every respect. Then aged fifty, tall and strongly built, he strode through the courts of Melbourne with a heavy tread that echoed along the corridors. He was no 'dasher' among barristers, but a steady, conservative man who prepared his cases meticulously and delivered his addresses in court with a deep, resonant voice. His junior would be Henry Winneke, still a young man but one who was destined for greatness as Chief Justice of Victoria and, later Governor of the State of Victoria. Knighted along the way, Winneke was always known for his down-to-earth attitude, he got on well with ordinary people, and it was he who played a key role in formulating the tactics later used in fighting the case.

It would not be cheap, Nolan warned Jenkins, but the Kyneton man said he and his wife had decided on a policy of win-at-all-costs. Nolan, like his rival solicitor Jack Galbally, now made hasty preparations for the upcoming case. Finding witnesses to that fateful night of 22 June 1945, might be no easy task. As they were to learn, all three nurses involved in the delivery of the two babies were no longer at the Kyneton hospital and even Dr Gerald Loughran had left the town.

Why this sudden exodus from Kyneton? Gerald Loughran, now thirty-two, had lived in Kyneton most of his life, following his father into the established practice in the town. He was well-liked, prosperous and had every reason to stay. Even today, thirty-five years later, some people still argue that Gerald Loughran got out because he wanted to avoid the controversy that he knew was coming. On the other hand, Loughran made no secret of his departure, made no effort to disguise that he was going. Noel Jenkins, who knew the doctor well, says, 'he wasn't the type of man that would back away from anything. He always gave me the impression he would relish getting into it.'

Mrs Jenkins agrees: 'You don't just take off to places like that. That was part of their plans. We knew they were leaving.'

Part of the explanation probably lies with his wife, Patricia, a woman who liked to travel and was obviously unhappy in Kyneton. She hated the winter weather and had always been attracted to life in more tropical climes, more exotic places. Added to that, it was common gossip around the town that Patricia Loughran preferred the independence of living further away from her husband's family.

As for the three nurses, the explanation for their departure is reasonably simple. All had been assigned to the Kyneton Hospital under wartime arrangements and it was understandable that they would leave for other parts when free to do so. Elizabeth Lockhart left in October 1945, just months after the Japanese surrender and long before the rumours of 'mixed babies' came back to the hospital. Tessie Atkinson stayed on until July 1947, returning to Melbourne to be closer to the man with whom she had fallen in love. She even gave up nursing because the night shift limited her time with the same man who later became her husband.

Olive Cass left Kyneton less than eight weeks later to further her career in nursing, a calling to which she has dedicated her whole life. She did not sever her links with the hospital and willingly returned on several occasions as a relieving sister when they were short-staffed.

Bernard Nolan found it surprisingly easy to find the three nurses who had been in the maternity ward that night. Sister Lockhart was now working at St Andrew's Hospital in East Melbourne; Olive Cass was also working in Melbourne and living in the northern suburb of Strathmore; Tessie Atkinson had quit nursing and was staying at her parents' home in a western suburb, Braybrook. She had taken a job at Melbourne's biggest retail store, the Myer Emporium, and was working behind the glove counter when young solicitor Joseph Wren approached and asked her to make a statement for the court case.

The young Tessie Atkinson was so nervous and overcome by the occasion that she thought he was John Wren the gambler, the man whose name was always in the news, and she could not understand why he would be involved in a case about babies. Even though she was very flustered she decided instantly not to get involved and she politely but firmly told Joseph Wren, who, in fact, was a son of John Wren, that she had no intention of swearing any affidavits.

Olive Cass was more forthcoming. She swore in her affidavit that both babies were placed in cots tagged with their mother's names and no mistake could have been made. Elizabeth Lockhart agreed, but also added, 'I did not carry the babies out of the ward, nor do I remember either of the other sisters doing so.'

Nolan must have realized that a vital witness was undoubtedly Dr Gerald Loughran, the man who had delivered the two babies and had also carried out the only blood tests on the Jenkins parents and young Nola. He was not so easy to find. On 20 August, Nolan obtained an adjournment of seven days to give him extra time. Then he won a further adjournment to 21 September, telling Mr Justice Barry that he had encountered difficulty finding Dr Loughran.

The task of finding Gerald Loughran should not have been so very demanding. When the doctor was eventually located he was holidaying with his in-laws in Broome, Western Australia: the McDaniels, probably the best known family in the whole town. Their patriarch, going by the most unlikely name of Daniel McDaniel, had gone to sea as a young man and been fortunate enough to survive a shipwreck in a wild storm off the Western Australian coastline. After that experience he decided to stay ashore and became one of the pioneers of Broome's famous pearling industry. His only daughter, Patricia, married Gerald Loughran after they met while working together at a hospital in Melbourne.

Apart from his problem tracking down Dr Loughran, Nolan reported another cause for delay in preparing his case. Jessie Jenkins was due to have another baby in about three weeks.

On 21 September the public at last heard the Jenkins' side of the matter. Up till then, only the Morrison view of events had received any airing, either inside or outside court. On this day Nolan presented to the court detailed rebuttal of the Morrison claim to Nola, in the form of affidavits sworn by Noel and Jessie Jenkins.

The Jenkinses stated categorically they were convinced that fair-haired, blue-eyed Nola was their baby, for many reasons. They produced photographs of their two sons, Arthur, eleven, and Arnold, six, and listed family physical characteristics which they claimed Nola shared. They said blood tests taken by Dr Gerald Loughran showed that Nola could be their child.

In detail, Jessie Jenkins swore:

'My sons Arthur and Arnold had fair hair as babies and resembled Nola. My grandfather had very blue eyes and fair skin. My grandmother's family also had similar characteristics. My father had brown eyes but very fair skin and sandy hair. My mother had fair skin and hazel eyes, but dark hair, and I have fair skin and hazel eyes.'

Noel Jenkins swore that he, too, believed there were strong resemblances between Nola and her two brothers and his wife's grandfather.

Mr Justice Barry questioned their barrister, Henry Winneke,

about Dr Loughran's blood tests and asked whether the family planned to seek further blood tests. Winneke replied no. He said the Jenkinses had sought expert advice and were satisfied there was no blood test that could positively say whether Nola was a Morrison or a Jenkins. Such tests could be negative but could not be positive, Winneke argued. He went on to make an important point for his clients: the onus was on the Morrisons to prove two things. They must first establish that Nola's parents were not Noel and Jessie Jenkins and, second, that Gwen and Bill Morrison were.

Winneke told the court the Jenkinses were satisfied Nola was their child. They also took the view that it would be a tragedy for both children if they should be removed from the family circle in which each had been reared.

Mr Justice Barry asked, 'You don't claim any difficulty in having blood tests made?'

Mr Winneke, then probably summed up the whole crux of the argument on the Jenkins side. He told the judge:

> 'We are fully conscious that such arrangements could be made, if desired. But my clients are convinced that the child is theirs and they feel, on expert advice, that no test would prove the child was the Morrisons', it would only prove she was not the Jenkins', and irrespective of any scientific tests they would be loath to be convinced against what was their human judgement.'

The first of what were to be many surprising developments in the case came on this day when a layman joined the judge on the Bench. Mr Justice Barry introduced him as Dr Frederick Grantley Morgan, director of the Commonwealth Serum Laboratories, and announced that he would act as scientific assessor in the case. He quickly pointed out that Dr Morgan's participation in the hearing would be confined to 'assisting the court upon scientific questions' and it would be up to the judge himself to decide the case.

It was plain, however, that the scientist's presence in the court indicated the judge's strong belief that blood would be a key issue. He made the point himself:

> 'It appears from affidavits that have already been before me that the correct interpretation of blood group tests and the accurate assessment of the value of evidence upon that aspect may be of considerable importance in this case.'

It was barrister Henry Winneke who then supplied the second surprise of the day. He announced that Jessie Jenkins would be unavailable to give evidence for at least a fortnight. She had given birth, the day before, to a baby girl. In the same delivery room, at Kyneton Hospital, where this whole affair had begun.

6 TEARS IN COURT

Colleen Morrison was only five years old when the case began, yet it is something she has never forgotten. Like any little girl she remembers only a few striking details, like the clothes her mother wore to court and the tears. There were to be many tears.

On the day that the case really got under way, Wednesday, 29 September 1948, Colleen sat in the Supreme Court in Melbourne between her mother and her grandmother as Mr Justice John Vincent William Barry (known to his mates as Jack) strode in at precisely 10.30 a.m. For someone of such tender years, Colleen Morrison's memory is remarkably accurate. Her mother was dressed in the smartest outfit she owned, a grey suit and a big black hat. 'I remember sitting in a courtroom. I can still see Mum in the witness box. Nanna was sitting beside me. Nanna was crying and Mum was crying.'

Gwen Morrison had managed to bottle up her emotions extremely well during the agonizing period of half an hour or so before the judge entered. When she was finally called, as the first witness in the case, her control slipped and she burst into tears on her way into the witness box. She sobbed through the taking of the oath and she was still crying when the tall, imposing barrister for the Jenkinses, Ted Hudson, rose to commence the action. He had to pause and wait, and his first question of this historic trial was to be a sympathetic: 'Are you in a position to answer questions yet?'

Gwen Morrison replied in a halting, weak voice: 'I am alright, thanks.'

Lined up beside Hudson, KC, was his junior, Henry Winneke, a redoubtable talent about to make his mark as a courtroom strategist. Briefing them was Noel Jenkins' old shooting mate, solicitor Bernard Nolan.

At the other end of the Bar table from the rather dour, conservative Hudson, was the Morrisons' KC. Solicitor Jack Galbally had chosen well. Leading his team was fifty-year-old Robert Vincent Monahan, witty, urbane, erudite, and blessed with the sense of humour and retentive memory for amusing anecdotes that could be called upon to keep an entire courtroom in his thrall. Monahan was called to the bar in 1922, and had steadily built his reputation in the 1930s, a period he once jokingly described as 'when barristers were so hard up we were taking in each other's washing'. By the time he figured in another sensational case, a murder trial known as 'the Pyjama Girl case', in the mid-forties, Monahan's name was a household word.

He had remarkable success in criminal cases and, as a dedicated opponent of hanging, he was proud to boast on his retirement that he lost only one client to the gallows. To give Monahan his due, he faced an uphill battle then. The defendant, one Tommy Johnson, had axed two men to death in a dosshouse in a maniacal fit of rage. Johnson had been trying to pick race winners when his concentration was disturbed by another dosser chopping firewood in the room above. They argued, Johnson went berserk, grabbed the axe and killed the man. The second victim was unfortunate enough to hear the ruckus and arrive on the scene before Johnson had time to calm down. He went the same way. As he stood on the trap, the noose around his neck, Johnson was asked if he had any last words. The illiterate, half-mad Johnson outdid the eloquence of his brilliant courtroom advocate with these immortal final words: 'Hang on till I finish this fag.' It was a story that Rob Monahan often told, part in amusement and partly to illustrate the futility of capital punishment.

Monahan's junior was Charles Augustine Sweeney, a more serious man but another fine speaker. Not only had Galbally secured the services of two of Victoria's most outstanding barristers, he had also managed to convince them that justice demanded that the Morrisons win this case. Such was their acceptance of the Morrison cause that both Monahan and Sweeney agreed to waive all fees.

Seated in the court were most of the key witnesses: Bill Morrison, Amelia Williams and nursing sisters Olive Cass, Elizabeth Lockhart and Tessie Atkinson. Dr Gerald Loughran was missing. Noel Jenkins was seated noticeably apart from his adversaries, the Morrisons. He cast a lonely figure in the court, his wife Jessie still absent in Kyneton Hospital with the latest addition to the family, daughter Helen.

Mr Justice Barry was a relative newcomer to the Bench, having sat on his first case only eighteen months earlier. At forty-five, he was the youngest judge of the Supreme Court and had made a spectacular rise through the legal ranks of his State. It is not too much to say that here was one of the finest minds in the country. Barry had been a great champion of the individual's rights and a man not frightened to defend unpopular causes. Such was his versatility as a lawyer that it was not uncommon for him to appear in the Criminal Court to defend a client on a murder charge one day, spend the next in the High Court arguing some involved constitutional issue and finish the week in the Arbitration Court dealing with industrial law. Little wonder, too, that he was one of the highest-paid barristers in practice before ascending to the Bench.

Jack Barry had many friends and admirers inside the Labor Party hierarchy but they had been too few in number when it really mattered, when a plum job, a seat on the High Court of Australia, fell vacant in 1946. Arthur Calwell, later Federal Leader of the Opposition, backed Barry for the position but Dr Herbert Vere Evatt, then Attorney-General, had the numbers and swung them behind a more conservative candidate, Queensland's Chief Justice, Sir William Webb.

No one was to know it at the time, of course, but Webb's appointment ahead of Barry was to ultimately have far-reaching effects on the lives of Nola Jenkins and Johanne Lee Morrison. Barry was unlucky to have missed out on the High Court role and the court itself was unfortunate to have missed out on the talents of John Vincent William Barry.

Above: The hint of what was to come was far away when this picture was taken on 23 January 1937.

The local newspaper, the *Sunraysia Daily*, reported: 'On the arm of Major Chanter (Trentham Cliffs Station), Miss Gwen Alberta Logan made a dainty picture as she entered St Margaret's Mildura, for her marriage to William Henry Morrison.'

Flanking the couple are Gwen's sister Gloria (described as very striking in her gown of soft shaded lemon georgette) and Ted Mayall, who attended the groom as best man.

Gloria was later to marry policeman George Bock in the same church.

Below: Where it all began. The old bluestone hospital on the hill, overlooking Kyneton, where Nola Jenkins and Lee Morrison were born on 22 June 1945.

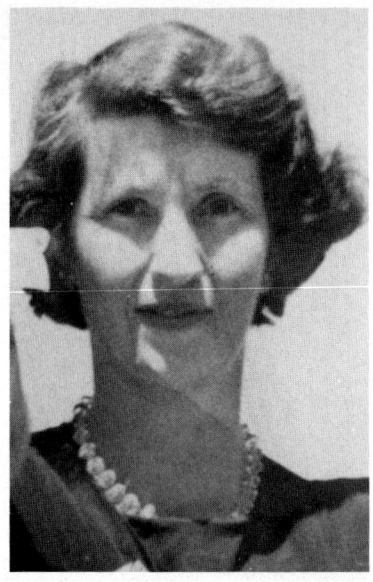

Above left: Gwen Morrison
Above right: Jessie Jenkins
Below: The front page story that changed two families' lives. *Truth*, the racy tabloid weekly, broke the exclusive news of the Morrisons' claim to Nola Jenkins.

Above: Whose baby? Lee Morrison, just weeks after her birth, in the arms of her brother Blair with sister Colleen. By now the family were starting to have terrible doubts.
Below: Gwen Morrison with her first daughter, Colleen, and the proud grandmother Amelia Williams. Gwen is 28 and her mother 47.

Above: Although a battler, Bill Morrison always managed to dress right up with the fashion. Gwen, too, was a smart dresser and young Blair, their first child, was being groomed in the same style.
Below left: The man who delivered the babies, Dr Gerald Loughran. The second generation Kyneton man left for Singapore as the case began. What he had to tell of the night of the births would have been invaluable.
Below right: Gwen Morrison's brother-in-law, policeman George Bock, on the tennis courts in Woomelang with his doubles partner Dot Dettmann. Bock was the man the Morrisons turned to when they left Kyneton and began their court case. Dot Dettmann firmly believes the Morrisons were right. Gwen Morrison was one of her closest friends during their stay in Woomelang.

The characteristics which made Jack Barry one of the great jurists of the land were not immediately apparent to the witnesses sitting in his court for the 'Whose Baby' case, as it was soon to be dubbed. Barry spoke quietly, often to the extent where people were straining forward to hear his words. At this stage, too, there was no sign yet of the ferocity with which he could cross-examine a recalcitrant witness. Before the case was much older, some would feel the lash of his tongue.

Barry obviously grasped from the beginning the impact this matter — the ugly public contest over two small children — was going to have on many people. There were those intimately concerned; the parents, the two girls, their brothers and sisters and other relatives. There were also the legal precedents which might be set and a mass of public opinion which would soon rear up. One of the judge's first moves was to order that a shorthand writer take notes of the case. 'Having regard to the history of the matter...' he explained, '...this is a matter which requires there should be a proper record.'

Another surprise was then to emerge which caused Jack Barry's hackles to rise and give those newcomers to his court a taste of his tougher side. Hudson, KC, for Noel and Jessie Jenkins, rose and pointed out that Dr Gerald Loughran was not in the court and, in fact, there was little likelihood of him ever appearing. Hudson explained that an urgent telegram had been sent to the doctor in Broome, Western Australia, telling him that his presence was required for cross-examination. The cable read: 'Advise when convenient for you to be present.'

Loughran had finally been traced to his wife's parents' home in Broome and it was his wife who replied to the urgent summons. The answer was blunt: 'Doctor unavailable. Leaving Australia. Patricia Loughran.'

Barry was plainly unhappy with this cavalier attitude. He rounded on Hudson and demanded: 'Do I understand from this no further efforts will be made to procure the attendance of Dr Loughran?'

Hudson: I do not know what further...
Barry: The answer is very imprecise. The telegram merely says

that the doctor is unavailable, is leaving Australia, not that he has left.
Hudson: That is in accordance with the advice we previously received, that he is going to Singapore. I do not know that there is any reason to challenge the bona fide of that.
Barry: Except that it would have been much better if the lady had indicated his date of departure.
Hudson: I thank Your Honour for the suggestion.

In Loughran's absence, the court had to make do with an affidavit he had sworn in Broome and mailed to the hearing. It was read out by Hudson's junior, Winneke, and stated, in part:

'I, at the request of Mr and Mrs Jenkins made blood tests of them and the child Nola... in the course of my practice I have had considerable experience in making blood tests and considering the results thereof... although the records of the said blood tests are inaccessible to me, from my recollection of the same I say that the child Nola could be the child of the union between Mr and Mrs Jenkins.'

Loughran did not say so in the affidavit, but in an earlier message sent to the Jenkins' solicitor, Bernard Nolan, the doctor had been more specific about the blood tests he had carried out. He told Nolan, 'Test made by myself showed child could be of Jenkins parentage according to main blood groups...'

'According to main blood groups.' Was that a proper scientific yardstick to prove parentage conclusively? On one side the Morrisons had lined up some of the country's foremost experts in blood testing. The Jenkinses were standing by the opinion of a country GP.

Wasn't the simple way out for the Jenkinses to take Nola and themselves along for more expert testing? Bernard Nolan swore to the court that he made 'strenuous efforts' to find out just how efficient blood tests would be. And he said he contacted four highly qualified experts but was unable to find anyone 'competent and willing' to test his clients and Nola. All that aside, the Jenkinses did not need blood tests to convince themselves that Nola was their child. They were utterly convinced and regarded the Morrisons as being strangely obsessed with the desire to take their Nola. Finally, they reasoned that even if — and it was unthinkable anyway — even if Nola was not their child, it was too late to tear their family apart.

Many years later, when both girls had grown up, Jessie Jenkins was to recall:

> 'You've got to remember they were not week-old, or fortnight-old, or four-week-old babies. It had gone until the children had become part of the family and I could never quite see why they had this obsession, and it was an obsession, about wanting Nola as theirs. I did sit down and think, "What if it had happened?" And I thought, "Well, the only child I've ever known is Nola." She was mine in every respect of the word. Well, I was fortunate enough, I suppose, that I was quite sure she was mine and I was convinced of that. And the tests did prove us OK.'

After her tearful entry into the witness box, Gwen Morrison was soon to shatter any illusions that she might have been a mixed-up, emotional housewife. She answered questions quickly and concisely and demonstrated a memory of remarkable clarity. Mr Justice Barry, who would rely greatly on the demeanour of witnesses in forming the fragments of his judgement, quickly assessed her as a woman of some character and considerable reliability. It had not escaped his appreciation that the woman in the witness box had a great deal to lose if she was not believed. Her reputation, her morality, was on trial.

Gwen Morrison, under slow, patient cross-examination by the opposition barrister Hudson, revealed that she had spent two days in the hospital as a result of a false alarm, about ten days before the birth of her daughter on Friday 22 June 1945.

Hudson: When you went there, I suppose we may take it that you took all the proper clothing for the expected baby?
Gwen Morrison: Yes, my clothing was left there in the hospital

when I went there the first time.
Hudson: I suppose you took all the usual clothing, including the rug for the baby?
Morrison: Yes.
Hudson: Were all the garments marked with your name?
Morrison: Yes.
Hudson: Coming to the morning of the 22nd of June, I gather from your affidavits, that you lost consciousness; that is to say you ceased to become aware of what was going on around you?
Morrison: I don't think I ever lost consciousness.
Hudson: You were aware of all that was going on throughout, that is your belief?
Morrison: Yes.

Already Hudson had zeroed in on two key issues in the case: name tags for the babies and Gwen Morrison's state of consciousness when her daughter was born.

Gwen Morrison said Sister Cass had shown her to her bed in the labour ward and she later saw Sister Atkinson in the ward. She told the court she chatted briefly to Sister Atkinson, who then left the ward and she did not see her again.

Hudson: According to what you swear, Sister Atkinson was not in the room for a substantial time before your baby was born?
Gwen Morrison: No, I didn't see Sister Atkinson when the baby was born.
Hudson: She was in the room for a substantial time before the baby was born?
Morrison: I don't remember seeing her there at all.
Hudson: You could see very easily all that was going on in the room?
Morrison: A screen was put up. Until the screen was put up I could, yes.
Hudson: After the screen was put up you could not see what was going on behind the screen?
Morrison: I could see the shadows behind the screen. It was only a thin screen, made of thin material.

Hudson: The screen was between the bed you occupied and the bed that Mrs Jenkins subsequently occupied?
Morrison: Yes.
Hudson: On your side of the screen there was a cot placed by Sister Cass, was there?
Morrison: No, there was not.
Hudson: Did you see, either through the screen or by any other means, a cot placed on the other side of the screen, or near Mrs Jenkins?
Morrison: I seem to remember when I went there, before the screen was put there, that there was a bassinet against the far wall, one of those folding types, a canvas sort of thing.
Hudson: A wire cot was in the room, I suggest, one of those wire cots on wheels, either one or two of those. Did you see them?
Morrison: No.
Hudson: Will you swear there was no wire cot in that room during the period you were there up to the birth of your child?
Morrison: Yes, I will swear that definitely.
Hudson: You have seen Sister Cass's affidavit?
Morrison: Yes.
Hudson: You realize she has sworn that there were cots alongside these beds?
Morrison: Yes.
Hudson: Are you prepared to deny that?
Morrison: Yes.
Hudson: Did you see any signs of clothing that was brought into the hospital by you? Did you see it in the labour ward?
Morrison: No.
Hudson: Are you prepared to swear that during the time when you were giving birth to your baby and the period that followed it, up to the time when the baby left the room, that there was no other sister present besides Sister Cass and Sister Lockhart?
Morrison: Yes.
Hudson: In particular, during that period, Sister Atkinson was not in the room?
Morrison: No, I don't recollect seeing her there.

Hudson: And you are prepared to swear she was not there?
Morrison: Yes.

Two definite and critical differences of opinion were now obvious to the court, Sisters Cass and Lockhart had sworn in their affidavits that Sister Atkinson was present for the births, Cass had further sworn that cots were ready beside the beds to take the newborn infants. Gwen Morrison was now saying under oath that they were wrong on both counts. Obviously Sister Atkinson was going to be a vital witness in sorting out the truth of what happened in the labour ward that night.

Hudson continued his cross-examination, leading Gwen Morrison through the birth of her daughter.

Hudson: After your child had been delivered, you have told us you were still aware of what was going on?
Gwen Morrison: Yes.
Hudson: Who was assisting the doctor in the actual delivery of your child?
Morrison: Sister Lockhart.
Hudson: Can you tell us who took the baby after it was delivered?
Morrison: No, I have no idea.
Hudson: When the baby was actually delivered who took it from the doctor?
Morrison: The baby was born and was just left on the bed.
Hudson: How long was it on the bed?
Morrison: I cannot say, it was not very long.
Hudson: About how long?
Morrison: It is very hard to tell under these circumstances. About five minutes.
Hudson: Up to the time of it being taken away the only sister who had anything to do with you and the birth of your baby was Sister Lockhart?
Morrison: Yes.
Hudson: Sister Cass had nothing to do with it, nothing to do with the actual birth?
Morrison: No.

Gwen Morrison would not be swayed on two points: that the doctor was not present for the actual delivery of her child, he was still with Jessie Jenkins, and that Sister Lockhart was the only Sister there with her.

Gwen Morrison was now to relive the most critical moment of the night of the births, the moment when she saw the two babies being carried out of the labour ward under the arms of one nurse. Oddly enough, she was to be the only one present that night who would offer any recollection whatsoever of seeing a baby or babies being taken from the room.

Hudson: By whom was your baby taken out?
Gwen Morrison: The sister had her back turned to me and when the doctor asked her if she had the baby tags or tabs, she said, 'Yes doctor.' I didn't see her face.
Hudson: You were lying on the bed, your baby has been put there, it remains there for about five minutes, you are completely aware of what is going on and the sister takes your baby off the bed from in front of your eyes and you cannot tell us which sister it was?
Morrison: No, I don't remember the incident of the baby going off my bed at all.
Hudson: What was the first you knew of the baby, the first you saw of the baby after it had gone off your bed?
Morrison: When the sister brought the baby into the room.
Hudson: During the five minutes that followed the birth, there was still only Sister Lockhart there?
Morrison: On my side, yes.
Hudson: Before your baby was delivered, you had seen Sister Cass on the other side of the screen, had you?
Morrison: Yes.
Hudson: Do you say you were able to see her through the screen?
Morrison: I could see the shadows and I could see the top of their heads over the top of the screen.
Hudson: That enables you to identify the sister as Sister Cass, is that what you say?
Morrison: Yes.

WHOSE BABY?

Hudson: There was only one Sister attending to Mrs Jenkins?
Morrison: Yes.
Hudson: Could you say what was done with Mrs Jenkins' baby after it was delivered, immediately after it was delivered?
Morrison: I remember seeing the shadow of the doctor holding the baby by the feet and tapping it on the back.
Hudson: Can you tell us what was done with it then?
Morrison: No. The doctor came round and attended to me then.
Hudson: You have a faint idea of a bassinet being there. Can you tell us whether the Jenkins' baby was put in that bassinet?
Morrison: No, I have no idea.
Hudson: This bassinet that you think was there, the canvas one, is it your recollection that it was on your side of the room or the other side of the room?
Morrison: On Mrs Jenkins' side.
Hudson: You are pretty definite that the cot for your baby had not been brought into the room up to the time your baby was born, are you?
Morrison: Yes.
Hudson: What was your child wrapped up in when it was put on the bed?
Morrison: It was not in anything. It was just as it was born.
Hudson: As far as you are able to say, it was taken out of the room just as it was born?
Morrison: No, it was wrapped in something when it was taken out.
Hudson: What enables you to say that?
Morrison: When the doctor made that remark, I looked up and I could see she had the two little bundles, one in each arm. She turned at the door, half turned, and I could see she had the two little bundles wrapped in something. I had had my hand over my eyes, but when the doctor made that remark, I looked up.
Hudson: I thought you told me you did not see your baby until it was subsequently brought back by a sister?
Morrison: I didn't see the babies, they were wrapped up when they went out.

Hudson: What is it you say, that the baby one minute is lying on your bed in a naked state, then the next minute you hear the doctor say something, you look up and you see a sister turn round at that time with two bundles in her arms?
Morrison: She turned sideways on at the door to open the door to get out.
Hudson: She was pushing her way through the door?
Morrison: Yes.
Hudson: She opened the door herself?
Morrison: Yes.
Hudson: To do that, she had to turn sideways?
Morrison: Just slightly.
Hudson: And you realized immediately that it was your baby going through the door with the sister?
Morrison: She had the two babies.
Hudson: Do you mean to say you don't know, or is it that you have forgotten, you were not able to recognize, or that you have recognized and have forgotten which of the sisters who had been in the room was carrying out these two babies?
Morrison: I don't know who took them out.
Hudson: Is it because you were not able to recognize who it was?
Morrison: I did not see her face.
Hudson: How far was she from you?
Morrison: Not far.
Hudson: Because you did not see her face you are not able to recognize which sister it was that you saw?
Morrison: I don't know who the sister was who took the babies out.
Hudson: Are you quite sure you saw anybody carrying the babies out?
Morrison: I am positive. I had my hands over my eyes quite a lot of the time and when the doctor spoke I looked up and saw her.
Hudson: You didn't notice the sister, whoever it was, come to the bed and take the baby off the bed?
Morrison: No, I was very embarrassed and had my hand over my eyes quite a lot.

Hudson: It was only the doctor's voice that made you take notice of the incident?
Morrison: Yes. I probably would not have noticed otherwise.

In Mr Justice Barry's copy of the courtroom transcript there are many pencil marks in the margin, indicating sections of the evidence that he considered of foremost importance. There are many marks during Gwen Morrison's cross-examination, some single strokes and others heavy, repeated markings alongside key answers. When Hudson moved on to the question of the missing bunny rug the judge made a series of thick, black scrawls in the margin beside it. The transcript shows, too, that Barry thought the missing rug important enough to enter into the questioning of Gwen Morrison himself.

What had happened was that Mrs Morrison had brought a rug for her newborn baby into the hospital when she was first admitted, nearly a fortnight earlier, with a false alarm. When she returned home that rug and the other Morrison baby clothes were left at the hospital for her eventual return.

Hudson: Do you know where the robe or blanket that you saw each of these babies wrapped in was obtained from?
Gwen Morrison: It was not my blanket, because they couldn't find my blanket until the next day.
Hudson: And you don't know where it was obtained from?
Morrison: No.
Barry: Did you say they couldn't find your blanket until the next day?
Morrison: Yes.
Hudson: Your blanket was found the next day, was it not?
Morrison: Yes, it was found around the hot pipes.
Hudson: You didn't see your blanket that night, but you did see it the next day?
Morrison: Yes, the sister came the next day and asked me did I bring one. I think it was Sister Walsh who asked me if I had brought a blanket for the baby.
Hudson: This blanket you brought had your name on it, I suppose?

Morrison: Yes.
Hudson: And it was brought to the hospital with the set of baby clothes?
Morrison: Yes.
Hudson: When was the baby first dressed? When you first saw the baby after it was dressed, it was dressed in the clothes you had brought?
Morrison: Yes.
Hudson: But at that stage it did not have any blanket?
Morrison: It had a blanket but it was not mine.
Hudson: Whose blanket was it?
Morrison: It belonged to the hospital.
Hudson: In your affidavit you said that either Sister Cass or Sister Lockhart took the two babies out, one in each arm. Do you adhere to that statement, that it was either Sister Cass or Sister Lockhart?
Morrison: They were the only two in the labour ward.
Hudson: When the sister went out of the room, whoever it was with the two babies, you were left without anybody attending to you?
Morrison: No, the doctor was there. He was with me for quite a while after the babies went out.
Hudson: But there was no sister there?
Morrison: I seem to remember Sister Lockhart still being there, standing there with the tray of instruments.
Hudson: Is it your impression, therefore, that it was Sister Cass?
Morrison: I didn't see anybody else there.

Olive Cass was not in court to hear the way the line of questioning was going. With the other two nurses she had been ordered out of the court before Gwen Morrison began giving evidence. Now she was sitting fidgeting outside, waiting her turn to be called and when that turn did come she would strenuously deny that she carried two babies under her arms from the labour ward.

Even today, thirty-eight years after the event, Olive Cass insists that it is preposterous to suggest that any conscientious nursing sister would carry two babies at the same time. On the eve of her retirement as deputy matron at a Melbourne hospital, she declared that carrying two babies went against everything she was taught as a young nurse. At the time of the case she swore in her affidavit that she believed no mistake occurred on the night in question. Many years later she is able to reflect that perhaps some mistake did occur in Kyneton Hospital, but she is convinced it did not happen while she was still on duty. Could the babies have been switched some time over the next twenty-four hours? Olive Cass wonders about that.

Ted Hudson, continuing his cross-examination of Gwen Morrison, established that there was a time gap of no more than thirty minutes between her baby being taken out to be bathed and then being returned to her bedside, wrapped snugly in a blanket.

Hudson: Who was it brought it back?
Gwen Morrison: I don't know.
Hudson: You knew Sister Cass, you knew Sister Atkinson and you knew Sister Lockhart?
Morrison: Yes.
Hudson: Was it any one of those three?
Morrison: I wouldn't like to say as I don't know.
Hudson: You have forgotten it, is that what you say?
Morrison: I have forgotten who brought the baby back, yes.
Hudson: You at that time noticed that the baby was dark-haired and dark-complexioned?
Morrison: Yes.
Hudson: May we take it that that was the baby that was brought back to you within half an hour, at the outside, of its birth and that you took away with you when you ultimately left the hospital?
Morrison: Yes.
Hudson: So that, if any mistake was made, in the transposition of these babies, it was prior to that time?
Morrison: Yes.

These last two questions and answers are both heavily marked in the judge's transcript and from this point on all legal counsel for the Jenkinses and the Morrisons, and Mr Justice Barry, concentrated on the possibility of a mix-up occurring around the time of birth or not long after. They appear to have discounted the affidavit of the Morrison grandmother, Amelia Williams, who swore that she was shown a fair-haired baby when she went to the hospital more than twelve hours after the birth. It is surprising that neither side saw fit to call the remarkable Mrs Williams as a witness. She may have shed some light on this odd twist to the mystery. Instead, all parties settled on the time of birth as the key period when a mix-up may have happened, to the exclusion of any other theory.

Hudson's questioning of Gwen Morrison on her mother's role in the case was perfunctory.

> *Hudson:* Had she seen the baby when she saw you on the day of that first visit?
> *Gwen Morrison:* She asked sister if she could have a look at the baby.
> *Hudson:* And she saw the baby?
> *Morrison:* Yes.
> *Hudson:* And she saw it closely?
> *Morrison:* Yes.
> *Hudson:* And you went on living in the same house with her for about how long afterwards?
> *Morrison:* About six weeks.
> *Hudson:* Did your mother make any comment on the difference in the colouring or features of that child compared with your other children, at that stage, during that six weeks?
> *Morrison:* She said when she saw the baby, when I brought it home, that that was not the baby she saw in hospital.

Gwen Morrison went on to explain that her mother continually pointed out that the new child was unlike the two older Morrisons, Blair and Colleen. When she left her mother's home to live closer to her husband's army camp it was she who took up the subject with her husband. Mrs Morrison said her husband was happy with the new baby and was unworried by suggestions that the wrong child may have been given to them. He simply did not believe it. She explained to the court that it was at least six months after the birth before she was able to convince him that something was amiss and they had blood tests carried out in August 1946.

She agreed with Mr Hudson that in January 1948, nearly eighteen months after the blood tests, she gave an interview to *Truth* newspaper, which then went on to publish the first account of the alleged mix-up of babies. Hudson's questions grew sharper, more barbed, as he pursued her motives for confiding such a story to a newspaper, rather than using some private method of reconciliation or settlement.

Hudson: You knew that the reporter was there to get matter to be published, did you not?
Gwen Morrison: I did not know whether they were going to publish it or not.
Hudson: But you believed they might?
Morrison: Yes.
Hudson: You did not object to them publishing it, you did not ask the reporter not to publish it?
Morrison: No.
Hudson: You did not consider that the publicity, the publication of all the details surrounding this alleged mistake, in a newspaper like *Truth*, would be of any benefit to the child?
Morrison: I certainly did not like the publicity.
Hudson: You would agree, would you not, that it was a very undesirable thing, from the point of view of the child, whose ever it was?
Morrison: Yes.
Hudson: Did you think you were going to achieve any purpose by having the story published?
Morrison: I had tried every other way of getting my baby back.
Hudson: Did you really think that by publishing the story, or allowing it to be published, that that would get you possession of Nola?
Morrison: I thought Mrs Jenkins might realize then that she did have the wrong baby.
Hudson: By reading it in the newspaper? By reading it in *Truth*?

Morrison: Well, she had seen me often enough and she would not talk about it with me.
Hudson: Are you serious when you say you thought when Mrs Jenkins read the details published in *Truth*, that she might then come to the view that she had your baby?
Morrison: I thought she might take me to court or do something about it.
Hudson: Did you not arrange with the *Truth* reporter to consult a certain solicitor?
Morrison: I think my husband did.
Hudson: Was not this the set-up: that you give them the story, they would give you assistance in the taking of court proceedings to recover the child?
Morrison: No, he didn't say that to me.
Hudson: What you say quite seriously is, that the purpose of having the story published was to bring Mrs Jenkins to the view that she should give you back this child?
Morrison: Yes.
Hudson: Why did you think the publication in *Truth* of such a statement, including these details, would achieve any more purpose with Mrs Jenkins than by writing out the facts and sending them to her?
Morrison: I tried to discuss it with her, but she did not want to discuss it.
Hudson: You never wrote to her?
Morrison: No.
Hudson: Will you tell us why you thought it might be more convincing to her if she read it in a newspaper of this type than if she read it in a statement of fact by you?
Morrison: I don't know.
Hudson: Or a statement of fact by your solicitor?
Morrison: I don't know. All I wanted was the one thing... to get my baby back.
Hudson: Within six days after the publication of the article on the 31st of January, of the substance of the evidence you have given here, you consulted your present solicitor did you not?
Morrison: Yes.
Hudson: Had you ever had Mr Galbally act for you before?

Morrison: No.
Hudson: May I ask who recommended him to you, who suggested him to you? Was it the *Truth* reporter?
Morrison: I never connected it with the *Truth* reporter.
Hudson: Who was it who recommended you should go to him?
Morrison: My husband came home and said Mr Galbally would like to take the case.

That was virtually the end of Hudson's cross-examination and soon after Gwen Morrison was told she could step down from the witness box. By today's standards Hudson, and his clients, the Jenkinses, had been most chivalrous in their attitude to Gwen Morrison. At no stage had the gentlemanly Hudson tried to introduce any inference that the mystery of the Morrison baby might be solved by suggesting that she had been unfaithful to her husband while he was in army camp.

This gloved approach was to continue throughout the case, and to be ultimately endorsed by Mr Justice Barry. One wonders whether Gwen Morrison, innocent though she most certainly was, would have escaped so lightly in the more recent era of Family Law Court squabbles and bitter custody cases. Certainly all those in the court that day had been impressed by this woman, her demeanour and her ability to remember events of three years before. The next witness was to prove a lot harder to handle. She didn't even remember being there.

7 THE NURSE WHO CANNOT REMEMBER

'Call Annie Teresa Atkinson!' The voice boomed outside the Supreme Court room into the foyer where Tessie Atkinson sat waiting, a bundle of nerves. She had been in such a state over the impending case that her employers, the Myer Emporium, had sent a store detective along with her to the court for moral support. She remembers that her parents were away in Sydney on holidays at the time and she felt most vulnerable. In fact, the tension had been building up, off and on, for a couple of years. Tessie first heard rumours of a mix-up of babies when she was still nursing in Kyneton, long before the case ever made the headlines. She recalls hearing stories around the town and then one day in the nurses' home she held a discussion with Sister Cass and others when someone mentioned a mix-up of babies and someone else said, 'We'll all find ourselves in court.' It was said half-jokingly, but now the joke was becoming reality.

She recalls the long walk to the witness box: 'I was shaking like a leaf, I always go to pieces and my legs get wobbly.'

Both groups of lawyers and, indeed the judge, were anxious to hear her version of events. Tessie was the only key witness not to have sworn an affidavit. No one knew what she would say, what answers she could provide. Perhaps here was the one person who held the key to the mystery. But, if everyone had expected much from Tessie Atkinson, they were to be bitterly disappointed and, before the day was out, the lawyers and the judge would experience utter frustration. It may have been nerves that made her mind go blank, but Tessie Atkinson's memory of the important night in question was sketchy to say the least.

Whose Baby?

The examination began promisingly enough. Mr Justice Barry drew from her that she had been a single certificate nurse, not qualified as a midwife, at Kyneton, but had now left the profession and was working as a clerk.

Barry: Do you recollect anything concerning the birth of a child to a Mrs Morrison and the birth of a child to a Mrs Jenkins?
Tessie Atkinson: I can remember that I was on night duty at that particular time and that there were two babies born on the one morning, I suppose it was.
Barry: In the early hours of the morning, was it?
Atkinson: Yes.
Barry: You had come on night duty, when?
Atkinson: At nine o'clock I think we came on.
Barry: What time did you go off?
Atkinson: Seven o'clock we used to go off in the morning.
Barry: What were your duties on the night when those two babies were born in the early morning?
Atkinson: Well, to assist if they needed me.
Barry: What was the general nature of your duties that night?
Atkinson: Well, mainly I looked after the medical and surgical patients which were down one end of the ward. It was my duty to look after them.
Barry: Was it a primary part of your duty to have to do confinements that might occur during the night?
Atkinson: At times I did, yes.
Barry: If you ranked your duties in some order of priority, what would be your first duties?
Atkinson: Well, midwifery cases came before anything else, mainly.
Barry: And although you did not have an obstetrical certificate, you did participate in work relating to confinement, did you?
Atkinson: Yes, at times. I had to assist.

So far Miss Atkinson had been a perfect witness, answering all His Honour's queries with unhesitant answers. The difficulty was

THE NURSE WHO CANNOT REMEMBER

to arise when they moved into any sort of detail.
Barry: Why did Sister Lockhart come on duty?
Tessie Atkinson: Well, Sister Cass felt she could not manage.
Barry: How did you become aware that Sister Cass was perturbed?
Atkinson: Well, I am not swearing to this, but I think Sister Cass came out and said, 'We will have to get Sister Lockhart.'
Barry: What else do you know about the events of that night?
Atkinson: I cannot remember anything.
Barry: Do you remember whether you were in the labour preparation ward?
Atkinson: I do not remember being there.
Barry: Do you remember whether you were in the labour ward?
Atkinson: No.
Barry: Does that mean you believe that you were not in the labour ward or labour room, whatever you call it? What do you call it?
Atkinson: It is possible I was there but I cannot remember being there.
Barry: Have you any memory of being there that night?
Atkinson: No, I have not.
Barry: Have you any memory of doing anything with respect to Mrs Morrison or Mrs Jenkins while they were in the labour ward?
Atkinson: No I cannot.
Barry: Do you recollect seeing Mrs Jenkins or Mrs Morrison before they went into the labour ward?
Atkinson: No, I would not know Mrs Jenkins if I saw her.
Barry: Do you recollect seeing them before you went off duty that night?
Atkinson: No, I do not.
Barry: Do you recollect seeing either of the two babies?
Atkinson: No.
Barry: You learned, I suppose, sometime during the morning before you went off duty that two babies had been born that night?
Atkinson: I think I would.

Barry: Did you see either of those babies?
Atkinson: Not that I can remember, no.
Barry: Did you ever have anything to do with either of the babies that was born on that night?
Atkinson: Well, I may have later. Sometimes when the babies would be bathed at night, I may have been there helping the midwifery sister with them. I might have been in the nursery.

Mr Justice Barry finally repeated an earlier question: 'Have you any memory of attending to either of the babies?'
'No, I have not.'
It was now the turn of Robert Vincent Monahan, KC, for the Morrisons, to make his first real entry into the proceedings. Monahan was a master cross-examiner, adept at coaxing rather than bullying the required answers from witnesses. His opener could not have been more polite: 'You call yourself *Miss* Atkinson now, I suppose, do you?'
'Yes,' she replied.
The barrister then painstakingly traced through her brief nursing career, establishing that she had joined the staff at Kyneton in February 1945, about four months before the double birth which was now the subject of this case.

Monahan: During that four months had you been called in to help with any confinements?
Tessie Atkinson: I could not answer truthfully to that.
Monahan: What is your belief? Have you any present belief?
Atkinson: I think I might have seen two or three babies born, it might have been more.
Monahan: Do you remember when the last baby was born prior to the occasion that you have spoken about, when Sister Cass was a bit troubled with the impending events?
Atkinson: No, I do not.
Monahan: Do you remember the Perry baby?
Atkinson: I can remember the name.
Monahan: The Hayes baby?
Atkinson: I cannot remember the Hayes baby, I can remember Mrs Hayes.

Monahan: Well, it appears from the evidence before His Honour, that the baby named Hayes was born on the 19th of June. A baby named Perry on the 20th of June and the two babies in question in this case on the 22nd of June. So there we have four babies which had been born in this hospital in a matter of three or four days?
Atkinson: Yes.

Tessie Atkinson explained to the patient Monahan that she had seen no births when she did her training in Melbourne so she had asked the matron in Kyneton if she could go down into the labour ward occasionally to watch some confinements. She said she was inquisitive and also considering doing the midwifery course.

Monahan: If anyone, for instance, said that at the time of the birth of the Morrison and Jenkins babies, it was your duty to take the baby when delivered and do certain things with it, that would not be your recollection of the position?
Atkinson: That would not be.

A further series of questions from Monahan and the judge left both them and the witness equally puzzled. By now Tessie Atkinson was thoroughly flustered and to one, long, involved question she replied, 'I am afraid I am very dumb.'

Then came the following exchange with the judge.

Barry: Are you aware of what has been said in affidavits by Sister Cass and Sister Lockhart in regard to this matter?
Atkinson: Am I?
Barry: Yes?
Atkinson: Yes, I am.
Barry: You are aware that both of them have sought to make it appear that it was your duty on the occasion in question to do certain things with the two babies?
Atkinson: Yes.
Barry: You do not agree?
Atkinson: I do not disagree, or agree.
Barry: Have you any recollection of ever attending on a

confinement or participating in the process of confining a woman?
Atkinson: Yes, at a later date than that I can.

What did Tessie Atkinson mean by that expression 'at a later date than that I can'? Mr Justice Barry was quick to pick her up on that point.

Barry: By the words 'than that' do you mean than the 22nd of June 1945? Is that what you mean?
Atkinson: No, I do not say that particular date.
Barry: Alright. Then that is the date with which we are concerned, and you seem to have had something in mind when you said 'at a later date than that I can'. That is what you said to me here today. What do you mean by the words 'than that'? The date was later than what?
Atkinson: I could not say later than any particular date.
Barry: You see, it was your own phrase. You are asked, 'Can you remember ever confining a woman?' and you volunteer, 'Yes, I can at a later date than that.' Now, I want to know what you mean by that answer?
Atkinson: Well, I never had before the date you are speaking of.
Barry: Now let us get this clear, and correct me if I am misunderstanding you. Do I understand you to mean that you cannot remember confining a woman or assisting in the process of confining a woman, before the occasion when these two babies were born?
Atkinson: No, I cannot.
Barry: But you can remember assisting in confining a woman subsequent to the date when these two babies were born. Is that what you mean?
Atkinson: You mean after?
Barry: Subsequent means after, yes.
Atkinson: Yes.
Barry: You cannot remember doing any confinements before that?

Atkinson: No.
Barry: But you can remember doing confinements after that?
Atkinson: After, yes.

This exhaustive exchange, dissecting one answer point by point, had tried the patience of everyone in that court. There was a collective sigh of relief when Mr Justice Barry looked at the time and declared that it was an appropriate time to adjourn for lunch. The court had been sitting for only two hours and twenty minutes but much had been crammed into that brief space.

Tessie Atkinson was not looking forward to another encounter with the man 'with the piercing blue eyes' when the court resumed after lunch. Mr Justice Barry had left a lasting impression on her and she was relieved to find the questioning taken up by the more friendly Robert Monahan, KC. She was less happy when he got right back on the track of her expression 'than that'.

Monahan: Well now, having regard to what you told His Honour, that is that you do actually remember being concerned yourself with a confinement at some time after the occasion of the birth of these two children, on that early morning in June 1945, do you now agree that when earlier in your evidence you spoke of something being later than that, that was what you were referring to? Do you follow the question?
Atkinson: No.

With that, Monahan obviously decided he had exhausted the subject and turned once again to the mislaid or misplaced Morrison bunny rug.

Monahan: There is some suggestion in the evidence that it was mislaid and could not be found at the actual time when the Morrison baby was born, but later it was found wrapped around some hot water pipe somewhere. Do you know anything about that?
Atkinson: No, I can't...
Monahan: You cannot remember anything about it?
Atkinson: No.

Monahan: Now up to the time when you left Kyneton, had you heard any local talk about the possibility of a mix-up having occurred in regard to the Jenkins and Morrison babies?
Atkinson: Yes, I had heard it mentioned.
Monahan: And had that come about in any official way by the secretary of the hospital?
Atkinson: No, never.
Monahan: Were any inquiries made of you by anyone who had a right to inquire?
Atkinson: No. No one ever inquired of me.
Monahan: Well then, may I take it you just heard it as something that was being talked about in the district?
Atkinson: Yes, quite outside the hospital.
Monahan: Well, when you heard this talk going around, did you discuss the possibility of there having been an error with anyone in the hospital?
Atkinson: No.
Monahan: And at the time you heard the rumours or the talk, did you have any better memory than you have today?
Atkinson: No, I think if I had remembered being there I would have said at the time, 'Yes, I was in the labour ward then.'
Mr Justice Barry: That causes me to intervene and ask you this: When you heard of the possibility that two babies had been mixed up, did you think you had anything to do with it, that you were in any way associated with the incident?
Atkinson: Definitely not.

The Jenkins' barrister, Ted Hudson, chose a different tack and immediately drew better results.

Hudson: Miss Atkinson, I suppose you are prepared to be definite as to this much, that on no occasion at the Kyneton Hospital did you carry out two babies at the same time in your arms from the labour ward?
Atkinson: I have never carried any baby out of the labour ward.
Hudson: You have never carried any baby out of the labour ward?

Atkinson: No.
Hudson: And I am told that the nursery was almost next door to the labour ward. Was that correct?
Atkinson: It was.
Hudson: You went out of the labour ward into the corridor?
Atkinson: And into the nursery.
Hudson: Next door?
Atkinson: Yes.
Hudson: And in this nursery there was a bench inset in which was a nickel-plated bath?
Atkinson: Yes.
Hudson: Was it in that bath that the babies of the hospital were bathed?
Atkinson: Yes.
Hudson: Perhaps at some stage, at all events, of your career there you had to do some of the bathing, did you?
Atkinson: Never a newborn baby, but later on when I had night duty and I was in the midwifery ward I bathed them many times.
Hudson: And there was no practice of bathing more than one at the same time?
Atkinson: No, you could not, the bath was not large enough for one thing.
Hudson: And apart from the occasions when a child was in with its mother, either for feeding purposes or for other purposes, generally all the babies in the hospital at the same time were kept in this nursery?
Atkinson: Yes.
Hudson: And were they kept in cots?
Atkinson: Yes.
Hudson: I am told that the principal type of cot that was in use at the hospital was a wire cot on wheels?
Atkinson: That is correct.
Hudson: And if you wanted to move a baby from one room to another it was wheeled, it was not taken out of its cot, the cot was wheeled from one room to the other?
Atkinson: No. The cot was not wheeled. The baby would be taken from the cot and taken into its mother, but not in the cot.

Hudson: You have seen a cot, or cots, in the labour ward have you not?
Atkinson: Yes.
Hudson: And may I ask you this, whether it was the practice during the period you are able to speak of — I know you are only definite in your recollection it was towards the end of your employment there — but during the period you have a recollection of assisting in the labour ward, the practice was it not, was to have the cot with the baby's clothes in it in the labour ward?
Atkinson: Yes, that was the practice.
Hudson: And after the child had been delivered it would be put into the cot wrapped in its bunny rug, or rug, or whatever it was?
Atkinson: Yes.
Hudson: Put in the cot, then wheeled out to the nursery, and then it would be bathed?
Atkinson: Yes.

Both Barry and Hudson questioned her about the role she, as a single certificate nurse, would be expected to play at a birth. Tessie Atkinson explained that as the assisting sister she would help the doctor with the patient during the actual birth. The doctor would remove the baby, sever and tie the umbilical cord, check that the baby was breathing normally and then either hand the baby to her or leave it on the bed for her to pick up. It was her job then to wrap the baby and place it in the cot beside the bed.

Hudson: On those occasions when you were assisting, I want to follow that procedure. After the baby has been put into the cot and wrapped in a blanket it is allowed to remain there some little while while you assist in cleaning up, is it not?
Atkinson: Yes.
Hudson: And at some stage, varying periods, no set period, at some stage later the cot with the baby is wheeled out of the labour ward into the nursery?
Atkinson: That is right.
Hudson: And in the stages when you were assisting in the

midwifery section did you frequently do that?
Atkinson: No, I have never taken a baby out of the labour ward to bathe it. If I have had to call the night sister to be present at the birth, the night sister always stayed on and bathed the baby for me. The midwifery sister, I should say.
Hudson: It was usually her function to take it out?
Atkinson: Yes.
Hudson: In the cot?
Atkinson: Yes.
Hudson: Well now, on the night when Mrs Morrison and Mrs Jenkins had these two babies of theirs, you were on night duty and Sister Cass was also on night duty was she not?
Atkinson: Yes.
Hudson: And at some stage you have told us Sister Cass asked you to call Sister Lockhart?
Atkinson: I don't remember Sister Cass asking me to call Sister Lockhart.
Hudson: You did call?
Atkinson: I don't remember whether I did or...
Hudson: Do you remember Sister Lockhart coming along?
Atkinson: I can remember she was there.
Hudson: And all three of you were assisting in this double birth, in the birth of these two babies?
Atkinson: I do not remember being in the labour ward. I can remember I was on duty.
Hudson: Supposing it is sworn, as it has been, that you were there on duty in the labour ward and assisting in the labour ward that night, would you contradict it?
Atkinson: No, I would not contradict it. I cannot say I was there.
Hudson: You just don't remember whether you were or whether you were not in the labour ward?
Atkinson: No, I cannot.
Hudson: You did not on any occasion hear Dr Loughran when you were in the labour ward say anything about not getting the babies mixed up?
Atkinson: No.
Hudson: You have not on any occasion seen any other sister

carry out babies from that ward in their arms?
Atkinson: No, I have never seen it.
Mr Justice Barry: Miss Atkinson, if you are young enough not to mind this question, how old are you?
Atkinson: Twenty-six.
Barry: Ordinarily have you a good memory?
Atkinson: Yes, perhaps in some things it is more vivid than in others. Some things are more vividly in my memory than others.
Barry: I suppose ordinarily where one confinement is going on that is an exciting business, is it not?
Atkinson: I think it is.
Barry: We may take it, I suppose, that if two confinements are going on at practically the same time, that is at least doubly exciting?
Atkinson: Yes, it would be.
Barry: Do you think it is possible that if you were present and two confinements were going on at practically the same time and two babies born within a few minutes of each other, that you would have forgotten such an incident? Do you really think if you were present and such events were happening that you would forget them?
Atkinson: It is not that I would forget them, but I might forget, perhaps, what I did or what time it happened.
Hudson: It is suggested that you were one of the nurses there. Now, do you think it is possible for you to have forgotten being present when such events were happening?
Atkinson: It must be, because I have forgotten being there, if I was there as the others say.
Barry: The two other nurses have given their version. I want to ask you to listen to what has been said. Sister Lockhart says that she administered an anaesthetic to Mrs Morrison and Dr Loughran delivered her baby. Sister Atkinson assisted at the delivery. Now, if that be accurate, do you think you could have forgotten that, seeing that that happened within five months of your going to the hospital?
Atkinson: I don't remember.
Barry: That means that if it is true you have forgotten it?

Atkinson: I cannot swear I was there and I cannot swear I was not there.
Barry: Sister Lockhart has sworn that you were there.
Atkinson: Well, she must have a better memory than I have.
Barry: Have you forgotten it or are you unwilling to remember it?
Atkinson: If I could stand here truthfully and say, 'Yes I remember being there,' I would do it right now. But I cannot.
Barry: Sister Cass says that 'when Mrs Jenkins' baby was born, Dr Loughran delivered the baby. I administered the anaesthetic and Sister Atkinson assisted at the delivery.' Does that stimulate your recollection in any way? Does that stimulate any recollections?
Atkinson: No, I have read their statements and I have tried to think about it.
Barry: The results of that is that Sister Lockhart is saying that you assisted at the delivery of Mrs Morrison and Sister Cass is saying you assisted at the delivery of Mrs Jenkins. Now, that involves, does it not, that if things went according to custom, you were the nurse who had the two babies, who picked them up from the bed?
Atkinson: I might have.
Barry: Well, if Sister Cass and Sister Lockhart are right, that is what it means does it not? That the nurse who gathered up the babies from the bed was yourself? Does it not mean that?
Atkinson: It appears so.
Barry: If the fact is that Sister Lockhart was giving the anaesthetic to Mrs Morrison she would not handle the baby would she?
Atkinson: It all depends how much anaesthetic the patient has been given. It does not go absolutely to routine. Everybody does not go to routine.

Mr Justice Barry now decided to spell out very clearly to Tessie Atkinson the seriousness of the situation from her point of view. If the evidence of the two other sisters was to be accepted, that neither of them handled the babies, and in fact she did, then Tessie Atkinson, through her weakness of memory, was leaving herself open to the gravest of accusations.

There was a pause, then Barry raised his usually soft-spoken voice. Looking straight at the witness he said, 'I think it should be pointed out to you, in your own interests, that it may be that at some stage of this case someone will suggest that you mixed up the two babies.' He continued, 'Can you see that that suggestion is open on this version?'

Tessie Atkinson replied simply, 'I can.'

The judge pressed on: 'Now, do you want to say anything about that?'

Her answer: 'I have nothing to say. I have not got anything to say.'

Her ordeal in the witness box was about to end and an ordeal it had been for the nervous young woman. Before she stepped down, however, Mr Justice Barry, very seriously, indicated that he was still hopeful her memory could be refreshed. He told her: 'Well, Miss Atkinson, you will leave this court now unless counsel wants you for some reason, but this matter will not conclude today. If you desire to give any further evidence, at any stage, you have only to communicate with my associate and the opportunity will be given to you.'

Tessie Atkinson knew what lay behind the judge's veiled comments. 'I have spoken the truth, every word of it, today,' she told him.

Barry had the last word: 'I am just intimating to you, the fact that you are leaving the box now does not mean you cannot come back to the box later, if you want to do so.'

Now a grandmother living in Melbourne, Tessie Atkinson can still remember walking down the street from the courtroom, still in a daze from the barrage of persistent, probing questions, and seeing the newsboys selling the evening paper.

The headlines in the *Herald* that night read: 'Nurse says she "can't remember".' Tessie says:

'The "can't remember" was in inverted commas. And it hit me then and I thought no one is going to believe me. I think that was the fact that people thought, "Oh well, she's telling lies." I've had to live with that, really, which has, I suppose, been embarrassing. I had no way to deny it. All I could say was, "Well I couldn't remember".'

8   THE DOCTOR DEPARTS

The slim, attractive, dark-haired Tessie Atkinson was replaced in the witness box by a shorter, plumper woman exuding a great deal more confidence. Katherine Olive Cass was a career nurse, proud of her calling and sure of her capabilities. She had done her midwifery training at the prestigious St Vincent's Hospital in Melbourne and, like the other nurses, had been stationed in Kyneton due to the wartime emergency arrangements. At thirty, she had been a nurse for more than a decade. Responsibility did not worry her at all and those who knew Olive Cass in her early years were not surprised to learn that she eventually spent her entire life in the profession.

Unlike Tessie Atkinson, Olive Cass had a clear recollection of the double birth, her role in the event, and what the others were supposed to do. Almost from the start she began contradicting some of the evidence given that morning by Gwen Morrison and she was equally forthright about Tessie Atkinson's part in both births.

Gwen Morrison recalled seeing only two sisters, Cass and Lockhart, in the labour ward at the time of the births. Atkinson could not remember even being there. Was she? Olive Cass had not the slightest doubt. She told the court that even if there had been only a single birth that night, Sister Atkinson, as the person on duty in the medical and surgical ward, would still have been required to assist in the labour ward.

Monahan, KC, began the questioning. It was less an interrogation than a relaxed, smooth trip in the memory of that fateful night. Monahan sought Olive Cass's view of Sister Atkinson's precise duties in the labour ward during confinements.

Monahan: What do you say her duties would have been in the case of there being but one confinement that night?
Olive Cass: She would have assisted the doctor during delivery.
Monahan: Just precisely what does that entail? Would you describe to us now what the sister who helps the doctor does from start to finish?
Cass: She would hold the patient in position while the doctor was delivering the baby. After the birth of the baby, after he had tied the cord and cut it, she would place it in the cot.
Monahan: Does the doctor hand it straight to her?
Cass: He may, or he may put it on the bed for the nurse to pick up, or he might hand it to her direct.
Monahan: What is the next thing she has to do?
Cass: Put the patient on her back.
Monahan: Well, she puts the baby somewhere?
Cass: She puts the baby in the baby's cot at the side of the bed.
Monahan: Is that the invariable practice, that the baby's cot is there?
Cass: Yes.
Monahan: Well, she puts the baby in its cot, it is still naked?
Cass: It is wrapped in a napkin and a blanket.
Monahan: Where does she get the napkin?
Cass: She has that ready on the bed for the baby to be wrapped in.
Monahan: Whose napkin is it?
Cass: The baby's napkin belonging to the mother.
Monahan: Then there is some other garment there, is there?
Cass: Yes, the hospital blanket is on the cot. It is tucked in over the baby afterwards to keep it warm.
Monahan: The hospital blanket then is part of the cot?
Cass: Yes.
Monahan: It is not part of the baby's gear at all?
Cass: Not that blanket.
Monahan: Where is the rest of the baby's clothing to be found at that moment?

Cass: One set of garments is placed in the cot before the delivery.
Monahan: What do they consist of?
Cass: A bunny rug, one singlet, one binder, one nightgown and one napkin.
Monahan: Is there any identifying mark on the garments or on the cot?
Cass: Yes, the mother bringing in each garment has it marked with her own name on it.
Monahan: Is there any identifying mark on the cot?
Cass: Yes, a tag with the surname of the mother.
Monahan: In this particular instance who did it?
Cass: I did it myself.
Monahan: What is this tag?
Cass: A piece of cardboard pinned on to the cot.
Monahan: Is that the general practice?
Cass: It was not the usual practice to tag the cots beforehand. Sometimes it was done later.

Another point of conflict was now arising. Throughout her evidence Sister Cass insisted that she personally tagged two cots in the labour ward with the names Morrison and Jenkins. The next nurse to give evidence, Elizabeth Lockhart, would swear that when she walked into the nearby nursery to bathe the two newborn babies, she found them lying in separate cots. There were no name tags on either cot.

Another mysterious reference to the name tags appears in the affidavit sworn by Sister Lockhart, just a matter of weeks earlier. On 14 September she outlined her recollections of what happened on the night the babies were born. Sometime during the swearing of that affidavit she inexplicably decided that she wanted an important correction made. The original statement read: 'Sister Atkinson took the baby, wrapped it in a blanket and placed it in a cot tagged with its name which was on Mrs Morrison's side of the screen.' The words 'tagged with its name which was on Mrs Morrison's side of the screen' were clearly struck out and Sister Lockhart initialled the alteration.

Had her memory of that night changed suddenly when she read

her affidavit before signing it?

Monahan turned yet again to the question of the missing Morrison bunny rug.

Monahan: Did you place the bunny rug with the name Morrison on it in the baby Morrison's cot on that occasion?
Olive Cass: As far as I can remember, I did.
Monahan: Do you remember Sister Walsh?
Cass: Yes.
Monahan: Do you remember anything about Sister Walsh finding the Morrison baby's blanket or bunny rug a couple of days later wrapped around a hot water pipe?
Cass: No.
Monahan: Did you never hear anything of the fact that the Morrison baby's blanket was missing?
Cass: No, I don't remember.
Monahan: On this particular occasion, I suppose that you recognized that you had a mere novice there to assist you in Sister Atkinson?
Cass: Yes.
Monahan: These two women had come in and you realized that during the course of the night they were both likely to be delivered of their children at approximately the same time, from the way the pains were going?
Cass: Yes.
Monahan: You were a bit frantic about that, I suppose? Alone there with a mere novice?
Cass: No, I was not a bit frantic.
Monahan: At all events, it was sufficiently worrying to get Sister Lockhart out of bed before her ordinary time?
Cass: Yes, I knew that I would need assistance.
Monahan: You say that on this particular occasion you were concerned principally with the delivery of the Jenkins baby?
Cass: Yes.
Monahan: You did not handle that baby in any way?
Cass: Not that I remember.
Monahan: Who did?
Cass: Sister Atkinson.

Monahan: Are you quite sure of that?
Cass: Yes.
Monahan: After she places the baby in the cot, what is her next duty if she does not take it out to bathe it?
Cass: To assist with the mother. The mother has to be sponged and moved into her own bed in her own room.
Monahan: Usually then, the cot would leave the ward roughly about half an hour after the baby has been delivered?
Cass: Yes.
Monahan: All that time, from the time the doctor has delivered it, the baby is in the cot where the sister has placed it?
Cass: Yes.
Monahan: Whose job is it to take the baby out of the ward?
Cass: Whoever is free.
Monahan: Well, you have said it is the senior nurse's job to wash the baby?
Cass: Yes.
Monahan: Is that the same one who has given the anaesthetic and who has had the supervision of the washing of the mother?
Cass: Yes.
Monahan: Is it her job then to wash the baby?
Cass: Yes.
Monahan: Does she take the baby out to wash it? Or does she hope to find it outside?
Cass: She may take it out.
Monahan: You do not remember whether you, in fact, wheeled out the ward cot in which the Jenkins baby was, or not?
Cass: I do not remember taking it out.
Monahan: Do you remember whether or not you washed the Jenkins baby?
Cass: No, I did not.
Monahan: But you could have done?
Cass: I did not bathe the babies, either of them.

Olive Cass gave a very simple explanation why neither she nor Sister Atkinson bathed the two babies that morning. By the time they had finished with the births and cleaning up afterwards it was long past 7 a.m., the time they were due to finish their shifts.

Monahan then asked her about the rumours of the mix-up which had swept through Kyneton and refused to go away.

Monahan: It grew apace did it not? Grew like a bushfire?
Cass: Yes.
Monahan: Did you not become alarmed?
Cass: No, I was perfectly satisfied as to what I had done that morning. I was not alarmed.
Monahan: You were perfectly satisfied that you yourself 'were in the clear'?
Cass: I knew what work I had done that morning.
Monahan: You reckoned you were in the clear because you had just left the baby there in its cot in the labour ward? You had not taken it out, that was your comforting reflection, was it not?
Cass: No. I knew that I had labelled the cots. I was not concerned about taking them out then.

Cross-examined by Ted Hudson, for the Jenkinses, Sister Cass repeated that she had personally tagged the cots.

Hudson: With the double birth taking place, was it necessary to take special precautions, did you consider?
Cass: Yes, that is why I tagged the cots.

Hudson got Olive Cass to outline where the two cots were in the labour ward in relation to the beds where the mothers gave birth. They were on separate sides of the screen, she told the court. The Jenkins cot was about six feet from Jessie Jenkins' bed and the other cot was against the side wall, near the bottom of Gwen Morrison's bed. Hudson, naturally trying to emphasize there had been no mix-up, then put the hypothetical question:

'Then, for the person who had handled the child at this stage, who had got these babies into the cot that was intended for the other, it would have been necessary to walk around the screen and go out of your way to put it in the wrong cot. Is that the position?'

Olive Cass gave him the answer he wanted: 'Yes.'

He questioned her about the types of cots and she recalled that one was a wire cot, with wheels, and the other was probably canvas and not on wheels. The canvas cots could be carried or pulled along on their legs. Mrs Morrison had sworn that she saw a nurse carry the two babies, one under each arm, from the labour ward. Hudson was now trying to show that with portable cots present in the ward there was little need to carry the infants. With that point established he moved on to the birthtimes.

Sister Cass described how Mrs Jenkins gave birth to her daughter first, about five minutes ahead of Mrs Morrison. Cass was administering ether to Mrs Jenkins during the birth and, on the other side of the screen, Sister Lockhart was taking care of Mrs Morrison.

Hudson: During this time were you able to see what was going on in the other bed or were you concentrating on what you were doing?
Cass: I could see a little, yes.
Hudson: Were you paying attention to Sister Lockhart?
Cass: Oh, I remember Sister Lockhart asking for the ether bottle and I passed that over to her.

Gwen Morrison never denied that she had been given ether that night but she insisted that it was merely a small amount and that at no stage did she lose consciousness. How much that brief encounter with the anaesthetic affected her faculties, her ability to see things clearly, will never be known.

Hudson then asked Sister Cass if she had concerned herself with what was going on behind the screen. 'No, Sister Lockhart was there.'

Hudson: Sister Lockhart and the doctor were there?
Cass: And Sister Atkinson.
Hudson: And Sister Atkinson?
Cass: Yes.
Hudson: Had Sister Atkinson done anything with the baby up to that stage?

Cass: Only put it in the cot.
Hudson: Have you any idea who washed the babies this night?
Cass: I have no idea.
Hudson: But there can be no doubt of this, that there would be two babies in the nursery that night who would require washing?
Cass: Yes.
Hudson: And what, anointing? Do you rub oil into them?
Cass: Yes.
Hudson: That in itself is an expert's job, is it?
Cass: Yes.
Hudson: To take a newborn baby and wash it and anoint it?
Cass: Yes.
Hudson: As far as you know the one person must have done the two babies that night?
Cass: Oh, I do not think so. There must have been another trained nurse on duty who could have done it.
Hudson: Was there? Have you any suggestions? You were there that night?
Cass: I do not remember, I was off duty.
Hudson: Then if you and Sister Atkinson went off duty, then it would be Sister Lockhart? She was the person available to wash the babies unless she got assistance from some other quarter?
Cass: Yes.
Hudson: Some nurse that was coming on duty that morning?
Cass: Yes.

Hudson rounded off his cross-examination by returning to the role of Tessie Atkinson.

Hudson: The person primarily responsible for looking after the babies as soon as they were born, and the doctor had satisfied himself that they were alive, was the assisting nurse?
Cass: Yes.
Hudson: Of the nurses in the ward, the only one who would have handled the two babies that night was Sister Atkinson?
Cass: Yes.

Olive Cass left the witness box. She had been a strong, believable witness, like Gwen Morrison, although there were blatant differences in their recollections of the events of 22 June 1945.

During the first day of the hearing, Mr Justice Barry accepted a report from his scientific assessor, Dr Grantley Morgan, on the value of blood grouping tests in establishing paternity and family relationships. Dr Morgan's report was complex but quickly boiled down the question the court wished to solve. He emphasized that for blood testing to be successful, the court would need samples from all four parents and the two children.

> 'It can be stated that comprehensive blood grouping tests carried out on the members of both families are likely to furnish evidence sufficient to solve the question before the court. A conservative estimate indicates that at least nine out of ten such cases would be solved by blood grouping tests.'

Dr Morgan went further. He assured the court that by using other factors they 'would enhance the probability of attaining a conclusive result'.

Dr Lucy Meredith Bryce was called briefly into the witness box and questioned on her opinion of Dr Morgan's estimate of the chances of solving parentage by blood group tests. She agreed that it would work in nine out of ten cases. This was Dr Bryce's second involvement in the case. She had been one of the blood experts consulted by the Morrisons back in 1946 and had, in fact, been forced to decline an invitation from the judge to sit as his assessor in the court because of her earlier involvement.

Dr Bryce's affidavit supported another from Dr Douglas John Thomas which stated that Johanne Lee Morrison could not be the child of William Morrison and Gwen Morrison.

Dr Bryce recorded that Lee Morrison's blood belonged to group B, type Rh1 and Rh2, and contained the factors M and N. Bill Morrison's belonged to group A, sub-group A1, type Rh1 and contained the factor N. His wife's belonged to group O, type Rh1 and her blood contained the factor M. Her conclusion: 'The possibility that the child Johanne Lee is the daughter of William

Henry Morrison and Alberta Gwen Morrison is therefore excluded...'

It was 4.30 in the afternoon when the court adjourned that day. Mr Justice Barry said the hearing would resume on 25 October, the long delay being necessary because Jessie Jenkins would need to recover from the birth of her daughter Helen.

There was a flurry among the law courts newsmen when the judge left the court. The case had been a front page story right from the outset and this day's evidence was dramatic enough for anyone. Although the intriguing battle for the two girls had captured the public imagination, not just around Australia but also in Britain, Europe and the United States, the public gallery in the court had been surprisingly lightly populated. There were two main reasons for this. The case was being heard in a borrowed out-of-the-way courtroom, the No. 2 High Court, in Melbourne's Little Bourke Street. The main Supreme Court building was having a facelift and a number of its courts were out of action. The other reason for the absence of spectators was that this was a civil action and it took a good criminal trial, a grisly murder or the like, to pack them in.

But if there were few people in the court that day, this was no true indication of the public's interest. The Morrison and Jenkins families and their postmen would tell a different story. Thousands of letters came from all over the world, supporting or denigrating them.

The Morrisons were warmly applauded for their brave stand by some of their correspondents and roundly condemned by others for wanting to part with their little dark-haired girl. The Jenkinses, too, had their backers, people who believed they were right to fight to the bitter end for Nola.

But the venom of some of the writers startled Noel and Jessie Jenkins. 'People didn't approve of what we were doing. They didn't agree with us fighting the case,' Noel Jenkins remembers.

The Jenkinses reckoned the letters were ninety-nine per cent in their favour but the one per cent could be devastating. Jessie Jenkins remembers opening up one envelope and finding a card edged in black, the kind of card you send to a home where someone has died. The anonymous ones irked Noel Jenkins.

'They would get stuck into you and call you lowdown blackguards and sign "Joe Blow". We would read it and say, "We think otherwise", and in the fire it would go.'

The newspapers had all found their own titles for the case. The *Age* settled on the rather conservative 'The Baby Case', while another paper went for 'The Mixed Babies Case', and a third used the title 'Wrong Baby Case' which almost prejudged the issue. The most catchy title, however, came from the pen of Tom Parrington, the doyen of the law courts press corps, who was covering the case for Melbourne's evening paper, the *Herald*. Parrington, an accomplished pianist who used to lead singalongs at a Melbourne club frequented by journalists, barristers and judges, dubbed the conflict the 'Whose Baby is Whose Case', after a popular song of the 1920s. Later, it was abbreviated to 'Whose Baby Case' and eventually all the papers abandoned their own names and fell into line. So, within a few short days, that title was appearing in papers all over the country and the public was quick to pick it up.

Sitting beside Tom Parrington on the crowded press bench was an intense young man who was on speaking terms with the judge and knew most of the barristers firsthand. At twenty-six, Laurie Power was establishing himself as a top Melbourne journalist, a stickler for the facts whose trademark throughout his career was accuracy. Power, now in his sixties, recalls being puzzled by the apparent mismatch in the leading barristers. 'Monahan was brilliant at the bar,' he says of the Morrison advocate. 'Hudson was quite tedious to listen to, a rather colourless character.' He still cannot understand why the Jenkins' solicitor, Bernard Nolan, chose Ted Hudson for such a dramatic, emotional case. He was better suited to the cold, logical, methodical examination of financial matters, in which he specialized.

Laurie Power says: 'Monahan had a great mind. He could offend a judge because he could overshadow the Bench. But, not Barry. Barry was more than a match for Monahan.'

Power has another strong impression left in his mind from his days in the courtroom. He has a clear picture of the two mothers, how they looked, how they acted. He recalls: 'Mrs Jenkins was tall and thin, an attractive woman. Mrs Morrison was shortish, more matronly. I can't recall at any stage the mothers talking to each other.' And, as for the fathers, they left no lasting impression at all. This was to be a case in which the mothers were predominant.

It was almost a month later, on Monday 25 October, when the newsmen got their next, brief taste of the case. Mr Justice Barry asked the barristers from both sides to consider and prepare legal arguments on whether he, as a Supreme Court judge, had the power to order Noel and Jessie Jenkins to submit themselves to blood tests. He quoted a judgment from the Supreme Court of South Dakota, USA, which ruled there was such power, and he also referred them to various English authorities on the question. He asked the barristers to consider a further argument: Should Nola be declared a temporary ward of the court.

So far, the judge had heard three varying versions of the events of the early hours of 22 June 1945, from Gwen Morrison, Tessie Atkinson and Olive Cass. Who was he to believe? His task would obviously be made simpler if the professional man, Dr Gerald Loughran, could be produced. It was now nearly a month since Barry had virtually demanded that the Jenkins' legal advisers find a way of terminating Loughran's travel plans and induce him to step into the witness box.

What had been going on? Did they follow his instructions or were they not at all enthusiastic about having him as a witness? For some reason anyway, it was not until 19 October — twenty days after Barry spoke — that the Nolan office dispatched this telegram to Loughran's in-laws in Broome, WA, the doctor's last known address: 'Advise date of departure from Australia of Dr Loughran. Urgent.'

The reply was back within twenty-four hours: 'Dr Loughran already left for Singapore.' So, Gerald Loughran was at sea, if he was not already setting up his new home and practice in Singapore. There was no question of extradition in this, a civil case, so the man who might have shed considerable light on the subject of the births and of the Jenkins blood test was never to appear. In fact, his departure from Broome severed his entire link with the case and he was to return to Australia on only brief occasions many years later.

WHOSE BABY?

Mrs Patricia Loughran says their departure at this unfortunate time was mere coincidence, nothing to do with the Morrison versus Jenkins case. He was not running from anything.

According to her they did not discuss what had happened that night or the court case because Gerald Loughran was strict in his attitude of never discussing medical matters in the family home. Whether he talked about it to his colleagues in Singapore is another question. Certainly they knew of his involvement in a controversy over babies. One Australian medico who had worked with Loughran in Singapore gained the impression that he was an honourable man who took the only decent way out when someone else, a subordinate, made a mistake at the hospital. Because he had been in charge, Gerald Loughran 'took the rap'.

9 A NURSE BREAKS DOWN

Elizabeth Grace Lockhart, the third and last sister present when the Jenkins and Morrison babies were born, strode into the witness box with some degree of self-assurance. Before too long she would be in tears. Sister Lockhart told the court she was called on duty to help with the double births and she personally tended to Mrs Morrison.

Monahan: What did that involve?
Elizabeth Lockhart: Administering a little anaesthetic with her pains.
Monahan: A little anaesthetic? What anaesthetic were you using?
Lockhart: Ether.
Monahan: You don't claim that she became anaesthetized?
Lockhart: No, it was not necessary at that time.
Monahan: What you are trying to describe, perhaps, is what the nurses describe as, what, a 'whiff'? Something that does not render her unconscious?
Lockhart: No.
Monahan: But renders her less susceptible to pain?
Lockhart: Yes.
Monahan: You would agree that she was conscious?
Lockhart: Yes.
Monahan: Throughout the whole delivery?
Lockhart: Not delivery, she was not being delivered at that time.
Monahan: Was she ever unconscious?

Lockhart: I should think so.
Monahan: Are you guessing, or do you really carry a recollection of this?
Lockhart: I certainly do.

Later Sister Lockhart was to vary her answer, saying she could not 'actually swear' that Mrs Morrison lost consciousness. She still thought that Gwen Morrison probably did pass out, briefly, perhaps for about three minutes. She had no hesitation in swearing that Tessie Atkinson had been present for the births.

Monahan: What was she doing?
Lockhart: She was there to take the babies and place them in their cots.
Monahan: You don't know what she did with the first baby, the Jenkins baby?
Lockhart: No.
Monahan: Did she ever handle Mrs Morrison's baby?
Lockhart: Sister Atkinson?
Monahan: Yes?
Lockhart: She took it from the bed, yes.
Monahan: What did she do with it?
Lockhart: What did she do with it? She put it in the cot.
Monahan: Where did she get the cot?
Lockhart: Where did she get it? It was there.
Monahan: What sort of cot?
Lockhart: A wire bassinet.
Monahan: Did you see a second cot in the labour ward?
Lockhart: I really can't remember that.
Monahan: You didn't see what became of the first baby?
Lockhart: No.
Monahan: One cot was there and you didn't see another cot at any time?
Lockhart: Well, I have no recollection of it.

Monahan led Sister Lockhart on to the time immediately after the births, the time when a mistake, if any, may have been made. She told him she could not remember the last time she saw Sister

Atkinson that morning or what Atkinson was doing at the time.

> *Monahan:* You don't remember, for instance, seeing her taking either of the babies out of the room?
> *Lockhart:* No.
> *Monahan:* Either in her arms or in the cot or in any way?
> *Lockhart:* No.
> *Monahan:* Did you wash either of these babies?
> *Lockhart:* I should think I would have, but I can't remember.
> *Monahan:* Do you remember Sister Cass, whether she stayed on after seven?
> *Lockhart:* Oh yes, I am sure she did.
> *Monahan:* Well, did she do any of the washing of the babies, of either of them?
> *Lockhart:* I don't think so. She would have other things to do to finish up.
> *Monahan:* Then who did? What is your belief? That you washed both of these newly born infants?
> *Lockhart:* I think it is quite probable that I did.
> *Monahan:* Is that your belief, that you washed them both?
> *Lockhart:* Yes.
> *Monahan:* And where did you pick them up from to wash them? Where did you find them?
> *Lockhart:* Well I haven't any memory about the further incidents of that night. It just seems to me that the first part of it seems to stick in my memory but the rest of it is...

Elizabeth Lockhart did not complete her answer. Her voice trailed off and she appeared to give a nervous giggle. Monahan, KC, was not amused.

> *Monahan:* I was asking you, and you appeared to find the question amusing, as to where you got these babies to wash them, where you picked them up from?
> *Lockhart:* Out of their cots.
> *Monahan:* Were they then in the nursery or in the labour ward?
> *Lockhart:* They would be in the nursery. I don't know as a matter of fact.

Monahan: Do you remember?
Lockhart: This other picture I have of going into the nursery and finding the babies in their cots was a separate one, and I don't remember if it was the same night or not, but as no other night happened when two people had babies together I think it must have been the same day.
Mr Justice Barry: Is it a memory of washing two newly born babies?
Elizabeth Lockhart? Yes, of going into the nursery and finding two babies waiting to be bathed.
Barry: Two babies that day who had never been bathed before?
Lockhart: Yes.
Monahan: And the mental picture, if I follow you, is that they were both in cots when you came upon them?
Lockhart: Yes.
Monahan: In similar cots?
Lockhart: Yes.
Monahan: Were there no identifying marks?
Lockhart: What, on the cots?
Monahan: Yes?
Lockhart: No, just the labels on the babies.
Monahan: Labels on the babies themselves, not on the cots? Where are the labels on the babies, around their wrists?
Lockhart: No.
Monahan: Where?
Lockhart: Just on the bunny rug.
Mr Justice Barry: On the bunny rug?
Monahan: On the bunny rug? What do you mean? The child's surname?
Lockhart: Oh yes.

Barry and Monahan sensed they were getting to the nub of the mystery. Cots, bunny rugs and labels. Could it now be solved?

Monahan: And you remember that the Morrison baby was in a bunny rug which, to the best of your belief, had been brought to the hospital by Mrs Morrison with the baby's name on it, is that right?

Lockhart: Yes, I suppose so.
Monahan: You don't think there is any mistake about that?
Lockhart: I couldn't swear to...
Monahan: I am suggesting that is where the mistake occurred. It may be His Honour will find that the Morrison baby's bunny rug was mislaid and was only discovered on the heating apparatus a couple of days later?
Lockhart: That won't make any difference.
Monahan: Why?
Lockhart: The babies were labelled with their names.
Monahan: On what?
Lockhart: On what was around... I can't swear...
Monahan: If the Morrison baby was in a hospital rug it would not have the Morrison surname on it. Will you answer that?
Lockhart: They were written labels pinned on the babies.
Mr Justice Barry: In whose handwriting?
Lockhart: Whoever was responsible for placing them there. I can't swear to whose handwriting it was on these.
Barry: Well, who is responsible for putting the label on the baby's rug, the baby's covering?
Lockhart: Whoever takes them into the nursery.
Barry: Is that the assistant, the nurse who assists the doctor at the delivery?
Lockhart: Is it her responsibility?
Barry: Yes?
Lockhart: Not necessarily.
Barry: Then whose responsibility would it be to write it out?
Lockhart: It would be either Sister Cass's or mine.
Barry: Did you write anything out?
Lockhart: No, I don't remember.
Barry: And when is this label prepared?
Lockhart: In the nursery.
Barry: After the birth?
Lockhart: Yes.
Barry: So at the stage when the child leaves the labour ward there is not any label on the child or on the rug in which the child is wrapped?
Lockhart: It is wrapped in its own bunny rug and napkin.

Barry: Then if that bunny rug is marked in some fashion which enables it to be identified, then the child is assumed to be the child of the mother who brought in that rug, is it?
Lockhart: Yes.
Barry: If you found a baby in a rug with the name of Mrs Jones on it and there was a Mrs Jones in the hospital who had just given birth to a baby, you would assume that it was Mrs Jones' baby?
Lockhart: Yes.
Barry: And you would make out a tag in the nursery 'Jones' and attach that to the baby?
Lockhart: Yes. You would know anyway. There is usually somebody at the birth who does these things.

Elizabeth Lockhart had taken the case to a sensational stage in just a few minutes. She had begun confidently but rapidly that confidence was eroding. Monahan and the judge had both extracted telling evidence from her. She had said there were no tags on the cots in the nursery when she went in to bathe the newborn babies. If Sister Cass had tagged the cots in the labour ward, and she had been adamant on that point, then did this mean the two babies were not wheeled from the ward to the nursery? Was Gwen Morrison's recollection of seeing a nurse with a baby under each arm correct after all?

Even if the babies had been carried and not wheeled from the labour ward it would have been difficult for them to be mixed up if each had been wearing its own, tagged bunny rug. But, was Gwen Morrison's tagged bunny rug misplaced in the turmoil of events that night and did her child leave the ward in a hospital rug? If so, there was certainly a greater chance for a mix-up to occur when the two babies were bathed.

Monahan had pinned great importance on the Morrison bunny rug, asking all three sisters if they could remember it being found sometime later wrapped around hot water pipes. He had even advanced it as the solution to the whole mystery with his earlier question to Sister Lockhart: 'I am suggesting that is where the mistake occurred. It may be His Honour will find that the Morrison baby's bunny rug was mislaid and was only discovered on the heating apparatus a couple of days later?'

Elizabeth Lockhart was soon to provide further insights into what went on in the ward that night. Monahan asked if she remembered seeing any nurse carry the two babies from the ward, one under each arm. Sister Lockhart replied, 'No.'

> *Monahan:* And she [Mrs Morrison] has also said that the doctor observed at that moment, 'Are you sure you have those babies tagged, sister?' Do you remember any observation made by the doctor to that effect?
> *Lockhart:* No. I would not swear to it, but I had the impression that he said something about getting them mixed up.
> *Monahan:* You have a belief that the doctor did?
> *Lockhart:* But he was only trying to be funny.
> *Monahan:* Perhaps if he was here he could tell us he was trying to be funny?
> *Lockhart:* That is the impression I got.
> *Monahan:* Is it your belief that the doctor sounded a warning note, whether in fun or not we cannot be sure, but you have that belief?
> *Lockhart:* Yes, I have that recollection.
> *Monahan:* Could your recollection carry you a step further and remember to whom he addressed that remark?
> *Lockhart:* No, I think it was just a general remark.
> *Monahan:* I am suggesting what might have been the occasion, that someone, one person, had both babies in her arms at the same time. That would be such an occasion as might provoke a remark of that sort?
> *Lockhart:* It certainly would, I should think.
> *Monahan:* Then does that help you to remember who that someone was?
> *Lockhart:* I certainly should remember if someone was taking two babies out of the labour ward in her arms.
> *Monahan:* Why would you remember? Would it be bad practice?
> *Lockhart:* Of course it would.
> *Monahan:* Then what you claim is that you didn't see how either baby left the labour ward? Your next recollection is that

you found the two newly borns in two cots in the nursery?
Lockhart: Yes.

Monahan switched his attention to another hospital, another incident almost three years later. It was the interview at St Andrew's Hospital, East Melbourne, between Sister Lockhart, ill in bed, and Frank Galbally, younger brother of the Morrison's solicitor. Galbally had gone to the hospital hoping to elicit Sister Lockhart's assistance as a witness in the Morrison action, but left a disappointed man. Now Monahan drew Sister Lockhart's attention to her conversation with Galbally and the glaring differences between what Galbally would swear she told him at that time and what she was now swearing herself in the court.

This new line of questioning caused obvious distress to Elizabeth Lockhart, who had been having a torrid time in the witness box anyway. The judge had to ask Sister Lockhart to raise her voice as it had dropped away from a firm, confident volume to a mere whisper.

> *Monahan:* Do you remember telling Mr Galbally something to the effect that you claimed that it would have been impossible for a mistake to occur?
> *Lockhart:* Well, I probably would say that, but I can't remember what I said.
> *Monahan:* Well, you could have told Mr Galbally that you had some recollection of dressing, what, one or both of the babies? Are you being helpful about this? Are you really trying to recall this conversation with Mr Galbally?
> *Lockhart:* Well, I can't remember. I was in bed at that time.
> *Mr Justice Barry:* You were in bed?
> *Lockhart:* Yes.
> *Monahan:* You were ill, were you?
> *Lockhart:* Yes.

Elizabeth Lockhart's voice faltered, she bowed her head and tears ran down her cheeks. The young woman had become increasingly edgy during the cross-examination but her sudden breakdown caught Monahan and the judge by surprise.

Monahan inquired, 'Are you feeling alright Sister?' He could barely hear her mumbled, 'Yes'.

Mr Justice Barry asked, 'Would you like to sit down, Sister? There is a chair there'. With that Elizabeth Lockhart slumped into the chair in the witness box, dabbing at her eyes with a handkerchief. Monahan paused for a few moments while she regained her composure, then asked, 'Would you rather have a rest, or get it over?' Sister Lockhart's voice picked up a little. 'Get it over,' she responded.

Monahan hastened through the rest of his cross-examination. He asked Sister Lockhart if she told Galbally that she had carried one of the babies from the ward. Her reply: 'No, I am afraid I would not have said that either.'

> *Monahan:* Do you remember him saying this, 'You have got nothing really to worry about because there can't be any criminal proceedings or you, yourself, cannot be made legally responsible'? To which you said, 'I don't care, I'm not going to say anything. I don't want to be mixed up in it at all.'
> *Lockhart:* I do remember saying I didn't want to be mixed up in it.

Ted Hudson, for the Jenkinses, took up the questioning. Throughout her evidence Sister Cass had referred to the babies being taken from the labour ward to the nursery inside their cots. Sister Lockhart would reveal a different means of transportation.

> *Hudson:* What was the practice as to how it was brought from the labour ward to the place where it was washed? How were the babies brought there?
> *Lockhart:* As far as I can remember, when they only had one baby they usually carried it out.
> *Hudson:* When they got out to the place where they were bathed, I understand there was only one basin for both children?
> *Lockhart:* That is so.

Hudson, in his patient, solemn style, now put forward his own theory on what Gwen Morrison might have really seen when she described a nurse leaving the labour ward with a tiny bundle under each arm.

> *Hudson:* Supposing you have two patients, would there be quite a couple of armfuls of soiled linen to be taken out after the cleaning up process had been going on? What would the linen be? The sheets, I suppose?
> *Lockhart:* If Mrs Morrison was still in the bed, only one sheet would be removed.
> *Hudson:* What about any of her attire? A nightdress or anything of that kind? Would that be soiled and taken away?
> *Lockhart:* Yes, it could be.
> *Hudson:* What about a certain amount of napkins and that sort of thing? Are they used?
> *Lockhart:* No, not very much, only if the mothers are out of the labour ward.
> *Hudson:* There would be a certain amount?
> *Lockhart:* Yes.

Hudson wound up with a few questions on the bathing of the two newborn babies.

> *Hudson:* One was taken out of the cot and bathed and put back into the cot and the other was taken out and bathed?
> *Lockhart:* Yes.
> *Hudson:* At that stage the child had a rug on with its name on?
> *Lockhart:* Yes.
> *Hudson:* And immediately afterwards it was in a cot that had its name on?
> *Lockhart:* Yes.
> *Hudson:* And wearing clothes that had its name on?
> *Lockhart:* Yes.

Elizabeth Lockhart answered a couple of further questions from Mr Justice Barry, then gratefully left the witness box and the court. She was not to know that there was another session with these searching examiners in store for her.

A NURSE BREAKS DOWN

With the conclusion of Sister Lockhart's evidence, the court now had three, often conflicting, stories from the nurses. The differences in their recollections ranged from the trivial to the crucial. The judge was going to have to pick his way through a minefield of possibilities. He had to decide firstly if a mix-up did take place and, secondly, if one or more of these three nurses was responsible.

A small human drama was enacted that day in the corridors outside the court. For the first time since the Morrisons stunned the Jenkinses with the first article in the *Truth* newspaper, the two mothers met face to face, their husbands alongside them. It was a meeting that neither side really wanted but one that was unavoidable in the cramped surroundings of the courtroom. Both sides were embarrassed but there was no open animosity. Noel Jenkins recalls: 'They went out that door and we went out that door, sort of thing. We sort of were passing, he and his retinue and me and my retinue.'

All eyes met and for a moment it looked as if no one would speak, just stare, but Noel Jenkins broke the spell with a formal 'G'day, Bill,' or 'How are you Bill?' and he remembers Bill Morrison responding with a similar brief, formal greeting. Morrison was on his way into the court to take his turn in the witness box. He was to be cross-examined by the brilliant young Henry Winneke, Hudson's junior in the case, who had remained in the background until this moment.

Winneke led Morrison through the early months after the birth of Johanne Lee when Gwen Morrison was insisting they had the wrong child but he was unconvinced.

> *Winneke:* I suppose there was a stage ultimately when you became satisfied in your mind that it was not your child. Could you tell me when you first definitely formed your opinion that the child was not yours?
>
> *Bill Morrison:* My wife mentioned it to me in the first place and I did not take any notice. I could see myself that at the time she could have had some grounds for her argument but I did not then go very far into the question as to whether the child was ours.

Winneke: Was it then that you were satisfied that the child was not yours?

Morrison: It was in between the two [blood] tests. I had my own ideas about it but I was not anxious to go on with the matter. We had had the child a long while.

Winneke: I take it that you are very fond of Johanne Lee and so is your wife?

Morrison: Yes.

Winneke: May we take it that Johanne Lee has been at all times brought up as an integral member of your family?

Morrison: Yes.

Winneke: At no stage has she ever been given cause to think that she was not a member of your family?

Morrison: No, at no time.

Winneke: There is no question that she unquestionably regards you as her father and your wife as her mother?

Morrison: No question whatsoever.

Winneke: And the other two children. Does she regard them as brother and sister respectively?

Morrison: Yes.

Winneke: Do the other two children believe that she is their sister?

Morrison: Yes.

Winneke: So that as far as your family circle is concerned, Johanne Lee always has been, and is now, an integral part of your family?

Morrison: That is true.

Winneke: And we may take it that you and your wife have a strong attachment for the child?

Morrison: Yes.

Winneke: Does she get on with the other two children as one of themselves?

Morrison: Yes.

Henry Winneke questioned Bill Morrison about the article which appeared in *Truth*, drawing from him the fact that it was through someone he knew at the newspaper that the story originated. However, like his wife Bill Morrison did not reveal to the court, nor was he ever asked directly, who that person was. Had they asked, Morrison could have explained that the man was journalist Frank Moffat, his wife's brother-in-law.

Morrison's own barrister, Robert Monahan, then rose and drew from his client an astonishing revelation. Not only did they hope to win Nola in this action, but they were hoping to keep Johanne Lee as well!

Monahan: I would like to ask a couple of questions Mr Morrison. You have been asked by my learned friend Mr Winneke about your attitude towards Johanne Lee. Do you want to keep her?
Bill Morrison: Yes.
Monahan: You are happy to have both children?
Morrison: Yes.
Monahan: You have told Mr Winneke that it did not need the *Truth* article to stimulate you into action. You always had intended to go on and fight it out when you could?
Morrison: That is right.
Monahan: Why was it that you did nothing about it till this year?
Morrison: My finances would not let me.
Monahan: What about your finances?
Morrison: The position is, I went to Mr Galbally about it. He said he would like to be certain one way or another and that if he was sure my case was definitely right he would take it up. He decided he would go ahead. I gathered that it would not cost me anything but he would look after my interests, but I would have to pay other costs.
Monahan: Out-of-pocket fees?
Morrison: Yes.
Monahan: The position is, Mr Galbally said if he was sure you were right he would take the case?
Morrison: Yes. And that he would need someone to assist and might be able to manage that for us.

To those who knew him, the action was typical of Jack Galbally. He might have had a thriving practice and his time undoubtedly was worth far more than the struggling spray painter Bill Morrison could afford, but Galbally was a man who had a soft spot for a battler and the Morrisons were not the only people to find themselves in receipt of his generosity. When Galbally took on the case, of course, there was no hint of the long and tortured course it would take but he never relented in his desire to see justice done for the Morrisons, even when that family were losing heart and feeling inclined to toss in the sponge.

10 TWO LITTLE GIRLS IN COURT

The witness that everyone was waiting to hear walked purposefully to the witness box, was sworn and immediately presented an aura of confidence and credibility. Much of the evidence so far had been favourable to the Morrison side. Ted Hudson, KC, was depending upon Jessie Jenkins, his star witness, to turn the case around. He had interviewed her at length and knew she would stand up well under pressure, a woman who would be able to resist walking into the traps that would be set for her by his clever opponent Robert Monahan.

Monahan's early questions covered family likenesses and Jessie Jenkins proved an expert on that subject, producing family pictures and swearing that Nola was a 'throwback' to Jessie's own grandfather, Robert John King, 'who had very blue eyes and a very fair skin'. She went even further. All of her grandfather's family had fair skin and blue eyes, so Nola was no misfit even though Noel Jenkins and Jessie herself had dark hair and brown eyes. There was an aunt, called Jane King, who was fair and an Uncle Sam who had blue eyes.

Monahan then got down to the hard issues and Jessie Jenkins remembers telling herself to remain calm and think clearly. She was an intelligent woman and Monahan soon realized she would be extremely difficult to pin down.

Monahan: I suppose I may take it that you have been greatly troubled over the situation that you two mothers may have been given the wrong babies?
Jessie Jenkins: Yes, naturally.

Monahan: And you have tried to convince yourself that there has been no mistake?
Jenkins: I didn't need any convincing. I knew there was no mistake.
Monahan: Well, have you had any comfort from your belief as to the similarities and so on in regard to the eyes of the person concerned?
Jenkins: The eyes are not altogether what count. There are lots of little things.
Monahan: It seems to be the thing upon which you have laid particular emphasis in your affidavit, doesn't it?
Jenkins: That is only because Mrs Morrison and Mrs Williams referred to the blue eyes and we consider that that has nothing to do with it.
Monahan: What else is there that you consider as having any real affirmative value?
Jenkins: Well, the whole structure of the baby's appearance, in so much as the head is similarly shaped, the ears are set similarly.
Monahan: Have you brought them [the other Jenkins children] here today?
Jenkins: No.
Monahan: Why not, His Honour might like to see them?
Jenkins: We thought if that was so we would have had some word. We don't want to do anything that is detrimental to their happiness in the future.

Monahan then asked Jessie Jenkins about her children's teeth and any noticeable gaps peculiar to them. That line of questioning leading nowhere, he moved on to the Morrison children and his key subject — blood.

Monahan: You have never seen the Morrison children, or have you ever sought to have a look at them, or wanted to see the other Morrison children?
Jenkins: I have seen them in the street occasionally, but I don't know Mrs Morrison very well at all. In fact...
Monahan: No, but have you ever taken any trouble to have a

look at the other Morrison children to see if they bear any similarity to Nola?
Jenkins: I can't say that I have.
Monahan: And might I ask why not?
Jenkins: For the simple reason it never occurred to me there was anything like this cropping up until the babies were fourteen months of age, and after that I never saw them. I never saw them very often.
Monahan: At the time this serious suggestion was made, it was put forward as a serious suggestion in the middle of 1946 wasn't it?
Jenkins: I suppose yes.
Monahan: At that time all the parties were living in Kyneton?
Jenkins: Yes.
Monahan: Why did you not endeavour to look at the Morrison children to see any striking dissimilarities between them and Nola?
Jenkins: For the reason that the only time I saw Mrs Morrison I thought the baby [Johanne Lee] was very like her. She is in one end of the town and we are at the other. I have no time. I only get up the street to do a few messages. It was only on rare occasions that I have seen her in the street.
Monahan: When this suggestion was made seriously, the wisdom of having this cleared up quickly was discussed and it was suggested that all parties should have blood tests made. Is that so?
Jenkins: That had nothing to do with me.
Monahan: Because you counted yourself out?
Jenkins: Oh no, I didn't. They didn't come to me. They went to my husband and we were sure we had our own.
Monahan: A very serious belief was entertained by the Morrisons that there had been a mistake?
Jenkins: Yes.
Monahan: And they wanted the thing cleared up as quickly as possible, the children then being old enough to be blood tested?
Jenkins: As far as I know there was no time limit on it.
Monahan: Did you ever hear that Mrs Morrison was only

waiting until the children were twelve months old?
Jenkins: No.

At last the question of blood tests had been put directly to the Jenkins. Why were they prepared to rely on the tests of their local GP, Gerald Loughran? And, most important, would they, if requested, submit to tests by experts to set the matter at rest?

> *Monahan:* You did hear that the Morrisons had had Johanne Lee blood tested?
> *Jenkins:* Only when my husband came home and told me.
> *Monahan:* And that the opinion had been expressed that she could not be their child?
> *Jenkins:* Only when...
> *Monahan:* You took up the attitude that you would not have any blood tests?
> *Jenkins:* No.
> *Monahan:* You didn't disclose in 1946 that you had been to Dr Loughran?
> *Jenkins:* Not to Mr Morrison, no.
> *Monahan:* You kept that to yourself, didn't you?
> *Jenkins:* Yes.
> *Monahan:* Do you believe in blood tests as being helpful in these matters?
> *Jenkins:* In so much as it helped back up our own opinion that we were quite satisfied we had our own child.
> *Monahan:* Has it come to your knowledge during these proceedings that, giving Dr Loughran's test its fullest weight and value, it proved nothing more than would be proved in four out of every five people?
> *Jenkins:* I don't know anything about the scientific side of these percentages. We just simply had it, as I said before.
> *Monahan:* Have you yet realized that?
> *Jenkins:* No.
> *Monahan:* That Dr Loughran's test, given its fullest value, proves nothing more than could be proved in relation to four out of every five people here in this court?

Jenkins: No, I have no idea of the percentages.
Monahan: In other words, that the groups are common to eighty per cent of the population of people who have been blood tested in this world?
Jenkins: As I said...
Monahan: That is not very much comfort to you, is it?
Jenkins: Oh, definitely.
Monahan: It is?
Jenkins: So far as we are concerned it is.
Monahan: Would not you like to know the real truth?
Jenkins: But I do know it. I know I have got my own baby.
Monahan: I suppose it follows that on any footing you would not want to receive Johanne Lee into your home? You don't regard her?
Jenkins: I don't regard her as my baby.
Monahan: And you don't want her?
Jenkins: I have got my baby and that is all I want.

The court was now seeing at close quarters the sort of woman Jessie Jenkins was and the determination, some would say stubbornness, that formed an integral part of her character. Noel Jenkins was cast in the same mould. Between them they were utterly convinced they had the right child and they didn't want to know about any doubts. Losing her would be unthinkable. Mr Justice Barry saw from the tenor of Jessie Jenkins' replies to Monahan that here was a woman who would not easily be persuaded to shift ground. He elected to enter the fray himself with a blunt, direct question.

Mr Justice Barry: Are you prepared to undergo a blood test?
Jessie Jenkins: I think we have had quite a lot of upset over this and we don't want to put the baby to any tests unless it is necessary and I can't see that it would shake any conviction of mine.
Barry: But you see, it is a question of the material the court must have to decide this matter. Are you prepared yourself to have a blood test done?
Jenkins: I would prefer not to.

Barry: Does that mean unless I order you to that you would not?
Jenkins: I don't wish to be disrespectful but I would like to go further into the matter before we did that.
Barry: Then, unless you are ordered by the court, you are not prepared to have a blood test?
Jenkins: Oh no.
Barry: You are aware it only means the scratching of the skin and the drawing off of a small quantity of blood? You realize that do you?
Jenkins: Yes.
Barry: And your unwillingness to have any test done on yourself or your child is not ascribable to any fear of physical injury by reason of the test?
Jenkins: No.

Ted Hudson, KC, rose slowly to his feet and immediately changed the subject. Blood, it seems, was low on his list of priorities. His first question was long and ponderous but it demanded a view from his client on the similarities between Nola and the other Jenkins children. Jessie Jenkins was happy to answer that:

Jessie Jenkins: Their heads are very similarly shaped, to begin with. Their ears sit very similarly. Their eyes, noses and foreheads. They eventually get the same hairline. The upper lip, the whole four of them have it very like their father's. It is rather unusual. It appears to me that they have a small blister on the upper lip.
Hudson: Was this little girl Nola breast-fed?
Jenkins: Yes.
Hudson: And you have succoured her and nursed her?
Jenkins: Yes.
Hudson: And she has been living with you and your other children right throughout?
Jenkins: Yes.
Hudson: Is she an affectionate child?
Jenkins: Oh definitely.

Hudson: And are the bonds of affection between her and you and your husband and the rest of the family noticeably strong?
Jenkins: The boys idolize her.
Mr Justice Barry: What is the new baby, a boy or a girl?
Jenkins: A girl.
Barry: What is the colour of the eyes of the new baby?
Jenkins: They could be a blue or they could be a grey. They are swinging between the two shades.
Hudson: Is Nola a very self-confident type or is she rather inclined to be shy?
Jenkins: At home she is boss of the house but when she is out she is rather inclined to hide behind me, the same as the boys did until they got to a certain stage and began to play with other children and that sort of thing.

Hudson asked nothing at all about blood, but Mr Justice Barry quickly returned to that subject.

Mr Justice Barry: You understand, do you, that the examination to ascertain your blood grouping that I spoke of was an examination under the supervision of the court? That was the form of examination I was inquiring whether you were prepared to submit to?
Jessie Jenkins: I see.
Barry: And you are unwilling to submit to that examination?
Jenkins: I would like to talk that over with my counsel and solicitors and make quite sure that that would be in order.
Barry: Yes. Well don't be afraid. At this stage you are perfectly entitled to indicate that you won't have it done.
Jenkins: Well I am.
Barry: I won't regard that as any disrespect to me.
Jenkins: Well, I am quite sure in my own mind that I have my own baby.
Barry: Whatever the reasons are, I want to get it for the purposes of record that you are not prepared to have an examination conducted under the supervision and direction of the court to determine what your blood grouping is?
Jenkins: I would definitely sooner leave it as we have it now.

Barry: And you are not prepared to submit the child to such an examination?
Jenkins: No.

Jessie Jenkins had stood her ground. When she left the witness box she left little doubt that her mind was made up. What could or would Mr Justice Barry do about it?

Noel Henry Jenkins soon found himself under the same line of questioning from Monahan. Monahan asked why Noel Jenkins had not informed Bill Morrison of the blood test the Jenkinses had had performed by Dr Gerald Loughran. 'I considered it,' Noel Jenkins told the court. 'Mr Morrison simply asked me if we would have blood tests taken in conjunction with them. I immediately interviewed my medical adviser and he suggested that we should have tests taken and under his direction we had them taken, and then when we had the results I saw Mr Morrison and simply said we were not interested in their case.'

The two men, barrister and builder, were about to become quite terse with each other as Monahan adopted a more aggressive approach.

Monahan: You have told us all that. Now what about answering my question, which was that seeing that you claimed to have had expert advice and blood tests taken before your second interview with Mr Morrison, if the position was as you say, why didn't you tell him so and say, 'We have had tests and our kiddie could be our child and this is the end of it'? Why didn't you tell him that?
Noel Jenkins: There is no reason why I didn't tell him, none actually. It was probably an overthought, overlook.
Monahan: Had you not been told that they were next door to useless?
Jenkins: No, that was never mentioned.
Monahan: Well that was not very comforting was it?
Jenkins: Yes, it was very comforting.
Monahan: What, just to prove that you were all in blood tests common to eighty per cent of mankind?
Jenkins: We didn't know that at the time.
Monahan: I have asked you. I think I have put it quite clearly.

Did you not realize, my question was that your tests were not worth much, and that was why you did not confide to Mr Morrison the fact that they had been taken?
Jenkins: At the time I saw Mr Morrison at the second interview I had no idea as to how far those tests were taken and I have no idea now.

Monahan asked if Dr Loughran had explained to the Jenkinses that the tests he carried out merely showed that the blood groups of Noel, Jessie and Nola were common to eighty per cent of people. Noel Jenkins replied: 'He simply told us that they were satisfactory. Whether they were common or anything else, I don't know. He said they were satisfactory, the groupings were satisfactory.'

Monahan: What you mean by that is that Nola could have been your child.
Jenkins: That is correct.
Monahan: Then if that were so, why was it that you didn't tell Mr Morrison of the fact? That was the question I asked.
Jenkins: There was no apparent reason, no reason at all.
Monahan: I am suggesting a reason, and that was that he went further and told you that it was very little comfort he could offer you because your groups happened to be common to eighty per cent of mankind?
Jenkins: No, that, no. He...
Monahan: He didn't tell you that?
Jenkins: No, definitely not.
Monahan: And since then I suppose you have discovered that your groups, yours, Mrs Jenkins' and Nola's, are common to eighty per cent of mankind? Is that correct?
Jenkins: Yes.
Monahan: So I suppose now we may take it you don't feel any great confidence in, what...?
Jenkins: Yes, just as confident as ever.
Monahan: Do you appreciate that since the matter has been placed before the court, in this matter, there are three different types of tests which can be used in an accumulative way, one

after the other, so that you can get almost certainty in regard to a matter which involves six individual persons? Do you appreciate that?
Jenkins: Yes, it is possible.
Monahan: And you don't want any certainty in this matter?
Jenkins: Why should we? We are quite certain now. All the certainty we want.
Monahan: Have you, in fact, not had a further blood test?
Jenkins: No sir. One and one only, Dr Loughran's.
Monahan: And you are going to stand on that, come what may?
Jenkins: Come what may, yes sir.

The next witness recited the oath as if he knew it backwards. He did, too, because Francis Eugene Joseph Galbally was now a newly qualified barrister, an impressive young man who was on the brink of a spectacular career in the courts of Victoria. Today, however, he was just a minor witness, called to give his account of his interview with Sister Lockhart, before the case began.

Galbally recounted how Sister Lockhart had been in bed ill when he asked her about the events of 22 June 1945, and her role in the births of babies Jenkins and Morrison. Galbally said he asked Sister Lockhart who took the babies out of the labour ward and she replied, 'I don't know.' He said he then asked her more directly, 'Did you?' and Elizabeth Lockhart replied, 'I took one of them out of the labour ward and another sister took another one.'

If Galbally's memory of this conversation was accurate, and he told the court he noted it down shortly after it occurred, this was the first and only clear reference to the babies being taken from the labour ward to the nursery. Galbally said he told Sister Lockhart: 'Mrs Morrison says that on this occasion Dr Loughran said to you, "Be careful not to get those two babies mixed up and see that they are tagged."' According to Galbally, Sister Lockhart replied, 'Oh, Dr Loughran was just being facetious as it was an extraordinary circumstance that the babies should be taken so closely together.'

The following day it was the lawyers' turn to be examined. Mr

Justice Barry had asked them to prepare their arguments on whether Nola should be declared a temporary ward of the court and on what power, if any, the court had to order blood tests from Nola and the Jenkins parents.

Unfortunately, Robert Monahan could not be present and had had to hand over the reins to his junior, Charles Sweeney. The versatile Monahan had switched from babies to racehorses, one of his great loves, appearing at a Victoria Racing Club committee hearing over a scandal involving the greatest jockey in the country, the legendary Darby Munro.

Ted Hudson, KC, had prepared well for the legal debate on two key issues close to the hearts of his clients. He vehemently opposed Nola being declared even a temporary ward of the court. That was yielding ground he could not afford and he reasoned that if she was made a ward of the court the next stop would be for the court, acting in the role of parents, to order a blood test against the wishes of the real parents.

Hudson was no less vehement in his argument that the court had no right whatsoever to force the Jenkinses to have blood tests against their will. The two matters were so important, so integral to his clients' case, that Hudson was to be on his feet for the entire day arguing against such court intervention.

He told Mr Justice Barry that nothing could justify the court taking steps to enforce blood tests. No court had the power to compel a person to become a guinea pig for a test or experiment. There were neither English nor American authorities for the proposition that such an order could be made. The only American decision on the matter had been against it, he argued.

Hudson also said that even if Mrs Morrison got the wrong baby, there was no proof that she had been given Mrs Jenkins' baby, or that Mrs Jenkins had been given Mrs Morrison's baby, because there were two other new babies in the hospital at the same time. Referring to these two other babies, the Hayes and Perry children, Hudson asked why — supposing the Morrisons did prove scientifically that Johanne Lee was not their child — they had to pick Nola Jenkins as theirs and not one of those other two. He suggested that the only answer was because Nola and Johanne Lee were born at the same time.

Mr Justice Barry replied that there was more to it than that. Other circumstances were involved, there was no evidence that the other two babies 'had been in juxtaposition'.

Hudson said that there was evidence that all four baby girls were in the same nursery. The Morrisons had not excluded the possibility that they might have the Hayes or Perry baby.

Another point he raised was the ultimate welfare of Nola, regardless of her parentage:

'Even if Your Honour thought there was some doubt, if you thought the parentage of this child was the Morrisons', I submit that it would be very unwise to do anything to disturb the family relationship of this child, which has been allowed to grow up with the Jenkins family for three and a half years. The correct approach in this case is to consider the welfare of the child.'

Mr Justice Barry replied, 'Would not the wise parent have a blood test taken to remove the doubt that has been cast upon the parentage of the child?'

Hudson: In this case there is a danger of grasping at the shadow for the substance. The search for scientific truth might be given a position of importance which is not merited.
Mr Justice Barry: The practical and obvious solution is to have the blood test.
Hudson: Where will that get you? The tests are the obvious solution to find the parentage and I agree that it is an important factor, but it is not in this case the predominant factor. I suggest that as far as the child is concerned, apart from anything that might be taken from the newspapers when she is grown up, she will be no worse off.
Barry: We do not know that. The question of inheritance might arise, and other things too, which might involve the proof of parentage. The question of parentage by blood tests can be decided only while the parents are alive.

Despite his careful preparation, Ted Hudson was not doing well.

He and the judge were quite clearly at loggerheads on the issue of blood testing. It was about this time that Noel Jenkins remembers being told that the case was as good as lost. He was stunned and only grateful that his wife was not there with him to hear the gloomy prediction. She had returned to Kyneton to look after the children.

The judge then heard Charles Sweeney, junior counsel for the Morrisons, attempting to counter Hudson's proposition that no matter what the true identity of the children, it was better that Nola should stay in her present, stable, happy environment.

Sweeney told the judge he should consider not only the present welfare of the child but also the future. Nola was entitled to the love and care of her true mother and father. 'Take the possibility of the future marriage of this child,' said Sweeney. 'The question of relationship may arise.'

Sweeney pointed out that although Noel and Jessie Jenkins might be confident that Nola was their own child, in later life Nola herself was certain to be told of this historic case. She then might not share the Jenkins' confidence, Sweeney said.

Noel casts his mind back to that black day, the day when his spirits were close to their lowest point:

> 'We walked out at lunchtime and they said to me, "We haven't got a hope of winning this case." I can remember saying, "There must be something we've slipped up on. There must be somebody that we can find that will alter his opinion".'

The lawyer merely shook his head.

> 'He said, "No, we haven't got a hope. Don't worry about it, we'll appeal and we'll win the next one." That came as a shock to me because I felt then that that was the end of the world, to lose it. I was down there on my own and it was the end of the world to me.'

Noel and Jessie Jenkins were a particularly close couple and there had never been any secrets between them, until that day. When Noel returned home in the evening he appeared outwardly cheerful, not giving his wife any hint of the anguish he was feeling inside. She would never be told what the lawyer had forecast.

Hundreds of thousands of words had been spoken about them, hundreds of thousands had been written, but up to that day the court had seen nothing of the two main players in this poignant drama. Nola Jenkins and Lee Morrison were three years and four months old and innocent of what was happening in Melbourne. On 28 October, Mr Justice Barry decided it was time for him to see the two children, whose future lives were at his discretion. He asked that they be brought before him in his private chambers on the following Friday, 5 November.

The first Tuesday in November is a very special day in Australia, the one day in the year when the whole country stops for a horse race. Not just any race, but the Melbourne Cup. Tuesday, 2 November 1948, is a day that will live in the memory of wounded punters, delighted bookmakers and a sixteen-year-old kid from the bush called Ray Neville who rode the outsider, Rimfire, to win the Cup on an 80 to 1 shot.

But, if all the rest of Australia stopped for this particular horse race, one man did not. Mr Justice Barry had chosen Cup Day for a largely unappreciated visit to Kyneton Hospital. Members of the hospital board were displeased when they heard he was coming. There had been enough bad publicity about the hospital already; they didn't need a visit from the judge drawing further attention to it. So the welcome they received was not overwhelming as Barry and his associate, Jim Edwards, toured the labour ward and nursery and took possession of certain documents.

Newspaper photographers were in abundance for the big day, Friday 5 November, the day when the two little girls would be paraded before the judge. They were not disappointed by the Morrisons. Little Johanne Lee was in her summer Sunday best as she was led into the court buildings by her mother for their appointment in the judge's chambers. Pictures of Lee taken that day show her a little overwhelmed by all the attention but also excited and curious. It was one of her rare visits to the big city.

Gwen Morrison had selected the prettiest of Lee's homemade dresses for the occasion. It was short-sleeved with a strip of lace across the top of the bodice and another touch of lace on the pocket. She had matching white shoes and socks, a bow in her hair and was clutching a full-sized handkerchief in her right hand. Gwen Morrison, in her familiar grey suit and black hat, was gripping her other hand.

The photographers missed Nola as she was hustled into the court precincts by the ever-protective Jessie Jenkins. Newsmen were not permitted to attend the remarkable ceremony which was about to take place in the judge's chambers. It was an awkward, tense time for both families as they sat in separate rooms, awaiting the judge's summons.

The Morrisons were called first, ushering a chirpy Lee ahead of them down the passage and into the dimly lit chambers. The door closed behind them. Jessie Jenkins tightened her grip on Nola's small hand. No one would prise her away from her mother. At home Nola ruled the roost, but here in this strange place, with her parents oddly subdued and speaking in hushed tones, she could sense the tension and clung close to her mother.

'It's your turn now, Mr Jenkins. The judge is ready for you.' The three of them filed out of the office behind the court orderly, crossed a courtyard and entered a long, narrow passage. In a masterstroke of insensitive timing, they were led virtually straight into two adults and a child leaving by the same corridor. The Morrisons!

Bitter adversaries face-to-face in such a tight space; would their antipathy towards each other finally break out? The crisis lasted only a moment; the two families brushed past each other, one man nodding to the other in a token sign of recognition.

Once inside, Jessie Jenkins remembers peering across the gloomy chambers and recognizing the judge, dressed informally in his street clothes, but not the other man who was seated nearby. They were motioned to a couple of comfortable chairs facing the judge and Nola perched on her mother's knee. Barry asked all the questions in a friendly, conversational fashion.

'He asked about her teeth. Nola had bad teeth, so did Helen,' Jessie Jenkins recalls. They were in the room for about half an hour before the judge finally asked a question which troubled the Jenkinses deeply. Noel Jenkins can almost remember Barry's exact words in that dark, book-lined room. 'What would you do if you had to give Nola over?' It was a question they could not possibly answer but it was a question that left them with a boding fear of the judge's intentions.

Barry detected a striking contrast in the two girls, not in their appearance so much as in their personalities. Lee Morrison struck him as being a bright, engaging little girl, not at all overawed by this mysterious meeting. Nola offered him nothing of her natural charm and, in fact, he had trouble getting a word out of her.

A short time later the judge saw the two girls for a second time, seated in the body of the court with their parents and he had the opportunity to compare them all together. Jessie Jenkins was aware of the presence of the Morrisons, just a few seats behind. Out of the corner of her right eye she could see Gwen Morrison and the dark-haired child beside her.

Also in the court that day were Sisters Lockhart, Cass and Atkinson, who were under orders to attend for further cross-examination. They were wondering what was going to happen next. Barry himself told the court that it was most unusual for him to recall witnesses, but then it was a most unusual case. The judge recounted his trip to Kyneton and said that the documents he had taken from the hospital had been sealed and later made available to the lawyers for both sides.

Sister Lockhart was first to be called. The judge questioned her about entries in the hospital's midwifery book and asked her if she had signed them. She denied that she had made the entries, which mistakenly listed the Morrison baby as having been born first. She also denied that she had signed the book, even though it clearly showed the name Lockhart. This issue took up a lot of the court's time, only to turn out to be a red herring. But it was yet another black mark against the hospital's efficiency. It was eventually cleared up nearly a week later when a fourth nurse, Sister Gwendoline Maud Walsh, revealed that it was she who had written the entries in the midwifery book and signed Lockhart's name as a matter of convenience. There was nothing sinister at all about it and the entry of the time of birth was a genuine mistake. Gwen Morrison's baby had indeed been the second born.

Mr Justice Barry questioned Elizabeth Lockhart once more about the method used at Kyneton to take the babies from the labour ward to the nursery. He had been given two versions by the nurses: Sister Cass swore they were always moved in cots, Sister Lockhart was equally firm that they were usually carried.

Barry: When the babies are taken from the nursery, when a newly born baby is taken from the nursery to its mother, is it carried by the nurse or wheeled in a bassinet?
Lockhart: Carried.
Barry: Carried in the nurse's arms?
Lockhart: Yes.
Barry: Out of the labour ward?
Lockhart: Out of the labour ward. Oh well, the usual practice up there was to carry it out.
Barry: That is that the bassinet that was in the labour ward was left there?
Lockhart: Yes.
Barry: The child was picked out of the bassinet and taken into the nursery?
Lockhart: Yes.
Barry: And the door that led out of the labour ward into the vestibule?
Lockhart: Yes.
Barry: Is a swing door, isn't it?
Lockhart: Yes.
Barry: A door which if your hands were occupied you would open by pushing your shoulder against it?
Lockhart: Yes.

The judge then turned to the possibility of a newborn baby being mixed up with one born twenty-four or more hours earlier. He asked Elizabeth Lockhart, 'Is there much difference between a newly born baby and a baby twenty-four-hours-old, from the point of view of telling the difference to a nurse or a mother?' She replied, 'Sometimes there is.' The answer was none too specific, so Barry persisted: 'Would you think it possible to mix up a newly born baby with a baby twenty-four-hours-old?' She answered, 'I don't think so.' Elizabeth Lockhart left the witness box and walked out of the 'Whose Baby Case' for the last time, but it was to leave unpleasant memories that would last a lifetime.

She did not abandon nursing despite the strain of her court appearances and the publicity. Elizabeth Lockhart eventually retired in 1978 and now lives quietly in the foothills of Melbourne's picturesque Dandenong Ranges.

Olive Cass made a brief return to the witness box for a series of questions from the judge which appeared to be designed merely to tie up a few loose ends in his own mind. Then she, too, walked out of the court and out of the case. Sister Cass admitted many years later that she had felt smeared by the whole affair and for a time she left Victoria and worked interstate because the name Cass immediately awakened people's memories of the 'Whose Baby Case'. She eventually returned and worked until her mid-sixties, retiring a few months early because of illness.

The third and last of the nurses, Tessie Atkinson, was to find her second encounter with Mr Justice Barry no more pleasant than the first. He greeted her with the remark: 'You have had an opportunity to think over lots of things since you were last here...' Barry then began probing the relationship between the three nurses and any possible animosity before or since the case began.

> *Barry:* Are you on quite good terms with Sister Cass and Sister Lockhart.
> *Tessie Atkinson:* I consider so, yes.
> *Barry:* You never had any quarrels with them?
> *Atkinson:* Never that I can remember.
> *Barry:* And you know of no reason why, do you, why they should say you were in the hospital labour ward at a double confinement if you were not there?
> *Atkinson:* I think if they said I was there they can probably remember me being there. I don't think they would say it if they did not remember me being there.
> *Barry:* Do you remember the first operation you saw?
> *Atkinson:* I would say no.
> *Barry:* Didn't that stick in your memory, the first time that you

saw a person operated on?
Atkinson: I can remember occasions when I have been in the operating theatre during my training, but I cannot remember the very first time.
Barry: Can't you remember the smell of ether?
Atkinson: I would not say that I do.
Barry: Sister, if a young nurse had been present at a double confinement, that being one of the first confinements she had ever seen, and she told you three or four years afterwards that she could not remember whether or not she had been present at it, would you believe her?
Atkinson: Yes I would.
Barry: The suggestion is not that you did wash the two babies, but you carried them out of the labour ward and put them in the bassinets?
Atkinson: I don't know whether I am correct, but I think you said earlier today that the door in the labour ward swung both ways. The larger door there will only go one way. As you are coming out of the labour ward you could not push it, you would have to pull it towards you. The double doors are certainly swing doors.
Barry: The customary thing is to push it with your shoulder, isn't it?
Atkinson: Maybe it would.
Barry: Coming in and out that would be the sensible kind of door to have, the kind of door that is opened by people who many times have their hands burdened and don't want, anyhow, to handle doorknobs. That is the kind of door it is, isn't it?
Atkinson: Yes, it is a very strong door.
Barry: However the babies were got out of the ward, whether they were taken out in bassinets or whether they were taken out in someone's arms, the person cast for the role of removing the babies out of the ward is you. That seems to be what the two sisters say. Sister Lockhart says that she found the two babies in their bassinets awaiting baths when she came into the nursery. You recall her saying that?
Atkinson: Yes.

Barry: Does that suggest to you that you might have been the person who brought them into the nursery?
Atkinson: I may have. If I did, I don't remember.

In his last questions to Tessie Atkinson, Mr Justice Barry harked back to her terrible lapse of memory of the events of 22 June.

Barry: Have you any recollection of being called into the labour ward?
Atkinson: Not any.
Barry: Not any?
Atkinson: No.
Barry: Have you thought over it since you were last here?
Atkinson: I felt very worried about it.
Barry: That has not brought back anything to your memory?
Atkinson: No.

There was no one happier than Tessie Atkinson to be finally excused from the witness box by her tormentor, Mr Justice Barry. He had been particularly tough on her, obviously finding it hard to accept that she could remember so little of such a momentous night.

Tessie Atkinson has a far better memory of some things. Thirty-five years after the case ended for her, she recalls the judge's 'piercing blue eyes' and his questions, mainly about the swinging door. 'I can remember, I can see him now,' she says. 'His eyes were so blue. Piercing blue eyes.' She is still bitter about the way the case was conducted and some of the things said in the court. She also has a pet theory about what happened in the Kyneton Hospital labour ward but she won't reveal it.

'I told the truth,' she insists. 'I still feel guilty about it all. Guilty because I was made the scapegoat. I'll never forget Judge Barry looking at me and asking which doors I went out. He probed and probed on that. I felt that it was me who got the flak for taking them out.'

Tessie Atkinson has fonder memories of the time she spent as a nurse in Kyneton, of the friendships formed and the fun they had even though it was wartime. 'We had a wonderfully happy time in

Kyneton. Gee, they were a comradely crowd. We used to go to dances together, not only two of us but the whole six or seven. It was a good atmosphere.'

Whatever friendships might have been forged between Sisters Cass, Lockhart and Atkinson at the Kyneton Hospital, they failed to survive the traumatic court case. After the three left the court that day they went their separate ways, never to meet again.

11 JUDGEMENT

Jack Barry was an angry man. The cause of his displeasure could be traced to the early days in the case when the first letters began to arrive. He regarded them then as a minor irritant, the work of a few misguided souls who saw fit to advise him on how to rule in this delicate matter. By now the case was virtually over, but the mail was reaching weighty proportions. No other case in Australian legal history had ever attracted such a flood of unsolicited advice.

Just before he began sitting on 12 November, the last court session before he would give his judgement, Barry complained bitterly to a couple of colleagues that he was heartily fed up with his unwanted correspondents. Later, he was formally to warn the letter writers to keep their noses out of judicial business.

Public interest had swelled as the case journeyed along and the letters came from all around the country, as well as a number from overseas. This last day, however, was dull, arousing little interest from anyone. It ended tamely, with Barry asking Hudson if he wished to present any further evidence. The answer being negative, he adjourned the case with the words: 'Very well, I will consider this matter.'

Thirteen days were to pass before Mr Justice Barry returned to the Supreme Court, on 25 November 1948, to deliver a judgement that had been awaited eagerly by all of Australia. The cream of Melbourne's legal society crowded into the court, anxious to hear the brilliant young judge's findings. They would be reported around the world and recorded, as the evening *Herald* put it, 'in law journals throughout the British Empire'.

136

Gwen Morrison leads Johanne Lee into court to be examined by Mr Justice Barry.

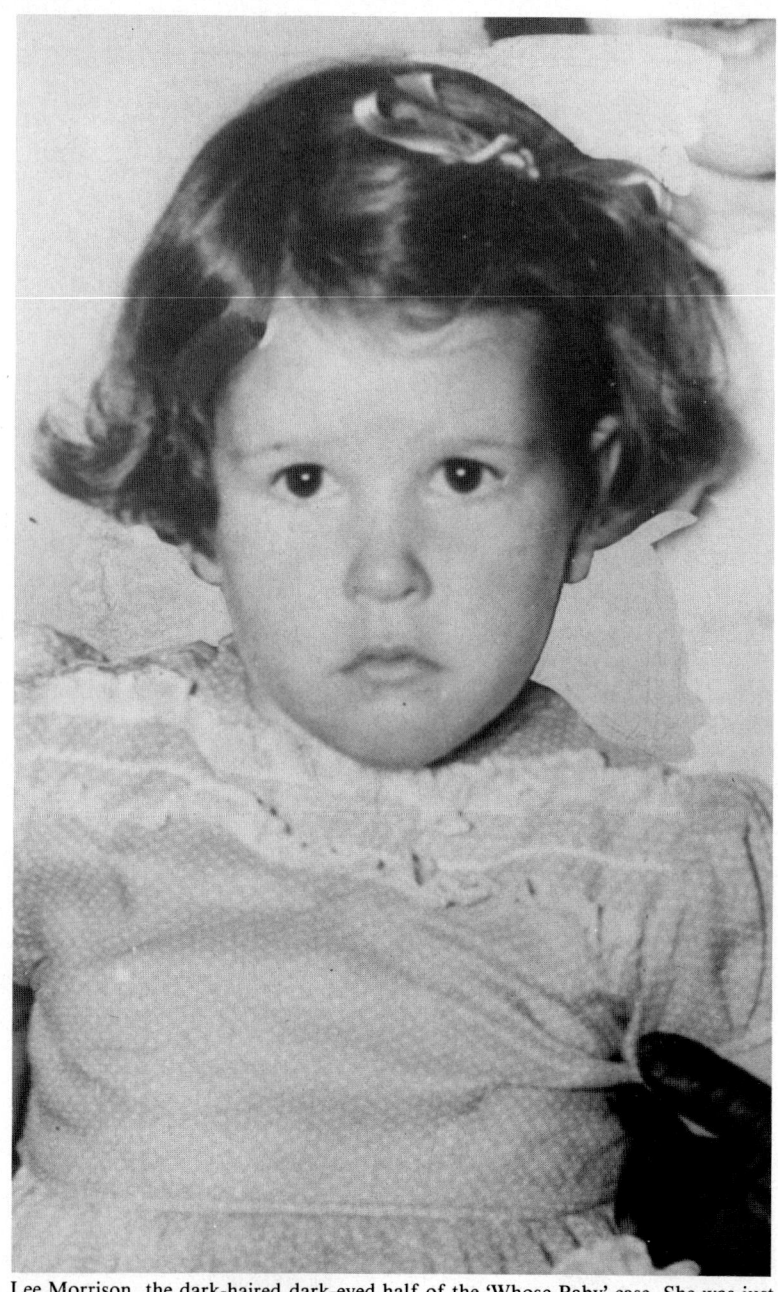

Lee Morrison, the dark-haired dark-eyed half of the 'Whose Baby' case. She was just over three years old when this picture was taken.

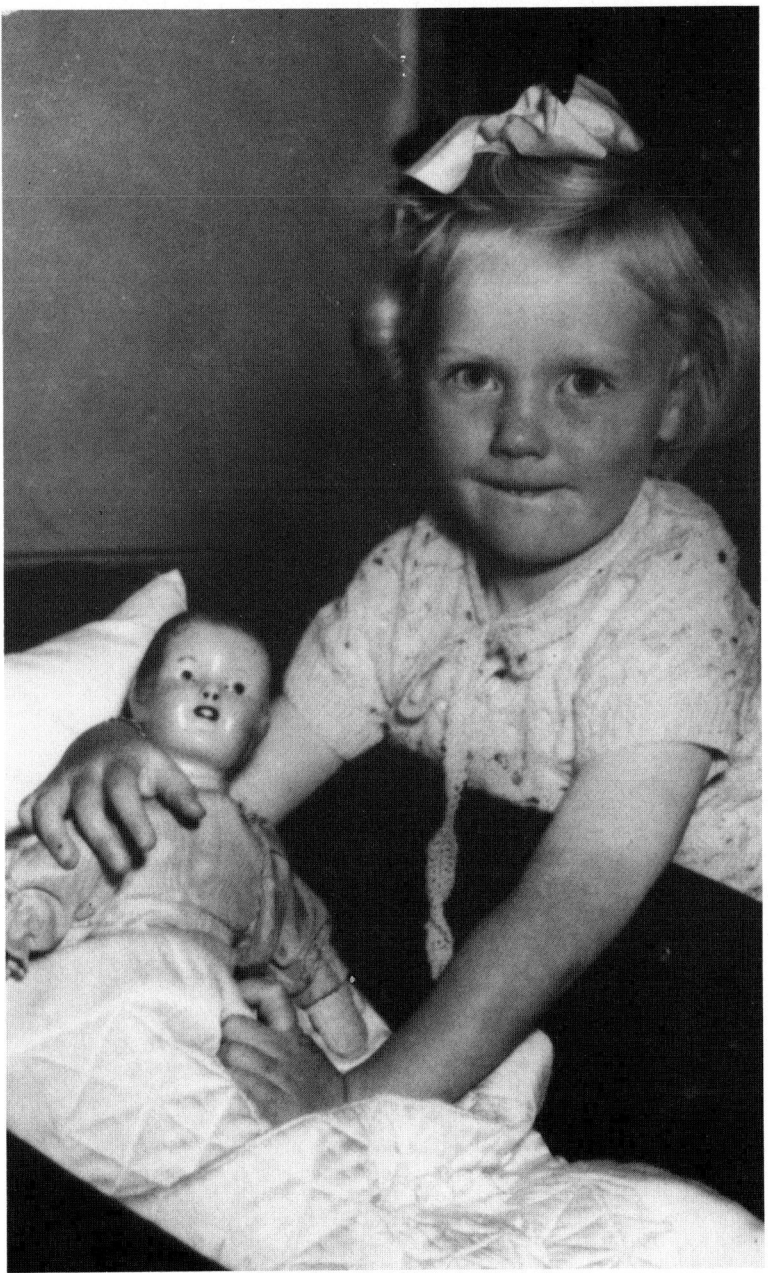
Nola Jenkins, aged 3, plays at home with her favourite doll.

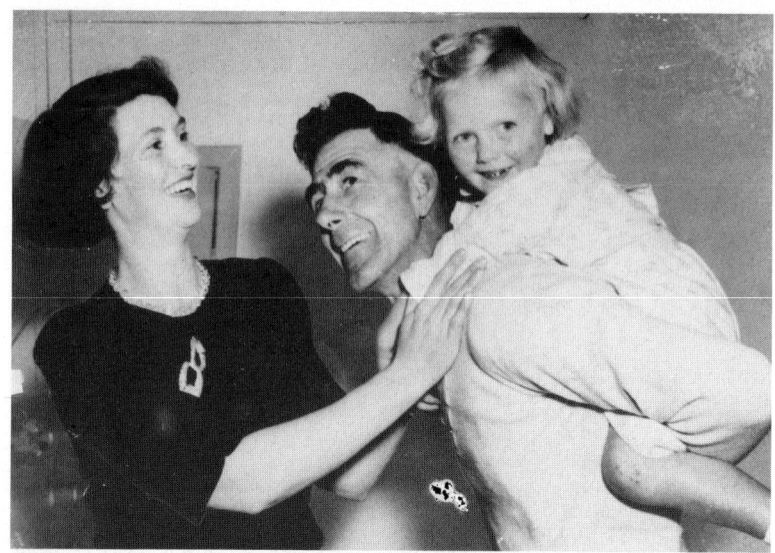

Above: The parents were showing a brave face—but only hours earlier Noel and Jessie Jenkins had heard bad news. They would lose their fun-loving Nola unless they submitted to a blood test. This was the first night that Mrs Jenkins had allowed photographs.
Below: They always had a special relationship, Bill and Lee Morrison. Even though he joined his wife in the fight for custody of Nola Jenkins, Bill Morrison had often sworn he would never give up Lee. On the day this picture was taken the Morrisons had been told they had virtually won their Supreme Court action for possession of Nola. Bill's comment was: 'If anyone wants us to give up Lee, they'll have to fight for her.'

Above: The night before her fifth birthday Nola Jenkins listens to a bedtime story from big brother Arthur. Arnold and sister Helen watch on.
Below: A treasured photo from the Morrison family album. Lee Morrison, five, and Colleen, seven, show off their matching dolls prams. As with all her clothes, Lee is wearing a dress made by her mother, Gwen.

Left: Bernard Nolan. He and Noel Jenkins became mates through their enthusiasm for shooting. Later Nolan was to act as solicitor for the Jenkins.
Centre: Mr Justice Barry. His judgement was brilliant but, much to his dismay, was to be overturned by higher courts.
Right: Solicitor Jack Galbally. At first he didn't believe the Morrisons but then he became their greatest ally.

Left: Ted Hudson. Senior counsel for the Jenkins. He argued that regardless of their parentage, the best interests of Nola and Lee would be served by them remaining with the families they knew and loved.
Centre: Barrister Henry Winneke played a key role in constructing the Jenkins' legal fight to keep Nola.
Right: The brilliant barrister Robert Monahan on his way into court. A man who could normally command a handsome fee, he gave his services free to the Morrisons.

Left: Charles Sweeney, barrister. He gave his services to the Morrisons for nothing and flew to London to prepare their case for the Privy Council.
Centre: Sir William Webb. It was left to him to make the final judgement in the High Court. His ruling—that Nola should remain with Noel and Jessie Jenkins.
Right: Mr Justice Lowe of the Victorian Supreme Court. Former Prime Minister Robert Menzies, once said: 'No man could be as wise as Charlie Lowe looks.'

Above: A picture that captures the spirit of togetherness of Noel, Jessie and Nola Jenkins. Taken when Nola was going on for four.

Below left: Five years old tomorrow, and still the fight goes on for the custody of this little girl. Nola Jenkins waves goodbye to a Melbourne *Herald* photographer on 21 June 1950.

Below right: A grim-faced Gwen Morrison at her mother's home in Kangaroo Flat, Bendigo, on 4 July 1950. Just a short time before she had learned that the case was finally lost. Jodhpur-clad Lee had no way of knowing, but the decision meant she would be staying with the Morrisons for ever. 'Lee will never suffer because of all this,' said Gwen Morrison. Then she added: 'I know that Nola will eventually come back to me.'

Above: The photographer taking this picture of a group of Woomelang mothers almost missed one of the key figures in the 'Whose Baby' case, and accidentally captured another. Top left and almost hidden is Gwen Morrison, beside her sister Gloria Bock, wearing the hat. Bottom right is Lee, who wasn't meant to be in the picture at all!
Below left: Almost five years old, Lee Morrison is developing into a remarkably pretty dark-haired girl. The public could never understand why anyone would want to give her up.
Below right: Nola in November 1948 with brother Arnold and 'friend'.

JUDGEMENT

Barry's task had been agonizing. Whatever his judgement, it would mean suffering for one of the families. He made no secret in later years that the case caused him great personal anguish and he had worried immensely about it. But, he always believed that the judgement he reached was correct and fair to all parties.

The judge was surprised, although he concealed the fact at the time, that not one of the four parents was present in the court. What he did not know was that the Jenkinses feared the worst, having been warned in advance by their legal team, and were loath to be present in the court where their emotions would be exposed to the public gaze. Bill and Gwen Morrison decided to stay at home, too, because they were equally concerned about the judgement going against them.

For them, there was also the question of money, something that had become increasingly embarrassing as the case went on. Every trip from distant Woomelang to Melbourne meant at least one day off work for Bill and, although Jack Galbally and the barristers were providing their services for nothing, there were other local costs eating into the Morrisons' meagre budget. Bill Morrison summed it up years later: 'There's got to be expenses and plenty of expenses for a working man. And while he's chasing that up he's neglecting his job, isn't he? You can't work.'

In his faint, almost inaudible voice, Barry made it clear almost immediately that in a case like this he would

> '... regard the welfare of the child as the first and paramount consideration ... and the rights of her parents in respect of her custody and upbringing are secondary and subordinate ...'

He moved quickly on to the nub of the case: Who were Nola Jenkins' real parents?

> 'It is obvious, I think, that in the circumstances of this case, the determination of the parentage of the child Nola is an essential element in deciding questions relating to her welfare. Tests to determine the blood groupings of Mr and Mrs Morrison and of the child Johanne Lee, who is in their possession, had established that the child Johanne Lee could not be the

137

progeny of a union between Mr and Mrs Morrison...'

Mr Justice Barry then quoted from the report to the court by Dr Grantley Morgan, the man he had appointed scientific assessor to sit on the bench beside him in this difficult case. Morgan had stated:

> 'In the blood of Johanne Lee a relatively uncommon combination of factors is involved. Therefore, she is the progeny of a mating which falls within a very restricted set of possible groupings. These total only 8.2 per cent of all matings in the Australian community. Blood grouping tests would provide a couple wrongly alleged to be the parents of Johanne Lee with an excellent chance of proving that she is not their child. Success can be expected with eleven out of twelve couples chosen at random in a statistically adequate series.'

Barry next dealt with Dr Gerald Loughran, the man who had delivered the two babies, who had carried out his own blood tests on Noel and Jessie Jenkins and Nola, and found that she 'could' be their child.

> 'An affidavit by Dr Loughran was filed but he was absent from Australia and was not available for cross-examination. This circumstance, the absence of any satisfactory evidence of his qualifications in the specialty and the manner in which the affidavit is expressed, leave me quite unprepared to give any weight to it.
>
> I furnished counsel for the parties with copies of Dr Morgan's reports, and made it plain that I considered it desirable that the blood groupings of Mr and Mrs Jenkins and the child Nola should be the subject of further tests. Mr and Mrs Jenkins were not agreeable for this to be done.
>
> In these circumstances, the questions arise, has the court the power to order such tests, and if the power exists, should it be exercised?'

The judge answered his own question a short time later: 'By virtue

JUDGEMENT

of their membership of the community, the obligation to give evidence attaches to all persons capable of doing so.'

During his major address in the case, the Jenkins' counsel, Ted Hudson, had argued that nothing could justify the court in enforcing blood tests. He said no court had the power to compel a person to become a guinea pig. Answering this point, Mr Justice Barry continued:

> 'The argument for the inviolability of the person rests upon the idea, of great vitality in British communities, that it is part of the security of the individual that he shall be free from any invasion of his physical integrity, unless he consents to it or it is done under lawful authority. Where there is conflict, however, the right of the individual must yield to the needs of the common good and the common good requires that justice shall be duly administered.'

The judge quoted various legal authorities on the question of the rights or otherwise of the individual to resist physical examination or testing before coming to his conclusion in this particular case.

> 'I hold... the Supreme Court of Victoria has the power to order Mr and Mrs Jenkins, although they are unwilling to do so, to submit to the harmless medical procedure necessary to enable a sufficient quantity of blood to be obtained to enable a test to be made to determine their blood groupings...'

Although Nola had not been declared a ward of the court, the judge said he considered the court did have the power to order similar blood tests on her. It seemed to those listening that morning that Mr Justice Barry was about to order Noel and Jessie Jenkins and Nola to undergo blood tests. He soon dispelled that impression.

> 'The existence of the power to make these orders is one thing; its exercise is another and different matter. It by no means follows that because the court has the power it must be

exercised, even if the court would be materially assisted in the performance of its duty by recourse to the examination.

The power is in the nature of a reserve power, and is based upon necessity, and it should be used sparingly and only when no other course will enable justice to be done.

Where the court is able to form a clear conclusion upon the evidence available to it and the affected parties, after full and ample opportunity to do so, have not yielded to the plainly expressed opinion of the court that they should undergo the physically harmless medical procedure necessary to enable the tests to be made, the court may proceed to deal with the matter upon the evidence before it.

For those reasons, and in view of the course I intend to take before giving a final pronouncement in this matter, I shall not order that samples of blood be supplied by the respondents [the Jenkinses] and the child Nola, and that blood grouping tests shall be made, but I shall make my findings upon the material I have before me.

This case is a most painful one, and it is perhaps unfortunate that doubts arose in the first place that led Mr and Mrs Morrison to feel that the baby given to Mrs Morrison was not her own.

It is certainly most regrettable that proceedings should not have come before the court until the two children affected by the court's decision have reached their present ages and formed their existing attachments.

Once their parentage has been openly questioned, however, common sense and human experience suggest that it is in the interests of the two children that the matter should be determined so far as it is within human capabilities to do so.'

It was very early in the case that the reporters covering it gave their own judgement. They sensed that Mr Justice Barry was being impressed by the Morrison case, as indeed they were themselves. The *Age*'s Laurie Power recalls: 'The Morrison case was far more convincing and we thought she would win. We felt there had been a mix-up and she'd get judgement.' Now, as Barry continued to read his lengthy decision, the reporters nodded to each other. They reckoned they had been right all along.

The judge told the court he believed the Morrison case rested upon two propositions. The first was that Nola was in fact their child. The second was that for her welfare she should be removed from the Jenkins' home and placed in the Morrisons' care. He said the order they sought from him could be granted only if they established both propositions.

He went on:

'To determine if the first proposition is sound it is necessary to examine four questions. They are as follows:

1. Was the female child to which Mrs Morrison gave birth on June 22, 1945, in the labour ward of the Kyneton District Hospital, the offspring of the union between her and her husband, William Henry Morrison?

2. Was the female child that was brought to Mrs Morrison before she left the labour ward the female child to which she had given birth about half an hour earlier?

3. If the female child so brought to her was not the child to which she had given birth, was there an opportunity for a mistake to be made by which some other female child could have been substituted for the child to which she had given birth?

4. If there was such an opportunity, what other child could have been mistakenly substituted for the child to which Mrs Morrison had given birth?'

Barry then went on to give these replies to his own questions:

'Legitimacy of Mrs Morrison's child:

Blood grouping tests have established that the child Johanne Lee, who was brought to Mrs Morrison before she returned to the hospital ward from the labour ward, could not be the child of a mating between Mr and Mrs Morrison, but that it could be the child of a mating between Mrs Morrison and some other male, other than her husband. It is necessary to say very little upon this aspect. Mrs Morrison's character has not been challenged and there is no ground for any suggestion that the child of which she was delivered was not begotten by her husband. She herself has sworn, "As I have never had sexual intercourse with any man other than my husband, Johanne Lee cannot be my daughter," and no question was directed to her in cross-examination upon that assertion. In accordance with accepted methods of legal reasoning, the court initially presumes that she has not committed adultery and that the child was legitimately begotten. These presumptions are fortified by the uncontradicted facts relating to her conduct, which show she was prompt in alleging a mistake has been made, that she submitted herself to tests to determine her blood grouping, and that she has been a party to the institution and pursuit of these proceedings. The only possible finding, therefore, is that the child to which Mrs Morrison gave birth of June 22, 1945, was the child of herself and her husband.

Was the child given to Mrs Morrison the child to which she had given birth?
According to Mrs Morrison, after her confinement, her baby and the other baby that had been born about the same time were taken from the ward, and within half an hour of the birth of her child, while she was still in the labour ward, a baby was brought to her, and it was that baby she took home with her when she left hospital. That child is Johanne Lee. Blood grouping tests have shown that she cannot be the child of a union between Mr and Mrs Morrison, and the conclusion reached upon the first question involved the further conclusion that the child brought to Mrs Morrison was not the child to which she had given birth shortly before.

Was there opportunity for mistake?
She [Mrs Morrison] has given a detailed account of the events that happened after she was admitted, and it is necessary for me to decide whether I can rely upon that version. Her condition as a woman in labour suggests immediately that her normal faculties for observation would be adversely affected, and accordingly I have scrutinised her testimony with great care. I was at pains to observe her while she was under cross-examination and she left me with the feeling that in the main

she narrated her actual recollection of events. A considerable part of her account is not contradicted and in respect of some matters of some significance her evidence is confirmed by Sister Lockhart, the sister who attended her during her confinement.

...It is necessary now to indicate the evidence given in respect of some matters by Sisters Cass and Lockhart that I reject. Sister Cass asserted that she placed a cot for Mrs Morrison's child on her side of the screen and a cot for Mrs Jenkins' baby on her side; that in each of these cots were placed the marked garments in which the baby was to be dressed and each cot bore a tag with the baby's name. I do not believe this evidence.

Mrs Morrison remembers only one cot in the ward and Sister Lockhart says there was only one cot there. Examination of the whole of the evidence on this aspect satisfies me that there was only one cot in the labour ward and that this cot was the only one usually there; that it was not tagged and did not contain garments with which to dress a baby.

Sister Cass also deposed that she prepared a second "set-up" in the labour ward for Mrs Jenkins' confinement. I do not accept this evidence. I think the only addition to the usual equipment of the labour ward was the bed that was pushed in with Mrs Jenkins on it. It is significant that Sister Cass remembered Sister Lockhart's asking for the ether bottle and that she passed it over to her. From this I infer there was only one ether bottle available for use, which would not have been the case had there been two complete "set-ups".

Sister Lockhart gave some inconclusive evidence to suggest that Mrs Morrison lost consciousness through the administration of an anaesthetic. I am satisfied to accept Mrs Morrison's evidence that she did not.

I have given careful consideration to the evidence of Sisters Cass and Lockhart concerning the part they allege was undertaken by Sister Atkinson, particularly in view of Sister Atkinson's professed failure to recall anything of the events of the night. It is quite incredible, if Sister Atkinson, a person completely inexperienced in midwifery, were in fact assisting at these two confinements which occurred practically simultaneously, that she would not carry a vivid recollection of the events. The versions given by the two midwives involve that neither of them handled a baby in the labour ward, and that the only person other than the doctor who did so was Sister Atkinson, who assisted the doctor at both deliveries.

I do not believe that Sister Atkinson assisted at the births; but the evidence satisfies me that it was she who took the babies out of the labour ward, through the lobby and into the nursery, which is outside the doors of the lobby and adjacent to the labour ward; that she there put the two babies in bassinets and went about her other duties elsewhere. I am satisfied that the babies were not wheeled out in the bassinets, but were carried out by Sister Atkinson in her arms, and that as she was leaving the labour ward, Dr Loughran made some remark for the purpose of directing attention to the possibility of confusing the identity of the two babies.

In view of Sister Lockhart's evidence that the usual practice where there was only one birth was to pick the baby up from the bassinet in the ward and carry it to the nursery and there place it in a cot, from which it was picked up to be bathed, I cannot accept Sister Cass's evidence that it was the usual practice to wheel the baby out of the labour ward in a cot or bassinet. In any event, the circumstances on this night were so unusual that it would be extremely unlikely that if there were any customary practices they would be adhered to, and it seems to me much more likely that the babies would be carried out of the ward as Mrs Morrison described.

My assessment of the reliability of the testimony of Sisters Cass, Lockhart and Atkinson may be gathered from what I have said. None of them impressed me as entirely frank, and I am satisfied that they have not given me their complete recollections of the events surrounding the births of these babies. Sister Cass was concerned to show that she took all precautions, and has, I think, described what ought to have been done rather than what actually occurred.

Sister Atkinson's claim that she has no memory at all of the events is at once too complete and too convenient to fail to arouse judicial incredulity. Sister Lockhart is less open to criticism for lack of candour than the other two sisters, but she also felt she had to show she was not at fault, and her evidence suffered accordingly.

The result is that where there is any conflict between these witnesses' evidence and Mrs Morrison's, I rely upon Mrs Morrison's version. The account given by Mrs Morrison has been shown to accord in its main outlines with the facts that are not in dispute.

Her statement that Dr Loughran said, "Are you sure you have those babies tagged?" is, in some measure confirmed by Sister Lockhart's recollection that, whether or not in fun, the doctor sounded a warning note.

In the result, therefore, I find Mrs Morrison a trustworthy and credible witness and I accept her account of the events in the labour ward, with this exception, that I consider her inference that the sister who carried out the babies was Sister Cass or Sister Lockhart was mistaken, and that the person who carried them out was Sister Atkinson.

The suggestion that she may have mistaken a sister taking out an armful of soiled linen for a sister carrying out two babies is ingenious, but I cannot accept it.

Upon the evidence before me, it appears that the two babies were left unattended in the nursery until Sister Lockhart entered to find they had not been bathed. The fact that they had not been bathed by the person who took them there is some indication that that person was Sister Atkinson, whose inexperience in these matters was such that she would not regard herself as expected to bathe newly born babies.

The probabilities are that Sister Cass, whose time of duty must have been past by the time she had taken Mrs Jenkins back to her room, considered she had finished her duties when she completed attending to Mrs Jenkins, and that she did not concern herself with the babies, but left that matter to Sister Lockhart, who was still on duty, or to any of the nurses coming on day duty.

It is clear that the two babies were bathed by Sister

Lockhart, who felt, not unnaturally, somewhat aggrieved at being left with the task. Sister Lockhart gives no reliable evidence that there was any identification of the babies on which she could rely. I have said I am satisfied that the bassinets in which she found the babies were not brought from the labour ward and thus, even if those bassinets were labelled, the effectiveness of that precaution depended upon Sister Atkinson having placed the babies she had brought from the labour ward in their right cots.

The conclusion to which this lengthy review of the evidence upon this aspect conducts me is that the circumstances surrounding the birth of Mrs Morrison's child were of an extraordinary kind, partaking of the nature of an emergency, and that there was not only the opportunity, but a very great likelihood that the identities of the two children might be confounded.

What other child could have been substituted for Mrs Morrison's?

It appears that between the 19th of June 1945, and the 22nd of June 1945, four female children were born at the Kyneton District Hospital. A female child was born on the 19th, another on the 20th, and two children, the circumstances of whose births has been examined, on the 22nd.

It was submitted by Mr Hudson that the evidence did not exclude the possibility that some baby other than Mrs Jenkins' child may have been mistakenly exchanged for Mrs Morrison's baby. I do not think there is any substance in this submission. It appears to me most unlikely that a mother of a child born on the 19th or 20th would fail to detect the mistake if a child born on the 22nd were brought to her.

If this be excluded as a possibility, the findings of fact I have set forth earlier leave open only one conclusion, and it is that the only baby that could have been exchanged for Mrs Morrison's baby was the baby born to Mrs Jenkins.'

The judge had now answered all the questions he had posed. He believed that Sister Atkinson carried both babies out of the labour ward in her arms. He believed the doctor warned her not to mix them up. He believed Sister Lockhart bathed them. He did not believe Sister Cass tagged two cots in the labour ward. If there had been a mix-up, and the judge obviously believed there had been, he left just one question unanswered. Just who did switch the babies?

Both families had placed much reliance on physical characteristics; hair colouring, the eyes, likenesses to other family members, even gaps in the teeth.

The judge did not share their faith in such matters. In fact, he dispensed with that in these three paragraphs:

'I saw each child in the company of the applicants [the Morrisons] and also in the company of the respondents [the Jenkinses] and I saw them together. I did not derive any assistance from this inspection. They are two attractive and well-developed children, but I was unable to observe any features of resemblance I could feel were of such a kind that I could place reliance upon them. This was not unexpected, for the better opinion of the authorities is that such evidence of resemblance is often fanciful and must be treated with great caution. For similar reasons, I have not obtained any assistance from the photographs that have been placed before me.

There are two other children of the marriage between Mr and Mrs Morrison, a boy aged about ten years and a girl of about five years, and Mr and Mrs Jenkins have two boys, aged eleven and six years respectively, and a child born during the currency of these proceedings. I was not asked to inspect these children and the result of my observation of Nola and Johanne Lee was so inconclusive that I felt no good purpose would be served by my doing so.

The applicants [the Morrisons] attached importance to the fact that the child Nola has blue eyes and the child Johanne Lee dark or brown eyes, whereas Mr and Mrs Morrison are both blue-eyed, and Mrs and Mrs Jenkins dark-eyed. I have no evidence before me from any experts in genetics that would enable me to give weight to these circumstances, and accordingly I do not rely upon them in arriving at my conclusions.'

Mr Justice Barry next moved on to discuss just what those conclusions were.

'The analysis of the evidence I have given establishes that Mrs Morrison gave birth to a female child begotten by her husband; that the circumstances surrounding the birth were such that there was an opportunity for that child to be mistakenly exchanged for a female child born to Mrs Jenkins at approximately the same time, and that the child which was given to Mrs Morrison as her child was, in fact, not the child to which she had given birth. The only conclusion reasonably open upon these facts is that Mrs Morrison was given Mrs Jenkins' baby and that Mrs Jenkins was given Mrs Morrison's baby.'

Reaching that conclusion from the jumble of evidence before him had been no easy task for Mr Justice Barry, but the harder part was still to come. He was a family man himself, with two teenage children, one of them a girl. Now he had to decide if it would be not only just, but in the best interest of Nola Jenkins, a child of three years and five months, to be taken from the home that she knew and loved and placed in the care of strangers.

'... I must consider what, in all aspects of the case, is best for the child's welfare in the fullest sense of that word. So far as is disclosed by the material before me, Mr and Mrs Morrison and Mr and Mrs Jenkins are all estimable citizens, and from the viewpoint of material benefits that the child would enjoy there is no substantial difference between the two families. Mr and Mrs Jenkins' economic position may be better than that of Mr and Mrs Morrison, but there is no reason to think that a child in the custody of either family would not be properly cared for and brought up as in a normal Australian family. The question that arises on this aspect, therefore, is whether the circumstances that the child Nola has grown up as a member of the Jenkins family, and is loved and cherished by those she believes to be her parents as their own child, should result in the denial of her custody to her true parents, who are not personally disqualified from being her custodians.

The decision of such a question is one of grave concern, but in arriving at it the court must act in conformity with the standards generally accepted in this community.

The first and most natural form of social group is the family composed of father, mother and children; it is the basis of Western civilised societies and, while the state exists for the common good of all individuals and families which compose it, the family exists primarily for the good of its individual members. The family is thus the fundamental unit in our society, and ordinarily where the parents are of blameless life, and desire the child to be with them and are able and willing to provide for the child's material and moral necessities, it is for her welfare to be with her real parents.

According to the custom of this community, parental responsibility does not end with the child's tender years; it extends through adolescence, and in actual family life, often into early maturity. Children bring great happiness, but they sometimes bring great sorrows and disappointments, and often it is the realisation that the person who brings these griefs is of the parents' flesh and blood that enables them to be endured. The assumption generally accepted in English-speaking communities and acted upon by the courts in matters such as this, that if there are no disqualifying factors, the proper place for a child is with its own parents and their other children, rests upon the experience of countless generations of the family as an institution in vicissitudes and tribulations as well as in good fortune and times of happiness.

After long and anxious consideration, therefore, I have come to the conclusion that the claim of those I hold to be the real parents should succeed. It is inevitable that the child will suffer grief by being removed from those she loves and by whom she is loved, but there is wisdom and comfort in the words of Eve J.'

Mr Justice Barry said that the learned judge Eve, in a case

concerning a seven-year-old girl who had been in the custody of relatives since infancy, had said:

> 'It was said that the little girl would be greatly distressed in parting from Mr and Mrs Jones. I can quite understand it may be so, but at her age, one knows from experience, how mercifully transient are the effects of parting and other sorrows and how soon the novelty of fresh surroundings and new associations effaces the recollections of former days and kind friends, and I cannot attach much weight to this aspect of the case.'

So it seemed that this was the argument that would win the day. But things were not to be quite so cut and dried. At this point the young, relatively inexperienced judge produced a surprise formula which would be hailed as eminently fair but was obviously the product of an immensely shrewd mind. Within the space of just a minute, he managed to shift the burden of deciding Nola's future back to the Jenkinses.

> 'The conclusions I have stated have been reached upon the evidence before me with full consciousness of their grave importance and with due regard to the heavy burden of persuasion resting upon the applicants. They have been reached, however, without knowledge of the blood groupings to which Mr and Mrs Jenkins and the child Nola belong. It was within the power of the respondents [the Jenkinses] to adduce this material evidence, which in its nature and form would be free from the defects and imperfections that so often mar narrations that proceed from human observation and human memory but, though fully apprised of its significance and importance, they refrained from doing so. The reports of Dr Morgan, confirmed by Dr Bryce, have been available to them, and show that if they are not the parents of Johanne Lee, the probabilities are very high that this fact can be proved to demonstration.
>
> I have decided to give them a final opportunity to submit further evidence in the form of properly verified scientific reports upon the blood groupings of themselves and the child

Nola and, for that purpose, I shall abstain from pronouncing a final order in this matter for seven days. If they decide to do so I shall be prepared to consider the matter in the light of that further evidence. Should they not adduce evidence of the kind indicated, I shall give judgement in accordance with the findings I have announced.'

On the face of it the decision was simple and fair. The Jenkinses were getting one last chance to help the court reach its decision. There was more to it than that, however. The judge was so sure that Nola was, indeed, a Morrison that he had really forced the Jenkinses into a corner where they could either confirm his judgement or appear utterly unreasonable in rejecting such a fair offer. It was a terrible dilemma for the Jenkinses. On one hand, they were convinced Nola was their own child, while on the other hand they did not want to learn anything that might indicate she was not. They had reared her for almost three and a half years and wanted to keep her, regardless. That Johanne Lee might be *their* daughter never appeared to concern them. The question of Johanne Lee had certainly been in the forefront of Mr Justice Barry's thoughts, and it was to her welfare he turned next.

'It is desirable, I think, to make it clear that the application before me relates only to the custody of the child Nola and is not concerned with the custody of the child Johanne Lee. Mr Morrison has sworn that he and his wife are very fond of Johanne Lee, who has never been given cause to think she is not a member of their family. Whether she will remain with Mr and Mrs Morrison, or will go to the custody of Mr and Mrs Jenkins, is not determined by any order I may make, but, in the event of a final order in favour of the applicants [the Morrisons], will depend upon arrangements between Mr and Mrs Morrison and Mr and Mrs Jenkins, or in default of such arrangements, upon an order of this court in proceedings other than those before me.'

So that was it. Unless the Jenkinses complied with his request for blood tests, Nola would be taken from them and given to the

Morrisons. But what of Johanne Lee, the other girl? Would there now be another court action to decide her future? Would the Jenkinses ever accept her and, more debatable, would the Morrisons let her go? The judgement left as many questions unanswered as it had attempted to answer.

The news was flashed over the radio within minutes of the judge leaving the bench. In Kyneton, there was public outrage and the townspeople were quick to show their allegiance. The Jenkinses were true blue locals; the Morrisons had been mere itinerants in the town. By nightfall, an enthusiastic team of collectors had amassed £133, a handsome sum in those days, to present to Noel Jenkins to help him keep fighting. Noel and Jessie put on a very brave front for the friends and relatives who called around at their home in Mitchell Street for a cup of tea and to offer some words of sympathy and encouragement.

If there had been even the slightest doubt that the Jenkinses would fight the case to its bitter end, it was dispelled in those first few hours after the judge's decision. Such was the strength and enthusiasm of their public support, that Noel and Jessie felt more than ever that the stand they had adopted was the only one for people of principle. But despite their outer show of strength, they were deeply troubled.

When the reporters from Melbourne arrived early that evening Noel was polite but firm, as always. There would be no interviews, he declared, although he and his wife made it perfectly clear that they considered the fight for Nola was far from finished. The newsmen were disappointed with their reluctance to speak but they got an unexpected bonus — Jessie Jenkins agreed to pose for pictures with Nola. There was no sign of grief or even uncertainty in the picture which appeared in the *Sun* the following morning. It was the first picture ever published of mother and daughter together and it showed a beautifully-groomed, attractive, dark-haired woman with a sullen little blonde girl on her knee. Nola remembers the picture being taken all those years ago, the photographers crowding around her, and a crystal clear memory of the outfit her mother was wearing, a black dress with large silver brooch in the shape of a bow. She must have wondered what all the fuss was about.

JUDGEMENT

While Kyneton's population of around 3,500 was smitten with fervour for the Jenkins' cause, there was little more than a ripple of excitement, at least publicly, in Woomelang. The Morrisons had been there for less than a year and were not that well known outside their intimate group of friends.

During the long ordeal leading up to this day of decision, Gwen Morrison had found a true friend and confidante in Marge McIntosh, whose parents owned a garage and general store in Woomelang. Marge, then in her mid-twenties, grew very close to Gwen Morrison in the months before the case began. They lived in homes separated by only a narrow back lane and Gwen was always popping in and out when she needed someone to talk to and lately that had been a daily occurrence. Marge McIntosh will never forget the evening of 25 November 1948, and the jubilation in the Morrison household. 'Gwen was just beside herself when Barry ruled that Nola was her child,' she recalls.

With the case all but clinched in her favour, Gwen Morrison was a different woman that night, far removed from the tragic figure who used to slip into the McIntosh home during the case, confiding her fears and anxiety. 'Before they got the paper she would come across and talk to me. It was getting her down. It was a terrible thing for her. She used to dread to read what was happening with the case,' says Marge. The entire Morrison clan appeared to go through great anguish, according to Marge McIntosh. 'It was really hell for them. Gwen was deeply distressed. She'd weep. She was desperate.'

It was an uncharacteristically outspoken Gwen Morrison who chatted to newsmen the following day. Perhaps her triumph in court had uncorked the hidden feelings but she certainly said some things she was later to regret. Interviewed in her home, feeling at last at ease with herself, the normally reserved housewife declared that she now planned to keep both girls. She said she was eager to see four children in the house instead of three and she would not discuss the possibility of parting with Lee. Backing her up, Bill Morrison declared: 'If anyone wants us to give up Lee, they'll have to fight for her. She's mine. She's not like the other children. They'll bow to me. But Lee has a will of her own. She's the only one who'll stand up to me.' Gwen Morrison nodded her agreement. 'Lee is daddy's girl. She is ours and we are going to keep her.'

The Morrisons must have been carried away with the euphoria of their apparent success, but their outspoken comments about Lee's future caused consternation in two quarters when they appeared in print that weekend. The Jenkinses had needed little convincing that the Morrisons were fanatical in their desire to win at all costs, and this latest claim to both children snuffed out any flicker of hope that there might, after all, be some sort of compromise or dignified settlement between Noel and Jessie Jenkins and Bill and Gwen Morrison.

From that moment, it was going to be eye-for-eye and tooth-for-tooth and eventually some of the legal infighting would get tough. The Jenkins' lawyers were later to attack the Morrisons on two new fronts, those of Gwen Morrison's fidelity and Bill Morrison's tardiness in settling debts.

The other person who greeted the Morrisons' bold statements with dismay was none other than Jack Galbally, the man who had taken their cause to heart. He did not anticipate that their exultant claim to both children would assist his case in any way. In fact, he could see it doing just the opposite.

The following Monday saw Noel and Jessie Jenkins closeted with their solicitor Bernard Nolan in his Melbourne office for the most important decision of the entire case. Would they or would they not accede to the judge's request that they have blood tests? They were still smarting over the Morrison comments about rearing both Nola and Lee. Jessie Jenkins says, with feeling:

> 'I could never quite see why they had this obsession, and it was an obsession, about wanting Nola as theirs. I did sit down and think, "What if it had happened?" And I thought, well, the only child I've ever known is Nola. She was mine in every respect of the word. Well, I was fortunate enough, I suppose, that I was quite sure she was mine and I was convinced of that.'

Noel Jenkins and his wife saw it as yet another example of the obsessive nature of this other family which had intruded on their lives. Would they stop at nothing? Noel Jenkins says with a trace of bitterness:

'I have no idea what went through their minds, or why they got that way, but it became an obsession with them. What created it, or what started it, we'll never know. They weren't people that we knew.'

It was no surprise then that the Jenkinses emerged from their legal conference determined on their future course of action. There would be no blood tests.

They left the Nolan office after a long, solemn discussion to find that the Morrisons had had a major change of heart. Now they were willing to hand over Lee in exchange for Nola. Their sudden reversal was no doubt due to a blunt telephone conversation with solicitor Jack Galbally earlier that day. After it, Galbally issued a statement on Mrs Morrison's behalf.

Galbally said that Gwen Morrison had suggested that the two families go away for a holiday together with the children and exchange them during that period. He quoted her as saying that she would give up Johanne Lee and had no desire to have any further litigation if she got back Nola. As soon as Nola was handed over to her, Mrs Morrison said, she would return Johanne Lee at once, although she would be loath to part with a lovely little girl who was one of the family.

The statement had a lawyer's ring to it, very different from Gwen Morrison's usual style and bearing no resemblance whatever to the fighting, defiant words of the same woman just a couple of days earlier. In precise language it set out Mrs Morrison's acceptance that she would have no right to retain Johanne Lee if she got back her own daughter. Mrs Morrison was also quoted as saying it would be a very sad parting and as a mother she could understand how Mrs Jenkins would feel. Mothers should have their own children. She and Mr Morrison had sought every means to avoid litigation. They wanted only what was right and proper in the interests of the children. It would be in the interests of the little girls if the parents went away together with the children for a holiday during the changeover. Both children would thus become accustomed to their real parents. The result would be that when the holiday ended, and it was time to go home, the children would have forgotten their earlier surroundings and would not notice the change. She hoped Mrs Jenkins would have the same approach.

It was wishful thinking and came three years too late. It seems hardly plausible that the suggestion came from the Morrison household, rather it smacked of the fair-minded Jack Galbally seeking an honourable way out for both families. Years later, Bill Morrison was to insist that he and his wife bore no animosity towards the Jenkinses, through all their confrontations, but his words had a hollow ring to them.

Blair Morrison, the eldest of the Morrison children, was ten when the famous court case was on. His parents kept it from them, he recalls, but there were some things they could not hide. 'Financially, it really hurt,' he says. 'There was a big problem as far as finance was concerned.' Even though their legal fees were being waived, the Morrisons were feeling the pinch over associated costs. Blair remembers how his mother had scrimped and saved a 'few bob a week' to pay into his bank, perhaps towards his future education. It had steadily mounted and the young boy was proud of his bank account. 'I know I had five pound in the bank at Woomelang. Five pound. Mother had to go to Melbourne for the case, didn't have any money, so she had to take that out.'

On the morning of Wednesday 1 December, Bill and Gwen Morrison were in buoyant spirits as they waved goodbye to a few close friends in Woomelang and set off on the long drive to Melbourne. They wanted to be in court the following morning for what they were certain was going to be a judgement in their favour. At last Nola would be their child. They left behind them the little dark-haired girl waving madly as the car drove off, the girl who had always regarded them as Mum and Dad.

Mr Justice Barry was punctual and most businesslike the following morning. He took his seat in the court at precisely 10 a.m. and immediately directed a question at Ted Hudson, counsel for the Jenkinses. 'Is there anything you desire to inform the court?' Hudson replied: 'If Your Honour pleases, my clients do not propose to undergo any further blood tests, and therefore they have no further evidence to offer to the court.'

JUDGEMENT

Before the judge could make his final, formal judgement awarding custody of Nola to the Morrisons, Hudson made it perfectly clear that for his clients the fight was only just beginning. He told Barry: 'My clients intend to test Your Honour's judgement. I propose to ask for a stay of proceedings.'

The judge then gave a brief summary of his earlier findings, including the major point that Gwen Morrison and Jessie Jenkins had been given the wrong children at birth. He explained that because of the emotional nature of the case he had taken great care to be scrupulously fair to the losers.

'I abstained from pronouncing judgement when I stated my findings, in order to give Mr and Mrs Jenkins a final opportunity to do what I considered they should have done at a very much earlier stage. The court has shown this unusual indulgence to Mr and Mrs Jenkins because it is important not only that justice should be done, but that it should manifestly and undoubtedly appear to be done. I realize that until memories faded the carrying out of the order would bring unhappiness to the child and would cause grief and distress to Mr and Mrs Jenkins...'

Mr Justice Barry then referred to his efforts to persuade Noel and Jessie to have voluntary blood tests:

'Had those tests been made and the result of them rendered it necessary for me to reconsider my findings, of course I would have done that, but if those tests were consistent with and confirmatory of my own findings, as I expected they would be, I felt that Mr and Mrs Jenkins should then, as sensible people, realize that it had been established with as much certainty as is humanly possible, that a mistaken exchange of the babies had occurred, and that although my findings caused sorrow to them they were findings which were just and in accordance with the evidence...

In deciding that the welfare of the child Nola required her to be with her true parents I was not insensible to the argument that the two children were happy with their present custodians, and that on a sentimental approach there was much to be said for letting well alone. I am concerned, however, not merely with the present happiness of a child aged three and a half years; I must look further ahead and consider the child as a member of this community who, all going well, will grow through childhood to adolescence and to womanhood, and to whom it may be of great importance as she grows older, to be able to say with certainty that she is with her true father and mother.

It is her welfare in the broader sense and not her present happiness, important though that is, with which the court is concerned... I order that the respondents give the custody of the child Nola to the applicants.'

They were the words the Morrisons had been waiting to hear. However, there was a disappointment for them. Hudson gave notice that the Jenkinses would appeal and the judge agreed to grant a stay of his order. Nola would continue to live with Noel and Jessie Jenkins until the appeal went to the Full Bench of the Supreme Court.

Mr Justice Barry had a last matter to deal with before he left the court that day.

'I have been the recipient of a number of letters in connection with this case. People who write letters to judges are extremely foolish. It does not assist the administration of justice; the judge, it is obvious, cannot acknowledge them in any way. It is an extremely undesirable practice and it is one to which no responsible citizen would have recourse.'

The formal order issued by Mr Justice Barry that December morning sounds cold and unemotional, the legal terminology far removed from the human aspects of this extraordinary case.

'It is ordered that the said child called Nola shall be delivered up by the said Noel Henry Jenkins and Jessie Jenkins to the said Alberta Gwen Morrison and William Henry Morrison and thereafter the said Alberta Gwen Morrison and William

JUDGEMENT

Henry Morrison shall have the custody and upbringing of the said child called Nola, and the manner in which the said child called Nola is to be delivered up reserved for future discussion.'

12 THE LIONESS AND HER CUB

'I still want to be Johanne's other mummy — and I want Mrs Jenkins to be Nola's other mummy for the rest of her life.' Gwen Morrison was still in a daze as she left the Supreme Court in triumph. She knew she had won and the fact that the Jenkinses were going to appeal had failed to sink in. She actually approached an eager reporter and offered him a statement on behalf of the Morrison family, victors in the historic action. She told him:

> 'I just want to say that I hope there won't be any need for more court cases. We are prepared to give back Johanne. We will miss her terribly as she's a wonderful child — I don't know how we are going to do it, but I realize we can't keep them both.'

The reporter was having difficulty keeping up as Gwen Morrison poured out her feelings.

> 'I knew all along that the girls had been mixed — from the time I left the hospital. When I saw the brown eyes I felt it beyond any shadow of doubt. Now I want Mrs Jenkins to know that I want her to come and see Nola whenever she likes. Our house will be open at any time to the Jenkins and I hope Mrs Jenkins will continue to take the same interest in Nola and display the same love. I hope we can do the same with Johanne. I want to be able to go and see her often and I want to continue to take an interest in her welfare.'

Gwen Morrison said she hoped to have Nola home for Christmas, a forlorn wish as the appeal would not go ahead until February. Her husband was less enthusiastic about the court victory and the future exchange of the two girls. Lee was precious to him but he had stuck by his wife despite serious misgivings about the whole affair. 'I had to stick with my wife's side,' he recalled years later, 'no matter what way I thought about it.'

From the Jenkinses there was silence. They had deliberately snubbed the final day of the court case and were already making plans for their appeal. Within seven days it had been lodged and solicitor Bernard Nolan listed sixteen grounds, including harsh criticism of the manner in which Mr Justice Barry conducted the case. One ground of appeal even suggested that the judge had favoured the presentation of the case for the Morrisons 'to such a degree as to be likely to cause a miscarriage of justice'.

Nolan also claimed that the judgement was against the weight of evidence, the judge was wrong in holding that the Morrisons had established that Nola was their child and that the judge was also wrong in rejecting the evidence of Sister Cass. He went on to claim that it would not be in Nola's welfare to be taken from the Jenkinses and the Morrisons had no right to expect judgement in their favour after delaying so long in taking court action.

Christmas 1948, was not a happy time for either family. The Morrisons had won an enormous victory, against the odds, but their jaunty attitude immediately after the Barry judgement soon gave way to doubts and fears. Bill Morrison, a battler at the best of times and something of a novice when it came to handling financial matters, found that he and his family were deeply in debt. Galbally, Monahan and Sweeney had all given their legal skills for nothing, but there were other expenses relating to the case which mounted all the time.

The Christmas presents that year, simple and inexpensive, were the best Gwen Morrison could manage from a few shillings she had saved. There was money owing to local stores and even some unhappy creditors left behind in Kyneton were pressing the Morrisons for settlement. On top of their money woes, they were becoming increasingly aware that even if they defeated the Jenkinses in the appeal case ahead, they faced the very real prospect of parting with Lee. As they watched her face light up on Christmas morning, after Santa Claus had been, Bill and Gwen Morrison were racked by the enormity of what they had set in motion. It was only then, watching Lee and realizing how much they loved her, that it dawned on them that they would be losers in this fight, no matter what.

Noel and Jessie Jenkins shared the financial problems of their rivals. They were paying all their legal fees themselves. Mr Justice Barry had ordered each family to meet their own costs but ruled that the losers, the Jenkinses, should pay for the shorthand writers. That alone amounted to about £50, a hefty sum. Added to that were their own legal fees which brought up a total of around £400, more than most men could earn in a year. And the appeal was still to come.

Within eighteen months both families were facing the prospect of legal costs running into thousands of pounds, amounts far beyond their means. Fortunately for Noel and Jessie Jenkins the townsfolk of Kyneton were still giving enthusiastically to the local fund to aid their cause and the couple themselves trimmed their household budget wherever they could. There were bare boards, though beautifully polished, in the Jenkins home and most of the furniture was handmade by builder Noel.

The 'Whose Baby Case' was sending ripples of unease through the maternity wings of hospitals around Australia. Suddenly everything and everyone was being tagged. It even got to the ridiculous stage where newborn babies were having their names scrawled across their tiny pink chests in letters six inches high.

On Friday, 4 February 1949, the Chief Justice, Sir Edmund Herring, Mr Justice Lowe and Mr Justice Fullagar began hearing the Jenkins' appeal. There was no sign of a Jenkins in the court but Gwen Morrison was there, a lonely figure sitting apart from the other spectators. There was a dull beginning to the appeal, compared with such a sensational trial, with the three judges going through the affidavits and transcript of the Barry case. But, if it was boring to most, Gwen Morrison was not among them. She seemed to hang on every word.

Herring, one of the great chief justices of Victoria, had returned to the Bench after a distinguished spell in the services during the war. A scholarly man, he took life and himself very seriously. Fullagar was a more jovial man, a popular, sociable character. Then there was Charlie Lowe, who looked more serious than any of his fellow judges but concealed beneath his severe countenance a delightful sense of humour. Some people remember him as the target of one of the finer asides from lawyer and later Prime Minister Robert Menzies: 'No man can be as wise as Charlie Lowe looks.' Because Lowe affected such a stern appearance, his witticisms in court often brought a bigger laugh than they perhaps deserved. However, there was deserved laughter in his court one day when a chap trying to avoid jury service told Lowe he couldn't possibly attend because 'my wife is about to conceive a baby'. Lowe did not change expression as he replied: 'It seems to me appropriate that the husband be present.'

Ted Hudson, appearing again for the Jenkinses, concentrated his attack on Mr Justice Barry and his handling of the Supreme Court case. He argued that Barry had not been justified in reaching his decision on the evidence before him but had instead based it on guesswork. He further criticized Barry for having participated in the case, rather than acting as an adjudicator.

Hudson said it was a departure from tradition and against one of the essentials of justice.

> 'When he came to assess the value of the witnesses, he became too close to the case and was not detached in his attitude. He was disposed to resent the attitude of the Jenkins to blood tests and his vision therefore became clouded.'

Hudson moved on to the human side, the fate of Nola, now aged three years and eight months. 'Nola Jenkins would be exchanging a certainty of happiness for uncertainty if the order that she be handed over to the custody of the Morrisons was carried out,' he told the three judges. The change would cause grave discontinuity and leave a vivid impression in the child's life, he warned. There was no certainty that the other children in the Morrison family would make her future life happy.

A key issue in the whole case, said Hudson, was whether there had been one or two cots in the labour ward the night Nola and

Johanne Lee were born. 'I submit there is no evidence to show there was only one cot in the ward. The evidence also showed the baby was clothed in a marked garment when first born,' he said. Hudson argued that it was most improbable that Mrs Morrison's baby was left naked on her bed after being born, as she had testified, especially as it was early morning in the middle of winter.

When it came to Robert Monahan's turn to take up the case for the Morrisons, he quoted legal authorities supporting the view that courts of appeal should not disturb the findings of a trial judge on the credibility of witnesses, unless they were satisfied he was plainly wrong. The trial judge had the advantage of seeing the witnesses, judging their demeanour and the manner in which they had given their evidence. Monahan said that in the matter of the cots, Mr Justice Barry had believed Gwen Morrison, who had testified that there was only one cot in the labour ward, and rejected the evidence of Sister Cass, who swore there were two.

After four days of legal argument there was good news for the Morrisons. The court rejected a number of important grounds of the Jenkins' appeal, mainly related to the way in which Mr Justice Barry had conducted the case. It rejected the argument put forward by Hudson that Barry had participated in the conduct of the case and also rejected his submission that the Morrisons had delayed too long in taking court action.

The Jenkinses were not too downhearted by this setback. By now they believed that public support was welling behind them. Why, just that day, the volunteer firemen of the central district of Victoria had presented them with a cheque for £136 towards their legal costs. Noel Jenkins was being rewarded for all those twenty years of service he had given to his local fire brigade.

Day five saw Robert Monahan trying to demolish what he had always regarded as Ted Hudson's pet red herring — the theory that even if there had been a mix-up of babies at Kyneton Hospital, there was no evidence that Mrs Morrison got Mrs Jenkins' baby. She might have been given the Hayes baby or the Perry baby, born a couple of days earlier. Monahan said this theory was rubbish and quoted the evidence of Sister Lockhart that she did not think it possible for a mother to mistake a newborn baby for one born twenty-four hours earlier.

Monahan said it was even more unlikely that a mother could mistake a newborn baby for one born seventy-two and forty-eight hours earlier, as in the case of the Hayes and Perry babies. He argued that Mrs Hayes and Mrs Perry would certainly have known their own children and immediately detected any mistake. If necessary, if the court needed to be convinced, he said, it would be a simple matter to obtain affidavits from those two mothers that they were satisfied they had their own babies.

Henry Winneke, junior counsel for the Jenkinses, interrupted to point out that it was a little late in the proceedings to be introducing new affidavits. None of the three judges pursued the matter so Monahan, naturally, let it drop. Many months later he was to find that red herring still bobbing up and he was to regret not having finally laid it to rest there and then.

Monahan was critical of the Jenkins' attitude: 'Right throughout the proceedings the attitude of the Morrisons was to get at the truth by blood tests, but apparently the attitude of the other side was the opposite.' Winneke was on his feet immediately, protesting that his clients were being misrepresented.

> *Winneke:* The attitude of Mrs Jenkins was that she was certain she had her own baby, and no matter what anyone else said she was convinced Nola was her child.
> *Sir Edmund Herring:* Even if a blood test showed that Nola could not possibly be their child?
> *Winneke:* She would still consider that Nola was her child. She was her mother, had brought her up and considered she should not be handed over to the Morrisons. That was why she refused to have a blood test.

It was at this stage of the appeal that the judges gave a broad hint as to the way they were thinking, led by the Chief Justice, who told the barristers: 'We have to consider the welfare of the children.' Mr Justice Lowe agreed:

> *Mr Justice Lowe:* What is troubling me is that in the absence of

blood tests of Nola it might subsequently be found out that Nola might have a blood constituent incompatible with that of the Morrisons. In the meantime what would happen to Johanne Lee? We have to determine this case on the paramount basis of consideration of the welfare of the child.
Monahan: Which child?
Lowe: Nola, in this case. What the court has to determine is the welfare of Nola and no one is representing Nola.

The court adjourned that day with the three judges reserving their decision. The Jenkins' barristers were delighted with the turn in events and that night solicitor Bernard Nolan told Noel Jenkins: 'I reckon we've won!'

For the Morrisons and the Jenkinses there were now forty-two days of waiting, feeling helpless, wondering if some small point had been overlooked which might have helped their case. For the Jenkinses there was that simple, straightforward, overriding fear that they would have Nola taken forcibly from them. Noel managed to brave it out in public and even at home he was the one who stayed dry-eyed. Deep inside, though, he was distressed to see what this awful case was doing to his vibrant young wife. She seemed to be ageing each day.

For the Morrisons there were many problems to ponder. Small wonder then that they could think or speak of little else than the case. Would they lose Nola after such a brief taste of victory? If they did retain Nola, what on earth would they do about Lee? How could they part with her? Finally, there was the money. If the judges ruled against them they would be financially ruined. How could a man earning seven pounds a week suddenly find hundreds for solicitors?

Even though they feared the worst, the Morrisons felt compelled to be there to hear the judge's words for themselves, so again they made the tedious eight-hour car trip to Melbourne from Woomelang. Bill and Gwen Morrison were waiting in the court on 25 March 1949, when the three judges marched in with their prepared judgements. Noel and Jessie Jenkins had, again, deliberately stayed away. Noel had decided his wife could not stand the strain of hearing the judgement in public, with spectators staring at her.

That morning he went through the pretence of working, turning up on the job and going through the motions while his mind was far away. At 10 o'clock he had had enough. He jumped in the car and drove home to be by his wife's side when the result came. They had to wait until 12.15, surrounded by relatives and a few close friends. Mrs Jenkins' mother had come across from the nearby town of Woodend to offer moral support, along with Jessie's favourite aunt from just a few streets away.

A neighbour arrived excitedly at the door of the Jenkins' home with the message from Melbourne, telephoned through a few moments before by Bernard Nolan. Noel and the neighbour spoke briefly at the door before he turned to his wife. His smile told it all. He announced triumphantly, 'We've won. All the judges backed us.'

Gwen Morrison was in tears, standing forlornly in the street outside the court.

'How do you feel, Mrs Morrison?' she was asked.

'This has been a terrible reverse,' she replied. 'Terrible. We're back where we started.'

Gwen Morrison had fought back the tears for more than an hour inside the courtroom, even when she knew in her heart that the case was slipping away. The Chief Justice had delivered a fairly lengthy finding, ending with the plain, unmistakeable words: 'In my opinion the appeal should be allowed.' Mr Justice Lowe took precisely 161 words to destroy what hopes she had left, ending his judgement with: 'I agree that the proper order to make in this case is that proposed by the Chief Justice.' That was it, the case was lost.

Still, the losing mother had to sit through the final, third judgement, and Mr Justice Fullagar would more than make up for the brevity of his colleague Lowe. His judgement seemed to go on for ever, but it had the same disheartening conclusion: 'I agree that the appeal should be allowed.'

Even as she stood on the footpath, just minutes after her hopes had been dashed, Gwen Morrison was thinking ahead, thinking of what the next step would be. She could not countenance defeat, not when she was positive she was right. Jessie Jenkins had her child, she would not be convinced otherwise. Standing nearby was her solicitor Jack Galbally, obviously and visibly upset. Would there be an appeal? 'It is completely up to Mr and Mrs Morrison,' he replied slowly, 'but I can say that trying to stop this fight is like trying to come between a lioness and her cub.'

Gwen Morrison said her greatest concern was for the two girls. 'They are growing older every day and we feel that a decision beyond all reasonable doubt must be reached soon. Every week that passes increases the risk that they will learn what is going on.' She said that she and her husband were anxious to appeal to a higher court but everything depended upon money. 'My husband and I are in comparatively humble circumstances and we are not sure what we will be able to do.'

The three judges had not yet ruled on costs, but it seemed almost a formality that the decision would go against the losers and the Morrisons would have to pay. Henry Winneke, junior counsel for the Jenkinses, had offered them an easy way out, but one which merely antagonized the proud Morrisons. Winneke had told the court that if the Morrisons gave an undertaking that the case would go no further, his clients were willing to limit the amount of costs to actual out-of-pocket expenses. Gwen Morrison was furious. It was as if he was trying to buy them off!

By mid-afternoon the Jenkins' home was full of happy confusion, crowded with relatives and friends all eager to congratulate the winners. The postman had delivered a stack of telegrams and for the first time in months Noel Jenkins saw his wife's eyes smiling once more. 'The people of Kyneton have been wonderful to us,' Noel declared. 'They have given us so much help that I'm not even sure myself how much it is. Every now and then, just when things were looking black and I was down in the dumps, someone would hand me a cheque for fifty pound or so, just to cheer me up. About twenty different organizations here in Kyneton helped us.'

Jessie Jenkins was ecstatic.

'I'm so happy I don't know how to put it into words. It goes too deep for words. All I can say is that we were sure all along that we had our own baby and now we can keep her. I don't want to gloat over anyone. But I'm so thankful that the court decided as it did. The relief of knowing she is ours, after two and a half years of rumours and uncertainty, is too big to describe. It's like lifting a huge load from us all.'

Noel clipped in: 'We're not planning any celebration. It is enough for us to know that we have got Nola. Ever since she was born, my wife has thought there is no one in the world like her.'

Although she did not feel much like talking, Gwen Morrison forced her mind to concentrate on the future. They returned stony-faced to Galbally's office for a post mortem. There she told him she wanted the fight to go on, if they could possibly afford it. She went further: to abandon the case now would be to shun her duty as a mother. She had to make every endeavour to have Nola removed from the Jenkins' household and returned to her.

In an interview that night, Galbally described seeing off the shattered mother:

'When she left by car to return to Woomelang, Mrs Morrison was in a very distressed condition. She saw her hopes dashed. It was a very big shock to this woman, who had been fighting ever since she came out of hospital to get what she believes to be her own flesh and blood. Mr Morrison's resources are limited. He is an artisan and has three small children. Mr and Mrs Morrison are already faced with the possibility of an order for substantial costs against them.'

Even Galbally was dismayed that all three judges had ruled against the Morrisons, largely on the basis that for such a serious step to be taken, the removal of Nola from the Jenkinses, the court needed absolute proof of her true identity. Mere probability was not nearly enough, the judges had noted.

Sir Edmund Herring warned of the tragic results if the child was removed from one family circle to another and then, at some later date, it should be decided that she belonged with the original family after all.

'It might be a different matter if the evidence was such that there could be no possible doubt that she really is their child. No such thing, however, can be said of the evidence in the present case. However convincing on the balance of probabilities the proof may be, it is not such as to conclude the matter beyond all possible doubt.'

Mr Justice Lowe had continued the theme. 'I could not be satisfied to the standard of practical certainty that Nola was the child of the Morrisons without knowing the blood groupings of all four female children born within the forty-eight hours, and of their parents.'

Mr Justice Fullagar disagreed with the original case judge, Mr Justice Barry, in his assessment of Gwen Morrison as a witness. Barry had accepted Mrs Morrison's version of events almost in their entirety. He was wrong, said Fullagar, pointing out that it was necessary to consider 'the condition and probable position in bed of Mrs Morrison, and to remember that she had had some ether'.

Fullagar went further: 'The delay, and the fact that the taking of these proceedings was not entirely spontaneous, seemed to me to demand a very cautious approach to Mrs Morrison's evidence.'

He drew attention to the apparent conflict in evidence between Gwen Morrison and her mother, Amelia Williams. Gwen Morrison had sworn that the baby she was given shortly after the birth was dark-haired and dark-skinned. Amelia Williams claimed she had been shown a fair child when she visited the hospital nursery some hours later. If the babies had been mixed at birth, as Gwen Morrison appeared to be suggesting, then why was her mother not shown the dark child in the nursery?

Fullagar said the court must be aware of the affect it would have on Jessie Jenkins if Nola was taken from the mother 'who has suckled Nola and reared her for three and a half years, and who will probably not be persuaded that Nola is not her child by a whole army of doctors and lawyers'.

He continued:

'No order changing Nola's custody should be made unless it is established as a matter of practical certainty that Nola is the child of Mr and Mrs Morrison, and perhaps not even then. If there is even the slightest room for doubt, no order, in my opinion, ought to be made. And I consider it quite impossible to say that there is not considerable room for doubt.'

The judge warned of the potential dangers of introducing 'a stranger' into a family.

'We do not know, and cannot decide, whether Nola is to be added to, or substituted for, Johanne in the Morrison household, and nobody can forsee how the other children will receive either a substitution or an addition. It seems to me to be altogether a chancy and dangerous business. It must not be overlooked that the present position is not merely that Nola has a happy home, but that she has a happy home with persons who believe that she is their child and whom she regards as her father and mother.'

Fullagar moved on to discuss the two adults most deeply involved in the courtroom drama, the mothers Jessie Jenkins and Gwen Morrison.

'With regard to Mrs Jenkins, it is only necessary to say that although her feelings cannot, of course, be a dominant consideration, no court could, as I think, simply ignore the grief which the taking of Nola from her might, not improbably, cause to her. Nor is her grief likely to be "mercifully transient". Practically speaking, the extremely intimate relation of mother and child has subsisted for three and a half years between Mrs Morrison and Johanne, just as it has between Mrs Jenkins and Nola. Mrs Morrison says that she has a great affection for Johanne; she can have only a potential affection at this moment for Nola, whom she does not know. Unless there is some element in this case which the evidence does not disclose, it is not easy to imagine her being willing to part with Johanne. And, if she is not willing to part with Johanne, it is not altogether easy to understand her desire to take Nola from

Mrs Jenkins. In saying this I intend not the slightest reflection upon Mrs Morrison.

The truth almost certainly is that the complex situation in its entirety and in all its aspects had never been fully considered or appreciated by the applicants when they launched these proceedings in 1948.'

With that last sentence Mr Justice Fullagar exposed for the first time the basic weakness, the vital flaw, in the Morrison approach to the whole tragic affair. They wanted Nola, they did not want to part with Lee, and they could not have it both ways.

At home that evening Jack Barry made no attempt to hide his feelings. The judge who had ruled for the Morrisons in the original case was not merely miffed that his judgement had been overturned. He felt outraged. He told his daughter Joan the three judges had been 'cowardly' in not backing up his order to force the Jenkinses to hand over Nola.

13   A BREATHTAKING VERDICT

The Jenkins' victory was shortlived. Only a few days went past before the news reached them that the Morrisons were determined to appeal and yet another court case was on the way, this time in the High Court of Australia, the highest court in the land. Bernard Nolan, the man who had once so smugly dismissed the Morrison claim to Nola as a 'lot of hot air that will soon blow over,' now took off the velvet gloves. He devised a new strategy to bring the Morrisons to an abrupt halt. Money, he reasoned, was the real weakness in their capacity to fight so he would use their lack of it to attempt to stifle further court action. It was a tough tactic but legitimate. He had to consider his own clients' welfare and there was no reason to believe they would ever be repaid their enormous court costs by the Morrisons.

Soon after the Morrisons won leave to appeal to the High Court, Nolan submitted an affidavit drawing attention to the family's poor financial record and urging the court to set a high security, higher than the usual £50, which the Morrisons would have to put up before their case could go ahead. He swore that the Morrisons had left Kyneton owing money to many traders and, in fact, there had been court judgements there against them on behalf of nine businesses, ranging from Shiltons Garage to Dales Mutual Store. The debts added up to nearly £53.

Unknown to Bill and Gwen Morrison, a bailiff's agent had been snooping into their affairs in Woomelang and his report found its way into the High Court. It did not paint a rosy picture of Bill Morrison's capacity to pay for any court costs, past, present or future. The agent said: 'I would say that his financial position is very poor, as I have on numerous occasions returned complaints and warrants of distress...'

Nolan warned the High Court that the Morrisons had not yet paid the shorthand costs from the Barry hearing or even one penny of more than £370 in legal costs owed to the Jenkinses. Bill Morrison responded with a plea to the High Court to hear his case, despite his hopeless financial position. He freely admitted that out of the seven pounds a week he was earning, twenty-five shillings a week went in rent and he had no assets whatsoever. 'I have no banking accounts either in my own name or in the names of my wife or children and my wife has no bank account or private means of any description. She is not employed and attends solely to home duties.'

Nolan's tactic failed. Morrison the battler was able to take his case to the Full Bench of the High Court. His eighteen grounds of appeal, worked out by Galbally, Monahan and Sweeney, included the view that the Supreme Court Full Bench had reached a decision that was against the weight of evidence and was wrong in law. To hear the appeal were five judges, the Chief Justice Sir John Latham, Mr Justice Rich, Mr Justice Dixon, Mr Justice McTiernan and Mr Justice Webb.

The historic case began on Thursday, 13 October 1949, in the High Court building in Melbourne, the same building where the Morrisons had triumphed in the first case before Mr Justice Barry. The hearing took just four days before the five men adjourned to consider their verdict. No one in the court during those four days formed any distinct impression of how the case was going. The judges seemed to accept and dismiss arguments from both sides.

Ted Hudson made his familiar point that the welfare of Nola was of more importance than her parentage and it was up to the Morrisons to make out a case that they could provide better advantages for the girl. He spoke glowingly of the home life provided by Noel and Jessie Jenkins and said Nola had become an intrinsic part of their family.

Charles Sweeney, junior counsel for the Morrisons, said it would be bordering on cruelty to leave Nola, now aged four and a half, with the wrong parents and then for her to learn some time later of her real status. Sweeney criticized the attitude of Jessie Jenkins. It was Nola or nothing as far as she was concerned, he said.

Hudson agreed that Jessie Jenkins had her heart set on keeping Nola. He said that as far as Johanne Lee was concerned, it was perfectly clear that Mrs Jenkins would never be satisfied if there was a change. The Chief Justice, Sir John Latham, replied, 'That is as broad as it is long. Mrs Morrison will never be satisfied if the change is not made.'

The Chief Justice referred to the innocent victims of this long and disturbing legal battle, Nola and Johanne Lee. 'These children are incompetent witnesses, they are four and a half. They are not parties, they are not witnesses, and yet they are more interested in the case than anyone else.'

Now, once again, both families would go through the agony of waiting while the judges considered the fate of the two girls. Jessie Jenkins was beginning to suffer small but frequent illnesses, things like bouts of the flu, severe colds and a general feeling of being 'run down'. She would barely be over one problem when another would strike and she'd be back in bed. Stories were going around the town that Noel Jenkins, proud, strong-willed, even obstinate, might clear off with Nola and the rest of the family if the court ruled against them. Certainly both parents were absolutely committed to keeping her.

Things were no better in Woomelang where Gwen Morrison, normally a reserved, composed woman, would suddenly burst into tears for no apparent reason. Her son Blair watched and worried as the days of waiting took their toll. Gwen's friend Vera Hatcher remembers sitting with her and watching Lee play outside in the garden one lovely, sunny afternoon. Vera had dropped across to the Morrison home because the court decision was expected any day and she was concerned about Gwen's health. As they sat there watching the kids outside, Gwen looked at Lee, turned to Vera Hatcher and asked her, 'Would you believe that any mother would not want her?'

With the sole exception of William Flood Webb, the High Court judges were men of exceptional ability. The Chief Justice, Sir John Latham, was a man who had risen to the very top of his profession against all the odds. From a modest family, he had worked his way through school and then university on scholarships and for a time took a job as a country school teacher before entering the law. He was afflicted with a nervous stammer, but like all the other obstacles he was able to overcome it. He took silk as a KC in 1922 and in the same year entered Federal Parliament. By 1925 he was Attorney-General and in 1929, when his Government lost office, Latham became Leader of the Opposition. Two years later he was deputy to Prime Minister Joe Lyons. Latham got out of politics in 1934 and was appointed Chief Justice of the High Court the following year. His appointment was criticized because of his political background but he showed fear or favour to no man in his strictly run court. Now aged seventy-two, John Latham was in his last years as Chief Justice.

There was no compulsory retirement age for judges in those days and that explains why Sir George Edward Rich was still taking his place on the Bench at the grand old age of eighty-six. He had served on the High Court for thirty-six years and was highly regarded as an academic with a beautiful turn of phrase and sense of humour. Rich had acted as Chief Justice in 1940 and 1941 when Latham took a government appointment as Australia's first minister to Japan.

The most distinguished judge on the High Court Bench was Sir Owen Dixon, sixty-three, a man regarded by many in his field as the finest jurist in the English-speaking world. After the Japanese bombed Pearl Harbour, Dixon had been sent to the United States as Australia's minister to Washington. He was eventually to succeed Latham as Chief Justice after first tackling the unenviable task of being United Nations mediator in the Kashmir dispute between India and Pakistan.

The youngest judge hearing this difficult case was Sir Edward Aloysius McTiernan, fifty-seven, a quietly spoken man who had earned appointment to the Bench when he was only thirty-eight. At the time he was regarded as too young and too inexperienced for such high office but he gained wide respect and acceptance by his performance in court.

Finally, there was Sir William Webb, sixty-two, the former

Chief Justice of Queensland who had been preferred for a position on the High Court ahead of none other than Jack Barry. Webb was a conservative character, kindly and affectionate. At the end of the war he had been president of the International Military Tribunal for the Far East and had conducted the war crimes trials of General Tojo and other Japanese leaders. Despite his wide experience, many thought Webb a poor choice for the High Court, not an intellectual of the stature of Dixon and Latham.

On the morning of Thursday 22 December, even though it was just three days before Christmas, Jessie Jenkins found herself unable to rise from bed. Worry, nervous tension and the flu had combined to make her feel at her lowest for months. She was also well aware that this day the vital decision on Nola's future would be delivered in the High Court in Melbourne. Gwen Morrison had been in court to hear the two previous decisions — one for and one against her — but this time she chose to stay away, the anguish of it all was too much to bear in public.

If the two mothers could or would not be present, there was no shortage of womenfolk to await the judges' verdict. Scores of women of all ages, some with their own daughters at their sides, packed out the public gallery long before the five judges filed in. There was already an air of drama but no one could have been prepared for the extraordinary chain of events that was to follow. People who were present in the court that day say it was a moment, an experience, they will never forget.

The five judges followed the established court tradition, each delivering his finding in order of seniority. The Chief Justice, Sir John Latham, led off. He found for the Morrisons.

Next was Mr Justice Rich. He ruled for the Jenkinses.

One all.

Mr Justice Dixon came down on the side of the Jenkinses.

Two to one.

Mr Justice McTiernan agreed with the Chief Justice. Another vote for the Morrisons.

The decision was tied at two all.

The result now hung on the judgement of William Webb and there was a hush as the most junior judge prepared to read his finding. The future lives of Lee and Nola rested in his hands.

Every eye in the room was upon him, the spectators straining forward for a better view, straining to hear. There was no need to call for silence, no one would dare break the spell. Not a whisper or a cough, or a sharp intake of breath as everyone waited. One mother's triumph would be the other's tragedy and every soul in the court knew it.

Mercifully, Webb came straight to the point: 'I would dismiss this appeal.' So the Jenkinses had won, three to two.

Jack Galbally, who had given so much of his time to the Morrisons, who had adopted their case as his own cause, could only sit there shaking his head as he heard those words. So close, it had been so close.

To lose was difficult enough to comprehend, but when the judge began giving his reasons, Galbally sat dumbstruck. This deciding judge had allowed himself to be finally swayed by the unlikeliest of all the theories which bedevilled this case. Webb told the court:

> 'If there had been only two infants in the Kyneton District Hospital on the 22nd June, 1945, namely those born on that day, this court would, I think, be obliged to restore the judgement of Barry and give the custody of Nola to the Morrisons as their child...'

Webb went on: '...there was no common ground that Mrs Morrison and Mrs Jenkins each received a newly born baby.' Incredibly, he had rejuvenated the theory that Mrs Morrison may have been given one of the two baby girls born a couple of days earlier. For the Morrison side it was heartbreaking to lose on such a point. Mr Justice Barry had dismissed it as irrelevant and Robert Monahan was convinced that he had banished it as a blatant red herring, conjured up by his opponent Ted Hudson in a moment of courtroom desperation.

Jack Galbally could not believe his ears. Here was Mr Justice Webb saying the Morrisons would have won but for the other two babies. How could he ever explain that to the woman who had gone through so much, for so long, to lose in such an unlikely manner? How would any mother mistake a newborn child for one a couple of days old? Well, the judge had an explanation for that. 'If Johanne was prematurely born (to Mrs Hayes or Mrs Perry) on the 20th June, or even on the 19th, she might have appeared newly born on the 22nd June.'

Galbally sat through the rest of Webb's judgement, then rose and walked sadly from the courtroom. He had the face of a man who had lost a personal fight for justice.

The telephone rang in the Morrison home in Woomelang and Gwen Morrison had to force herself to ease the receiver from its cradle. She burst into tears as Galbally broke the news as gently as he knew possible. Bill Morrison sank deeply into his chair. He knew they had lost.

Gwen beckoned him to the phone, she needed him to speak to the lawyer because the words would not come. The two men talked briefly and she heard her husband say something about a Privy Council appeal, and money, then he replaced the phone and came to her side. The Morrisons were alone again with their private grief.

In Mitchell Street, Kyneton, Jessie Jenkins had not stirred from her sick bed all morning. Suddenly there was banging on the door and an excited neighbour rushed inside to announce their victory. Noel Jenkins, still in his overalls from work, switched on the radio and they heard it for themselves. 'The world famous "Whose Baby Case" was decided by the Full High Court just minutes ago. The judges decided that Nola Jenkins will remain with Mr and Mrs Jenkins of Kyneton. It was a majority decision, three to two. The majority judges thought that, in the circumstances, the welfare of the child should decide the issue. The dissenting judges thought the question of parentage was the important factor.' There was just one sour note for the jubilant Jenkins family. The announcer wound up by saying the case might not yet be over. 'It can still go to the Privy Council.'

For the rest of the day there was bedlam in Mitchell Street as crowds of friends and relations turned up to congratulate Noel and his wife, who by now was already making a rapid recovery from her illness. They hardly had time to open the telegrams which poured in once again from their supporters across the land.

'Nola is ours,' Jessie Jenkins said proudly. 'It's the most wonderful Christmas present we could hope for, but while it means everything to us, I'm thinking of the Morrisons. It won't be so happy for them.' Noel was grateful that the decision had finally arrived after a wait of nine weeks. 'If the decision had not come this week we would have had a miserable Christmas,' he declared.

Jack Galbally was questioned that afternoon about the possibility of a further appeal, to the Privy Council in London. 'If Mrs Morrison could walk to London I have no doubt she would start this afternoon,' he said. 'There is only one thing that is stopping her — money.' Galbally estimated that the cost of taking their case to London would amount to several thousand pounds, a laughable proposition for the impecunious Morrisons.

Jessie Jenkins was right in her prediction that Christmas would not be happy for the Morrison family and it was, in fact, a photograph of her that helped to compound their misery. Jessie was pictured in the *Sun* newspaper the following morning hanging up the Christmas decorations with a bright-eyed, smiling, little blonde helper. Gwen Morrison saw the picture and wept again for Nola.

To try to bolster their spirits, the Morrisons set off for Gwen Morrison's mother's home on a small farm near Bendigo to spend their 1949 Christmas. While Gwen and Bill were bitterly unhappy, little Lee had one of the best Christmases of her entire life. Not only was she smothered with affection from a family which realized they had come so close to parting with her, but she was on the receiving end of scores of presents sent anonymously by people who were touched by the plight of the little dark-haired girl.

Even in her misery, Gwen Morrison was full of fight. Early on Christmas Eve she was asked if a Privy Council appeal was in the offing. She replied defiantly: 'We will even go to the King if our counsel advises it.' Later that day Bill Morrison backed her up: 'The High Court has not had the last word. We shall go to England for the next hearing.' His mother-in-law, Amelia Williams, joined in: 'We love Johanne but we do not believe she is of our blood. We believe the baby Jenkins is.' As she spoke, nine-year-old Blair tugged at Bill Morrison's shirtsleeves. 'Daddy, mummy is crying again,' he told his father, 'you'd better come and see her.' Sound asleep in the room next door, a brand new doll on each side of her pillow, was Johanne Lee Morrison, still blissfully unaware of the sorrow her birth had brought to her family.

The two High Court judges who had ruled in favour of the Morrisons had no doubt that Lee was, in fact, a stranger in the Morrison family. The Chief Justice, Sir John Latham, spelled it out very clearly: 'It is therefore clear that a mistake was made in the hospital and that Mrs Morrison was given the wrong baby.'

He dismissed any inference that Gwen Morrison's child may have been fathered by someone other than her husband: 'There is, in my opinion, no ground whatsoever for suggesting at this stage in the proceedings that Mrs Morrison had been unchaste and that the child which was born to her was not the child of her husband.'

Sir John dealt with the future welfare of Nola and Lee and the possible effects of separating Nola from the woman who had fought so hard to keep her.

> 'Nola is now a little over four years old. Doubtless a change of custody will cause her some temporary unhappiness. But upon a long view it is much better for her that she should be brought up in the family of those whom a court has found to be her parents. It is not at all certain that Mrs Jenkins would take Johanne Lee. The position of Mrs Jenkins is that she has become fond of Nola and that therefore Nola should be left with her. In my opinion, the effect of any order upon the feelings of Mrs Jenkins should not be taken into account in determining the custody of Nola...'

Sir John, unlike Mr Justice Webb, saw no strength in the theory that Mrs Morrison may have been given the baby girl born to Mrs Hayes or Mrs Perry. Mr Justice McTiernan also examined this theory minutely and discounted it. The judge worked out that the Hayes girl was at least fifty-five hours old when the Morrison and Jenkins children were born and the Perry infant was at least thirty-one hours old.

'They would have been more than once bathed, dressed, fed and have been in the possession of their mother. It is hardly probable that either would at that stage of her life have been placed with a woman not her mother.'

Ruling for the Morrisons, McTiernan concluded:

'The short facts proved by the evidence are that Mrs Morrison did not get her own baby; necessarily some other mother got her baby and Mrs Morrison got that other woman's baby. The only rational conclusion is that the other mother is Mrs Jenkins and that she got Mrs Morrison's baby and Mrs Morrison got her baby.'

Mr Justice Dixon and Mr Justice Rich both argued that the welfare of the child was paramount and to make any order they would need to be certain that Nola was the child of the Morrisons. No such certainty existed, they ruled, and both referred to the presence of the Hayes and Perry babies in the hospital at that time.

Mr Justice Dixon told the court:

'Nola has from birth been accepted by Mr and Mrs Jenkins as their own offspring... They have never doubted that she is their child and she has, of course, never doubted that they are her parents. At present her life and happiness are bound up with her membership of the family... If she is to be torn by judicial decree from this family life it can only be for a very strong reason... Not only is her happiness and welfare involved but so is that of the other child, Johanne Lee... What is to happen to her if the court were to transfer the custody of Nola to the Morrisons does not appear.'

Mr Justice Dixon gave some support to Webb's concern about the Hayes and Perry babies. Like his fellow judge, he referred to the fact that the Hayes or Perry children could have been born prematurely, thus making it more plausible to argue that one of them could have been mistaken for Gwen Morrison's newborn baby. Dixon summed up:

> 'I think when all the possibilities are taken into account there is too much uncertainty in the inference that Nola is the child of Mr and Mrs Morrison to warrant an order taking her from Mr and Mrs Jenkins...'

Mr Justice Rich concentrated on the welfare of the two children, Nola and Lee, because in his own words, 'I am not satisfied that the scientific evidence is infallible.' He told the court:

> 'No evidence, or none that is convincing, was led to prove that a change of custody would in any way benefit the child. On the contrary it appears that the present custody is satisfactory and conducive to the health, happiness and general wellbeing of the child... After this length of time a change of custody would wrench the child from its present happy and contented condition and throw it into an unknown place and among persons strangers to her.'

Speaking of the Hayes and Perry babies, the judge said 'the possibility of a mistake with either of these children cannot be excluded.' If this point, the theory based on the extra two babies, had angered Jack Galbally, it left the Morrisons' senior advocate, Robert Monahan, almost speechless with fury. Three times before he had sought to crush this implausible belief and three times he had won — or so he thought. Certainly Mr Justice Barry had agreed with him and dismissed it completely in the original case. Then, in the State Full Court, he had been left with the distinct impression that Hudson and Winneke had 'thrown in the towel' on the point when he had offered to produce affidavits from the other two mothers. Years later his recollection was that the State Full Court 'had stopped me and told me, "You needn't worry about that".' And hadn't he even been told in this final High Court hearing, by no less than the Chief Justice himself, that there was no need to raise again the question of the Hayes and Perry babies?

'Latham, the Chief Justice, had consulted with other members of the court and told me that I needn't worry about that matter,' Monahan recalled. 'And so I did not. Yet it was on this very point alone that a member of the High Court Bench, who made the majority of three, based his judgement in the High Court, and we lost the case.' Is it any wonder he was bitter at the end of that painful day in court?

The following day the spotlight switched to these two other babies. Could they really have been involved? Farmer Ted Perry found himself parrying newspapermen's questions and he was none too happy about it. Contacted on his farm at Redesdale, just north of Kyneton, Perry was emphatic that his girl could not have been part of any mix-up. 'Anyone can see that she's the living image of us,' he pronounced. Kyneton grocer Tom Hayes was equally dismissive of the claim, although he didn't get too upset about it. He admitted he'd been interviewed by solicitors involved in the case but no one seriously believed that his Margaret was not in her right home.

The Hayes family was to have ample opportunity to compare likenesses. Margaret was the fifth child in a family which eventually expanded to nine children. Her big brother Arthur, who took over the running of the family supermarket, says they were never in any doubt about Margaret. 'It was a non-event as far as we were concerned.' His mother, also Margaret, was so sceptical of the whole suggestion that she didn't even give blood tests a second thought. 'We didn't feel the need.'

New Year, 1950, produced a resolution from the Morrisons: they would try to take their case to the Privy Council in London. Within days they had begun to sell household goods, anything they thought could raise them a few pounds towards the legal costs. Even so, the position looked hopeless, they would never be able to muster the thousands that Jack Galbally had estimated would be needed. Their closest friends, Dot Dettmann, Marge McIntosh and Vera Hatcher, plus Gwen's sister Gloria and her husband, Constable George Bock, rallied to them and proposed a solution. On 22 February, Gwen Morrison made her plans known publicly. She would appeal to the Privy Council and would rely on donations from sympathizers to finance her cause.

The Woomelang friends had taken the lead of the Kyneton supporters of the Jenkins family and were already raising funds. A committee was formed comprising George Bock, as president, the Woomelang State School headmaster Ted O'Connor, Dot Dettmann, Bendigo dentist Thomas Williams, and a Perth stockbroker, Mr A. Greenwood.

Among the first to contribute was an anonymous 'Legal Observer' with £250. 'Wellwisher' gave £50, 'Medical Sympathizer' £25, H. Baxter of Timboon sent one pound and an L. Downing from Queensland sent two shillings. That gift of £250 was by far the biggest donation the Morrisons ever got and it led to wide speculation as to the identity of 'Legal Observer'. Could it have been John Vincent William Barry? If it was not the judge, then someone else must have felt strongly indeed about the case to part with what amounted to nearly a year's salary for the average Australian.

'For the sake of the two little girls I want this matter to go before the world's highest legal authority,' Gwen Morrison declared. 'I am not taking the matter to the Privy Council just to be stubborn. I am doing it for the sake of the two little girls, who may not be satisfied with the present indecision when they get older.' Mrs Morrison then came up with this ingenuous approach to her rivals: 'Mr and Mrs Jenkins could help us by having blood tests taken. This may convince them that the child Nola living with them is not their daughter. Blood tests have proved that Johanne Lee could not be our little girl.'

She did not have to wait long for an answer. Jessie Jenkins snapped back the following morning: 'I thought she was going to allow the case to lapse and spare us all from further worry.' Mrs Jenkins said she was griefstricken at the thought of another appeal but, if necessary, they would be in there fighting. Noel, as usual, backed her to the hilt: 'We're convinced she's our child, that we are in the right and that we will eventually win this case.'

Nola, by now aged four years and eight months, was developing remarkable family characteristics, he said. 'When Nola was born she took a long time to grow any hair and had the high forehead common to my family. She has developed a calcium deficiency like our baby Helen. My eldest son, Arthur, had that when he was younger.' Noel Jenkins ended with a plea: 'All we want is to live a quiet life and bring up our family.'

The war of words continued between the two families. Gwen Morrison offered gratuitously to share their new legal fund with the Jenkinses. She was rebuffed in a curt letter to the *Sun* by Noel Jenkins. 'In making these statements, Mrs Morrison, or no one on her behalf, has consulted myself or my wife and as we have no doubt whatever as to the parentage of our child we do not desire to be associated in any way with the public subscription being raised on her behalf.'

Noel Jenkins' friends in Kyneton quickly reopened their own fund and within weeks it had gathered hundreds of pounds. The secretary, hairdresser Charles Rogers, and president Bill Doran, a Kyneton electrician, said in a joint statement: 'We differ among ourselves on the dispute between the families but we all agree that Noel and Jessie Jenkins should not be denied the Privy Council justice, whatever that might be, through lack of money.'

Woomelang lagged way behind Kyneton in supporting its fighting family. Dot Dettmann, one of the hardest campaigners on the Morrison appeal committee, admits: 'It hardly ever got off the ground. You had to live there thirty years before you were even accepted.' Dot puts forward two reasons why the folk of Woomelang were reluctant to give: 'There wasn't much money around in those days and the wowsers probably frowned on Bill Morrison because he was the type of man who liked a drink.'

By now, figures of between £4,000 and £7,000 were being quoted as the likely costs for the losing side. Said Gwen Morrison: 'We are not well off, we are staking our whole life on winning. I know it is a gamble but I know there is no other course open to me.' The same day, friends of Jessie Jenkins let it be known that the young woman was being 'worn to a shadow' by worry.

Less than a week later, Gwen Morrison made 'one further and final appeal' to Noel and Jessie Jenkins:

'I am prepared to accept as final and conclusive the result of the proper and scientific blood test which could now be taken. I have no wish to incur the further expense of appeal to the Privy

Council, because if I lose that appeal it will mean ruin for me.'

The reply came from a tense Noel Jenkins: 'We will fight this case if it takes every penny we have in the world.' He and his wife sat together in the kitchen of their home, the children tucked up in bed, and spoke of the misery they were being forced to endure by the obdurate Morrisons. Said Noel: 'I've worried about the case and about my wife's health, and sometimes the strain is so great I can't even face my friends. Running away wouldn't help. I've kept away from people all day, I've seen no one.' People who knew Noel Jenkins well would never expect him to crack up under pressure, but now he was certainly on the verge of it. Jessie had been an early casualty and she was not getting any stronger under the constant pressure of a case that had now been strung out for twenty long months.

Holding Nola in her arms, just a month short of her fifth birthday, an emotional Jessie Jenkins poured out her feelings:

'It's become a heartbreak to go along the street. I don't like to go out. Arnold is old enough to read the stories himself. When the last case came on the children met him at the school gates and told him about it. He was very upset. The other children are coming on and I suppose it will affect them all their lives.'

On Monday, 29 May 1950, Jack Galbally caught a Qantas Constellation flight from Sydney to London. Although he was by now a Labor politician in Victoria's Legislative Council, he still found the time to make what he regarded as almost a sacred mission to the Privy Council. With him on the plane for the long and tiring flight to Britain was barrister Charles Sweeney, another man who had become attached to the case. Both of them had paid their own fares.

Already in London was an eminent barrister, Garfield Barwick, KC, a man who would make his mark on politics and the law in Australia in a brilliant, if at times controversial, career. Galbally had snapped up the opportunity to brief Barwick for the Morrisons. Not only was he one of the finest advocates in the legal world, he was in the right place at the right time. Barwick had been in London to represent the Australian banks against the Government which was bidding to nationalize them. Having him there on the spot meant a considerable saving in travelling costs for the Morrisons. The Jenkinses, too, chose a barrister already in London on other business, Alan Taylor, KC.

While the lawyers began the complicated processes involved in launching an appeal to the Privy Council, both families tried to keep their minds off the case and lead normal lives. When 22 June arrived, however, they were soon back in the public limelight. The press were on their doorsteps badgering them for pictures of Nola and Lee on their fifth birthdays. Touching pictures they were, too. Nola was sitting in her pyjamas being read a bedtime story by big brother Arthur, twelve, watched by her other brother, Arnold, then eight, and sister Helen, twenty-one months. Lee and sister Colleen were pictured helping Mum with the washing up at their grandmother's home at Kangaroo Flat. Gwen Morrison and her children were spending more and more time with Amelia Williams of late as Bill Morrison had taken a job in Birchip, another Mallee town near Woomelang. The family's links with Woomelang were about to be severed as Gwen Morrison's sister and her policeman husband George Bock were preparing for a transfer to Bass, more than 250 miles to the south, and they had been the Morrisons only real reason for living in the town. Already Gwen and her mother were planning for the family to settle permanently in Bendigo.

Five years old! It was an appalling situation for both families, but more so for the two innocent little girls, who knew nothing of the legal conferences going on in London which might decide their futures. At least this London manouevre would be the last, hopefully, in this long, sad saga. The Privy Council, composed of a panel of legal lords, was the ultimate arbiter in the British Commonwealth. What they decided would be the end of the matter, no matter how much one family might dispute their finding. By now the Morrisons' legal team had applied for leave to appeal, the first hurdle they had to surmount before an actual appeal could take place.

Noel Jenkins was having an awful nightmare. There was this

banging noise going on and on inside his head and a voice shrieking at him. Suddenly he was wide awake and he could hear the sounds more clearly. 'Wake up! Wake up!' He stumbled out of bed towards the window where he could just make out a shadowy figure through the blind. 'You've won! You've won!' he heard the hysterical voice shout. Now Noel was wide awake, shaking Jessie to break her out of her deep sleep. He lifted the blind and saw the beaming countenance of his mate Bill Doran, still shouting the news that had just been telephoned through from Melbourne. Doran, one of the chief fund-raisers for the Jenkins cause, was rushed inside. 'It's great news, Noel,' he announced. 'One of the newspaper blokes just rang up and told me. The Privy Council has knocked the Morrisons back. You've got Nola for sure now.'

It was 1.30 a.m. on Tuesday, 4 July. Twelve thousand miles away in London it was mid-afternoon on 3 July, and solicitor Jack Galbally was facing up to the unpalatable truth: the Morrisons had finally lost. The unbelievable case that had come his way more than two and a half years before and which he had come to believe was worth sacrificing part of his life for, had finally petered out in the most frustrating of defeats. The five law lords of the judicial committee of the Privy Council — Lord Simonds, Lord Normand, Lord Morton of Henryton, Lord MacDermott and Lord Reid — had taken just twenty minutes to reach their decision after listening to addresses from Garfield Barwick and Alan Taylor and examining tens of thousands of words of evidence. The Morrisons were denied leave to appeal.

After the formality of the Australian courts, the judicial committee was a marked contrast. Here in the home of British law, the accent was on informality. In the richly panelled, high-ceilinged council chamber of the Privy Council, the five law lords sat at a round table in boardroom fashion, facing the counsel for the two families. A newspaper report at the time said the lords 'fired questions incessantly and laughed frequently'.

Barwick had summed up the Morrison case by saying that if the High Court decision was not set aside, there would be a situation where parentage had been established yet blameless parents had been denied custody of their child. He criticized the Full Court of Victoria and the High Court for demanding standards of proof in this case which far outreached those required in criminal cases. The judges had apparently said to themselves: 'We will never make a decision in a matter like this if we have any doubts at all.' Barwick said this seemed to mean that a decision would never be given in cases of this kind.

Barwick told the law lords that the Morrison and Jenkins babies must have been switched within half an hour of their births. The High Court decision had ultimately hinged on the presence of the other two baby girls in Kyneton Hospital at the time, but Barwick dismissed this as irrelevant. He said for the Hayes or Perry babies to have been involved was almost impossible. Barwick also gave a warning: 'If leave [to appeal] is not granted the possibility of a fresh action cannot be ruled out. A fresh custody order would have to be sought in Victoria for this to take place.' The Jenkins' barrister, Alan Taylor, said that if the litigation continued, the costs involved would ensure that 'neither family would be in a position to bring up the child Nola.'

Lord Simonds, who presided over the hearing, admitted: 'This case is unique in so far as both the children are getting the same affection from both sets of parents. Would not a judge need to feel that a change would not only be not harmful to the children but would, indeed, be for their good welfare?' Lord Reid also wondered about the welfare of the two girls. 'Isn't a judge entitled to demand the highest possible standard of proof when the ages of the children involved are such that any alteration in the custody now might have disastrous effects on both households?'

The Jenkinses found it impossible to go back to bed after such a rousing awakening. They sat in their kitchen and waited for the children, particularly Nola, to wake up. More than ever they felt the need to have all four children around them on this great day. Jessie Jenkins, in the light of dawn, looked happier and healthier than her husband had seen her for many, many months. Jessie was jubilant: 'It's a nightmare over,' she rejoiced. 'Now we'll try to forget the whole, unhappy business. It's been a great strain for the past two years. We've never been free of it. There were times when we were very down. Then a letter would arrive from someone we didn't know, saying they were thinking of us and praying for us. It gave us a lift and let us feel we weren't alone. Although our legal adviser said he was confident there was always the worry that it could go the other way.' Noel joined in, smiling: 'You can be forty lengths ahead but you haven't won until you get past the post first.'

Jessie said they would take Nola aside when she was old enough to understand and explain the whole, controversial affair. 'Nola will have to know sooner or later and I would prefer that she learn it from me first.' Wellwishers began to arrive at the Jenkins' home with the dawn and there was a spirit of triumph in Kyneton that morning.

In Kangaroo Flat, just outside Bendigo, Gwen Morrison had sat with her mother, Amelia Williams, listening to the crackling shortwave radio broadcast from London. It was in a barely audible sentence from a British broadcaster that she managed to pick up the crushing news that the battle had been lost. In tears, for the first of many times that day, she had to be helped to her bed. Amelia Williams, trying desperately to buck her up, assured her daughter: 'Don't worry Gwen, she'll come to you. You'll get her back.'

Later that same morning Gwen Morrison swore: 'I'll never give up the fight for my child. She has the blood of my husband and me and we are certain she is our baby. I will never be far away from her.' It was all too much and she broke down again. Lee, playing in a corner of the room, rushed over and flung her arms around Gwen Morrison's neck to comfort her. Gwen looked down at the dark-haired girl and vowed:

'Lee will never suffer because of this. She will get everything a girl could wish for. But I will never be able to give her the love she would get from her own mother. I still can't believe that the lords have ruled against me and I don't think I ever will. I am absolutely certain that Nola is my daughter. Only her mother would have gone through what I have for her. I have done everything I can and I am utterly worn out from the strain and worry and hours of waiting.'

Whose Baby?

Gwen Morrison paused for a few moments in an attempt to compose herself.

'I have been saying all the time that I will not cry but I can't help it. Yesterday the strain of waiting was something awful. I could not concentrate because my mind was in England, wondering what was happening. Now I know and I don't know what is going to happen. The litigation has cost us all we own — all our savings, our home and everything we ever had. I have not seen the Jenkinses since the case began. I wish we could have been friends and solved this problem without all those heartbreaking court cases. I can only hope and pray that the years will bring me back my own little girl.'

Echoing her mother's words, spoken when they heard the news in the early hours of the morning, Gwen Morrison predicted: 'I know that Nola will eventually come back to me.'

14   A KNOCK ON THE DOOR

Bill Morrison was the only one to hear the knock, which was not surprising for it was a timid, half-hearted rap anyway. He opened the door, all eyes in the Morrison home turning in his direction and fixing on the figure standing in the darkened doorway.

'You'd better come in,' he said.

Gwen Morrison's prophetic words back in 1950 had come true. Nola Jenkins, the girl she claimed as her own daughter, had finally come home!

They all stared in her direction, Gwen Morrison, Bill, Colleen, Lee. No one spoke. Then, Nola and Lee's eyes met for the first time, and there was instant recognition between the two girls who had been born a few feet from each other and only moments apart in the Kyneton Hospital nineteen years earlier. As if by some strange understanding they switched their gaze to Gwen Morrison and found themselves comparing features. Had Nola at last found her real mother or had she made some ghastly mistake?

The visit to the Morrison home in Bendigo on that Wednesday night, 16 September 1964, was the climax of years of soul-searching by the blonde, blue-eyed half of the 'Whose Baby Case'. Nola Jenkins had never been able to leave that famous case behind her. Try as they might, her parents had been unable to protect her from the whispers, sneers and gossip, not to mention stares, of a small country town. Noel and Jessie Jenkins were loving parents, all that any child could ask for, but if they erred in their upbringing of Nola it was in their tendency to over-protect her.

Right from the day they learned that another family was trying to take Nola from them, the Jenkinses built up a wall around her. They tried not to give her special attention but it was impossible. Mrs Jenkins admits they were probably too eager to cosset Nola. 'I had to sort of protect her,' she says. 'The only thing that bothered me was people's inquisitiveness. It didn't matter where you went you had to shield the children, particularly Nola. You had to shield her from people who'd pry. And that was the most bothersome thing of the whole jolly lot.'

The Jenkinses knew that it was natural for people to make comparisons, but they found it hard to endure. 'I knew that they were comparing,' Jessie Jenkins says, 'I used to think to myself, "Oh, they are just stickybeaks," and take no notice of them. I've always found the best defence is offence. If they were being stickybeaks, I'd just walk straight up to them. I'd hope that I made them feel a little bit guilty or something.'

Despite the elaborate care they took to protect their children from the prying gossips of the town, Noel and Jessie Jenkins did not discuss the case with the youngsters, certainly not in their early years. Jessie explains: 'I didn't think it was the sort of thing you should worry them about. I suppose the boys knew. We just led as normal a life as we possibly could. We didn't let those sorts of things interfere with the children's fun and games.'

Arnold Jenkins, second in the family and three years older than Nola, remembers it differently.

'We were probably aware of the case all the time. I don't know if we were really ever told. It was just an ongoing thing. They may have tended to shield Nola a lot more. We weren't allowed to talk to anybody in the street. We had to go home, all those sorts of things. We weren't allowed to go to anybody's place to play unless they were vetted first. And because people tended to quiz you up, we weren't just allowed to go anywhere and had to go straight home.'

Mrs Jenkins remembers Nola being a particularly affectionate child, but one who demanded all of her attention, sometimes at a cost to others in the family. 'She wouldn't let me out of her sight,' says Mrs Jenkins. 'She didn't like the others getting in first.'

With the case behind them, the Jenkinses tended to relax more and the strict rules were eased. Although it was well and truly over, the case was far from forgotten, as Nola was to learn when she began school. She isn't exactly certain how she found out about her controversial birth and the aftermath, but thinks it was probably shortly after she started school.

> 'I think I always knew there was something different about me. I used to get teased about it. I didn't quite understand and I had a real temper. I was never much good with words, but I could always use my fists and feet. I suppose the teasing bothered me, but I didn't realize how much.'

At state school she received jibes like, 'Who are you?' and 'You don't know who you are!' Nola admits she used to hate going to school in those days. 'I can remember crying a lot so I could go home.' Coincidentally, almost every day in her primary school life, Nola would pass another little girl in the street, going to or from the nearby Catholic convent school. She and Nola knew each other, but neither was aware of their link with the past. The other girl was Margaret Hayes, born just two days earlier than Nola in the Kyneton Hospital in 1945. The presence of Margaret Hayes and the other baby girl in the hospital at that time had been the key factor in deciding Nola's future life — as a Jenkins and not a Morrison. Margaret Hayes was enjoying her school life. Unlike Nola no one even mentioned her tenuous link with the 'Whose Baby Case'. The people of Kyneton, young and old, had never taken seriously Mr Justice Webb's view of the case.

Nola could have expected some peace by the time she reached high school, but that was not to be the case. If anything, the children were more cruel, the taunts more barbed, and her sensitivity heightened as she moved into the critical adolescent years. She can remember it well. 'It was worse in high school. As I got older it affected my studies and I kept failing. I wasn't particularly interested in school. I wasn't particularly interested in anything.'

Arnold Jenkins watched Nola's battles at school, especially

those she had at high school.

> 'She used to get a terrific lot of teasing, particularly when she was in forms one and two. She had a bad time for a while, with kids, not adults. Children are cruel. I think she was probably a bit confused at times.'

Arnold was proud of the way his sister stood up to the pressures from her unkind schoolmates. He recalls that she would never shed a tear, except in rage. Never, ever, in feeling sorry for herself.

> 'Nola is a very strong-willed person. She doesn't cry. She only cries with rage. Nola never cries. I've seen her fling her bike on the road and dance with rage and bawl her eyes out, but that was because the bike wouldn't go properly.'

Nola hung on at school until she reached fourth form but she couldn't wait to leave when she turned sixteen. She had no real job to go to, but for a time she took care of the children of a cousin whose husband had died. Her only real interest was in dogs and in a certain young man who worked at a builder's yard in Kyneton. His name was Bernard Aloysius McGuane and he was two years older than Nola. They had often chatted when Nola passed the builder's yard on her way to school.

A friend's mother had kennels in Kyneton and Nola spent a lot of her idle time up there working on the dogs. Later she was to take a job in a poodle parlour in Melbourne, where she learned to clip poodles. Pretty soon, the fad for the breed spread to Kyneton and Mrs Jenkins found herself, somehow or other, the proud owner of three!

Doubts about her origins still bothered Nola and she sought reassurance from brother Arnold. She found it difficult to raise the subject with her parents because it seemed to cause them pain, particularly her mother. Arnold wasn't able to help her much when she questioned him about the mysterious other family, the Morrisons. 'Nola would say, "Well, what do they look like?" Or, she would say she would like to go to see them. But she'd never come straight out and say she had any doubts.'

Arnold himself had been unable to resist comparing Nola with his elder brother Arthur, his parents, and his little sister Helen. He agrees: 'She's not particularly like Arthur or I, or like Helen, actually.' However, he does point to strong likenesses with two of his mother's aunts, Else and Ethel. 'They are all small, dumpy ladies,' he says. 'Nola is very like Else and Ethel, especially if she gets her hair permed.'

Arnold says the whole Jenkins family formed a united front in their belief that Nola was one of them and did their best to convince her, too, that this was so. 'We believe that she is our sister anyway. We all have a good close bond between one another.' But, although the Jenkinses stick stoutly together, Arnold has noticed over the years the strain on his parents, most visibly on his mother. 'She suffered the most. She still gets very upset about it. She gets very, very upset. She has huge problems coping with it. But, then, she had a very bad time when it was on.'

Apart from the case itself, Jessie Jenkins also bore the brunt of Nola's tormented school days. Arnold says, 'I think Mum has a tendency to worry about what people will say, whether people will say she didn't do her best for Nola. She worries about Nola nonstop.'

Nola's move away from Kyneton to the anonymity of Melbourne was deliberate. She needed to establish herself away from the close family fold and she was hoping to become plain Nola Jenkins, not 'that Nola Jenkins' from the 'Whose Baby Case'. She had even seriously considered changing her name, wondering if it would bring peace of mind.

Arnold accepted Nola wholeheartedly as his sister, but he did wonder at times about what happened to the other girl, Johanne Lee Morrison. Even as a young boy he was aware of the other girl. One night he overheard an anguished conversation between his parents after the first judgement went against them and they seemed likely to lose Nola to the Morrisons. At that stage there was even a suggestion that the Morrisons could end up with both children.

Arnold remembers:

'When it looked like they were going to get Nola they weren't

> going to let her [Lee] go either, though. We were going to end up with nobody. They weren't going to let go of her but they wanted Nola. I can remember that. I wasn't supposed to be there, but I can remember Mum being really upset. I can remember it vividly. They didn't want to let the girl go, but they wanted Nola. They had been looking forward to having a four-child family.'

Arnold says his parents have always insisted that Nola is their rightful child, no argument.

> 'There never, ever has been any doubts in their minds or anything. That's it. We've never had any contact with the other girl. I always feel very sorry for her because she was always in the back seat and she must have had rather a bad life. I always sort of felt that she probably had a pretty rough go of it.'

But did Lee, as Arnold puts it, have a pretty rough go of it? Whereas Nola had many people rushing to reassure her that she was one of them, a true Jenkins, Lee had no such family umbrella to ward off her inner fears. Although they lost the long legal tussle, Bill and Gwen Morrison never for one moment considered that they might have been wrong. To them, it was as simple as black and white, Nola was the Morrison and Lee the Jenkins. And they made no pretence of otherwise.

There is no doubt that Lee was her father's favourite child, Jenkins or not, and that she was dearly loved by her mother, brother and sister. However, from the earliest age she can remember, Lee was fully aware that she was the odd one out in the family. Her eyes flash with anger as she declares unhesitatingly: 'I firmly believe the Jenkins were my parents.' Then she goes on, still vehement in tone:

> 'Work it out, there were two babies. Either my mother was a stupid woman, or a liar or something. I know I can't be Dad's daughter, that's a fact. Either Mum wasn't nice and went to all this trouble to cover up something like that. Now, that's just not on! So you have to look at it and say that she was right.

There's no way known that what Mum said wasn't right. It was quite right what she said, what she thought, what she felt. Once you believe that, there's only one thing left isn't there? I'm a Jenkins.'

Just as the Jenkins parents tried to bury the case in the backs of their minds, the Morrisons adopted similar tactics with their children. They just did not discuss it. The oldest child, Blair, had been twelve years old when the case was finally sent to the Privy Council in 1950, so he was well aware of all that was going on around him and the controversy surrounding his little dark-haired sister. Colleen was only seven, but she remembers being intrigued to overhear a whispered conversation between her parents about their fight for Nola.

Lee may have learned of her background from a relative or from other children, she cannot be sure exactly how she found out. 'I've always known about it,' she says. 'I don't know how or why, I've just known. I can't remember anyone sitting me down and telling me.'

Colleen believes her mother and father wanted to obliterate the memory of the case. 'Mum never ever discussed it, nor did Dad, not until we were teenagers. It was a bad time in their lives and they wanted to put it behind them.'

Blair says his parents were so distressed by the mere mention of the case that they turned their backs on large sums of money offered by magazines seeking their story. 'Mum was determined that nothing was going to be brought out. It was just going to be left to lie. There were opportunities to make some money out of it, right, and they desperately needed the money, but wouldn't do anything about it.'

Bill Morrison always believed the family had been right to fight to the bitter end for Nola, but once it was over he had many regrets. He hated the notoriety, but most of all he was bitter that he should have lost what to him was a clearcut, fundamental human right — that parents should have an inalienable claim to their own child.

Towards the end of his life Bill Morrison insisted that he and his wife had had no animosity towards the Jenkinses. 'No, we did not. Somebody made a mistake in our estimation and it was the hospital that did it. You can't blame the Jenkins for that. You can't blame anybody but the hospital for that.'

After the Privy Council moves had foundered, there had been some suggestions that the Morrisons could do it all again, retracing the agonizing path through the courts once more with a new action based on a different legal approach. It was never taken seriously, the Morrisons had had enough. A close friend of the Morrisons blames the case for turning them into nomads, moving from place to place, job to job, always seeking something different. Bill Morrison believed the expenses of the long, protracted court case had cost him the chance to become a success. But the truth is that he had always been a bit of a wanderer, even before he met and married Gwen. They moved from Kyneton to Woomelang before the first court case began, then on to Kangaroo Flat, Deniliquin, Ballarat and Bendigo. They liked these towns of central Victoria.

With every move came a new job. Sometimes panelbeating, occasionally as a barman, and between times, as a taxi driver. Blair Morrison, speaking of his father's restlessness, says: 'It was virtually after the case he started to become unsettled completely and couldn't settle down at all into a job. He was a fairly talented man. It was a bit unfortunate he couldn't get on the line and stick to it.'

Bill Morrison was a man with a short fuse to his temper and Blair blames this on a hangover from the lost case. The entire family were occasionally subjected to his bursts of anger and, ironically, Lee seemed to be the only person able to calm him down.

When he was feeling depressed, unhappy that he had not made more of his life, Bill Morrison would confide to his son that the wretched court case had done it, blighted his chances.

That temper of his certainly curtailed his advance up the ladder in a number of jobs. His brother-in-law Frank Moffat sums up Bill Morrison and his approach to life:

'Bill was a bit short-tempered at times and inclined to let his emotions rule him a bit. I always had the impression Bill projected his emotions into his work at times. I don't think he did himself justice. If he had a boss, he'd tell the boss what he thought of him smartly. But he was a darned good worker, he was very attached to his wife and kids and was a good mate to have.'

Typical of Bill Morrison was the way he lost his job as a barman at the Shamrock, Bendigo's landmark Victorian-style hotel. Telling the story against himself, Bill recalled that it was a scorching hot day and he felt sorry for the cook who was sweltering in the hot kitchen serving up counter lunches. 'How would you like a nice cold beer?' he asked the sweating chef.

'I'd love one,' was the quick reply, 'but the boss won't allow me to drink while I'm working.'

That didn't deter headstrong William Morrison. 'Bugger the boss, I'll bring you a pot.'

It was just Bill's luck that the boss chose to tour the kitchen just as he delivered the banned beer. The exchange of words that took place was almost as hot as the day itself, but the outcome was predictable. Bill Morrison was looking for another job.

Some years earlier he had teamed up with another publican at the Kangaroo Flat Hotel on the outskirts of Bendigo. This time the boss was a woman and a formidable one at that — Amelia Williams, his mother-in-law. Their working relationship could be imagined and it wasn't too long before they parted company. Asked years later about his mother-in-law, Bill Morrison raised his eyes skywards and answered: 'Cancel that one, cancel that one out. Some people are born lucky...'

Blair Morrison remembers one time at the pub when 'Ma' Williams and her son-in-law did stick together. A drunk in the bar was causing trouble, so Bill went to order him out. Before he could get there, Amelia Williams was on the spot, waving the kitchen poker under the drunk's nose and showing him the door.

The Morrisons eventually settled in Bendigo and Lee, along with her sister, went to the Catholic primary and secondary schools. Unlike Nola, Lee was able to settle into the background of school life, largely unrecognized as the girl in the 'Whose Baby Case'. There was no teasing for her and the few fights she had in her youth were mostly with her big sister Colleen, who was bigger in terms of years but smaller in stature and usually came off second-best. During those happy days at school, the convent girls usually mixed with the boys from the nearby Marist Brothers college. Among the youths that Lee met was John Nicholas Chant, a rugged individual who always seemed preoccupied with sport of some sort. Lee, like everyone else, knew him as Joe and thought him a likeable enough character, though she could not quite fathom why he wasted most of his time on football grounds or tennis courts.

Although Bill Morrison said he and his wife had decided to forget all about the past once the case was finally decided against them, he was not being entirely frank. Unknown to the Jenkinses, there was one person in Kyneton who was keeping a very close watch on the progress of young Nola. This anonymous woman friend of the Morrison clan sent frequent reports to Gwen and Bill about Nola and just how she was growing up. It did not do anything for Gwen Morrison's peace of mind to learn that some people in Kyneton now thought she was right after all, that Nola was the image of her.

One day, while her parents were out of the house, the inquisitive Colleen did what hosts of other children have done in years gone by. She decided to rummage through a drawer where she knew her mother kept a number of precious items, things that the children were never allowed to see. She made an amazing discovery. It was a picture of a blonde girl, dressed up for a party or a play. The picture was a hazy snap but it had been lovingly framed and was in a drawer that Gwen Morrison used every day. It did not take the bright youngster very long to piece together the last part of the family jigsaw.

When Lee herself learned of the treasured photograph of the blonde girl, the deep-seated doubts about her real position in the Morrison family were aggravated once again. Whenever she was unhappy at home she couldn't help but wonder if all those reassuring words from her mother, and particularly her father, meant anything. She knew they loved her, but why did they still cling to their link with a girl they had never known?

Colleen recalls the times when she and her mother would talk to Lee and try to make her feel part of the family. Lee was always the one to raise the question of her true parentage and force her reluctant parents to discuss it. 'Lee was happy in the environment she was in, most of the time,' Colleen says. 'But she'd get fed up with life at times.' It was then that the old, hated topic of Morrison-Jenkins would be dragged up.

Lee remembers her parents trying so hard to console her, frequently posing the same question: 'Are you happy?' The answer was mainly, 'Yes.' But it never solved Lee's inner torment. Sometimes Gwen or Bill Morrison would put it bluntly. Lee says they would ask her: 'Do you ever want to go down to Kyneton [to see the Jenkinses]?' And they would promise: 'If you ever want to go, we'll take you down.'

It would have been a simple matter, less than an hour's drive, but Lee always held back from the unknown. She knew they would be strangers to her, and she, perhaps, an unwanted vision from the past. Whenever her parents mentioned the subject, they were careful to avoid any discussion about Noel and Jessie Jenkins and they told Lee that if they drove her to Kyneton they would wait outside while she went in. They were not about to pay a social call on the other family.

While Gwen Morrison had no intention of ever setting foot inside the Jenkins' home, she had never given up hope of seeing Nola again. She could never go to Nola but Nola could come to her. Often her mother, Amelia Williams, reassured her: 'She'll come back to you one day Gwen.' Blair Morrison says his mother needed little convincing, she had a premonition herself that Nola would suddenly appear, uninvited, on her doorstep. 'She just knew she'd come and see her, that's all,' he explains. 'Mum knew that. She'd just say, "She'll come and see me one day."'

When Lee left school, she took a job as a receptionist for a real estate firm in Bendigo. Joe Chant was studying to become a teacher and although he was still a sports fanatic and Lee was not the slightest bit interested in football and the like, they began to see a lot of each other. Joe had always known of Lee's background, as his father had been friendly with someone connected with the Morrisons.

All the Morrison children, like their mother, were brought up

Catholics. Bill Morrison had little truck with organized religion but he respected his wife's beliefs and he was pleased to see the girls trained as 'ladies' by the Catholic schools. He expected much from both his daughters and Colleen, more than Lee, was very careful to behave herself in his presence. Lee had a way with her Dad, getting off lightly for misdeeds that would have earned the other kids a hiding. But, even she had to bow to his will once he had determined on something. Once, Colleen spent a good part of her hard-earned wages to have an expensive, fashionable, beehive hairstyle which was all the rage with the young women of Bendigo. When she paraded in front of her father, just before she went out for the night, he grumbled that it made her look 'cheap' and ordered her to comb it down. She did.

When Lee took up smoking, she did so openly in front of her father, himself almost a chain smoker. Colleen kept her smoking to herself for years, until one day Lee boldly offered her one in front of her father and asked him politely: 'You don't mind if Colleen has a cigarette, do you Dad?' He probably did, but he didn't demur.

Wednesday night, 16 September 1964, was nothing special for the Jenkins family back home in Kyneton. Their daughter was living in Melbourne and the 'Whose Baby Case' could not have been further from their minds. It had not been raised in the home for ages. Things were about to change. Within seventy-two hours they were to see their names, their daughter's name, and that tragic episode in their lives emblazoned in the newspaper headlines once more. The shock was to be delivered again by a paper they had come to hate, the Melbourne *Truth*, the racey weekly tabloid that had broken the first news of an alleged mix-up of babies and had trumpeted the story for years afterwards.

Nola had been introduced to *Truth* by a friend in Melbourne, someone she was later to regard as less than a friend because of the way things turned out. At that time, though, she was riddled with doubts about her real mother and father and she took little convincing that a meeting with the Morrisons would set her mind at rest.

Reporter Lawrie Francis was summoned by editor Bill

Williams and briefed on an amazing new development in the almost-forgotten 'Whose Baby Case'. He had to explain the whole background to the twenty-one-year-old reporter and then instructed him to visit Nola and find the Morrisons. It didn't take him long to do both, but when he returned to the editor's office he had bad news. One, Francis regarded Nola as being in no fit mental state to handle the trauma the editor had in mind. Two, Bill Morrison had been aggressive, unfriendly, and downright difficult.

The discussion inside the editor's office became somewhat terse. 'I told Bill Williams I'd prefer *Truth* didn't do the story,' Francis recalls.

> 'Nola had told me she'd been unhappy for several years and said she'd been contemplating suicide. I wasn't keen on doing the story because of her emotional state and because I contacted Mr Morrison by phone and told him what we wanted to do and he said, "We don't want her brought up." He didn't want it brought up anymore. It wasn't the best thing for the family. For those two reasons, I thought we were playing God a little too much.'

Williams, an off-beat newspaperman who used to write colourful prose under the scarcely unassuming byline of 'Bede Tracy, Melbourne's most exciting man', was not used to being told how to run his newspaper. 'Williams said to take her up. I got the distinct impression it was worth my job if I didn't go,' Francis says. Bill Williams could see great possibilities in the story and the fact that Nola had sought *Truth*'s help to find the Morrisons convinced him that he had every right to publish the story. Francis was dramatizing the risks involved. There was every chance that it would all climax with a reunion and a happy ending.

Four of them, Francis, a *Truth* photographer, Nola and her friend, set out for Bendigo by car on Wednesday morning. Francis recalls the cheerless trip. Nola hardly spoke, the friend said little more, and he and the photographer were reluctant to be on the assignment anyway. Once in Bendigo the next step was to persuade the Morrisons to see them. They found Bill Morrison, now working as a taxi driver, and Francis played his trump card. He told him that Nola was with them and was anxious to meet the family. It was too much for any father to resist, so a meeting was arranged for that evening at the Morrison home.

Bill Morrison had been waiting on the edge of his chair. His wife Gwen was shaking. An hour or so earlier she had telephoned Colleen, who was living in another part of town, and called her across. Colleen had been puzzled by the call and her mother's odd explanation, 'It's Lee.' Only when she walked in, a few moments before Nola, did her distressed mother explain the drama that was about to unfold. Even then, Gwen Morrison knew that the one person most likely to suffer as a result of Nola's visit was, naturally, Lee, and Colleen's help might be needed if there was any crisis.

Next to arrive into this emotionally charged room was Lee, just home from work, with her boyfriend Joe. It was not to be the first or last time that Joe would be at her side in a time of need.

Nola had been getting edgy enough on the trip up. By the time it came to walking up to that unknown front door her nerve had almost deserted her. Still, she had Francis, the photographer, and her friend at her side, so she grimly drove herself up the path and lightly tapped on the door. Bill Morrison was furious to see the two *Truth* men tagging close beside Nola. In almost the same breath that he invited Nola in, he dismissed them with a curt: 'You're not getting in here!' So Francis and his photographer were left stranded outside in the dark while the events they had come to record unfolded out of sight in the lounge of the Morrison home.

Everyone in the room that night thought that at last they were going to get all the answers. The 'Whose Baby Case' was to have a conclusion, nineteen years and three months after the two baby girls were born in Kyneton Hospital. The tension was almost unbearable, no one spoke, just stared. Lee was stunned by the other girl's face. 'There was Mum's child.'

They were all thunderstruck by the resemblance. In that instant, Lee decided that Gwen Morrison and Nola Jenkins were mother and daughter. 'She was the image of my mother.'

Nole knew from their looks what they were thinking, but she

could think of only one thing; getting out of that room as fast as possible.

> 'All I wanted to do was turn and run. I walked in the door but I wanted to be walking out the door. It seemed like an eternity. I was horribly embarrassed. All the way up in the car I'd been thinking, "What have I done to Mum and Dad?" You know, that was weighing on me heavily, because I just couldn't work out what was the next move. I got so rattled about the whole thing. I honestly didn't know what to do. I think everyone was just covered with embarrassment and feeling stupid.'

Colleen Morrison and Joe Chant needed only one glance to make up their minds. Says Colleen: 'I knew as soon as I saw her, Mum was right. I said to myself, "Right, she is a Morrison."'

Gwen Morrison finally broke the ice. She expressed her feelings, without words, in the simplest of ways. She walked across the room and kissed Nola on the cheek. Nola then remembered the bunch of flowers in her hand and passed them silently to her. With that, a formal, stilted conversation began and Bill Morrison carried out all the introductions. Nola, by now, was slowly recovering her wits, but she was still terribly nervous. Her greatest concern at that moment, apart from extricating herself as rapidly and as decently possible, was to console Lee, who was looking exactly how she felt at this unwanted, unexpected turn of events. Nola blurted out an apology to her, 'because I felt an intruder in her home'.

Certainly, Lee regarded her as one, and it was only her strict upbringing and respect for her parents that prevented her from saying so, in the blunt fashion she had learned from her father. It was, considering the circumstances, an eminently reasonable reaction. For years Johanne Lee Morrison had felt that her position in the family was held by default, despite her parents' constant love and reassurance. Now it seemed that this complete stranger, who had burst upon the scene, was going to finally confirm her worst fears and take away her niche among the Morrisons. She had always believed that she was really a Jenkins, but the Jenkinses hadn't wanted her. If she was eased out of the

Morrison family, what was left for her? On the surface, Nola found Lee to be polite, even friendly. The truth is, Lee was seething with resentment and wanted her out of the house.

Colleen watched her sister's expression. She knew what was going on in Lee's mind. The two sisters had never been very close, but in that room, that night, a new bond was forged between them. They were, finally, sisters.

As Nola chatted, rather too loudly and too forcefully, out of sheer nervousness, she was not creating a favourable impression with either Morrison sister. They just didn't like her. The harder Nola tried to be charming, the more she attempted to be entertaining, the more irritated Lee and Colleen became. Their parents were too overawed to notice the coolness between the three of them, even though Gwen Morrison had correctly suspected the meeting might be traumatic for Lee.

Gwen Morrison had just celebrated her fiftieth birthday and it had been sixteen years since she last set eyes on the girl she believed her own. For her, the meeting was a vindication of the stand she had taken, the tears she had shed, the money they had spent, the agonies they had gone through and the long, empty years of waiting and longing for her daughter to step through the door. Is it any wonder she was as nervous as Nola? The two of them found it difficult to carry out a conversation, so much so that Nola could form no clear impression of this woman who claimed to be her mother. 'I think I was too worried to form a lasting impression,' Nola recalls.

Nola took an instant liking to the down-to-earth Bill Morrison, who tried his best to make her feel at home. 'He was quite a nice bloke, very matter of fact.' Bill Morrison had not the slightest doubt that Nola was his daughter and the evidence before his eyes was compelling proof that he had been right to stand by his wife when she risked her reputation and fought their cause in the courts. Before Nola could make her exit, Bill Morrison exacted a promise from her that she would return again. She agreed and went a step further: next time she would stay a night with them.

The two men from *Truth* were waiting outside when Nola emerged, a little unsteady and uncertain about what she had just done. The whole showdown had taken just two hours but to Nola it seemed she had been inside, forcing the conversation along, for much, much longer. Her mouth was dry, she had a splitting headache and the last thing she was ready for was an interview with the eager *Truth* reporter. 'She seemed a little more at ease,' he remembers, 'but she was still hard to get information from.' Nola didn't tell much but there was still plenty of material for *Truth*. Francis was to write with feeling: 'When she returned to Melbourne with us she seemed a happier girl — a contrast to the troubled and stormy personal life she has led since leaving school three years ago.'

He quoted Nola as saying:

'I feel much lighter, much happier today. I'm grateful to *Truth* for making it possible for me to see Mr and Mrs Morrison. I think they were glad to see me. Mr Morrison said that when he used to drive through Kyneton he always looked around to see if he could see me. Perhaps now our two families can see each other to talk things over and break down the wall that seems to have been between them for almost twenty years.'

If Nola was hoping to effect a reconciliation, she had gone about it the wrong way. Her family still didn't know she had even been to Bendigo to see the Morrisons. Nor did they know of her link with the hated *Truth*. Arnold Jenkins wasn't quite so much in the dark. As his sister's confidante, he had known for years about her self-doubts and her occasional impulse to seek out the Morrisons. Just the same, he didn't really believe she would ever go through with it. 'She had been talking about it for a fair while but she hadn't mentioned it for a long time,' he says.

So, Arnold was just as unprepared as his parents when a friend knocked on their door on Friday and waved a copy of *Truth* under their noses. 'Look what's just come in,' he said excitedly. The headline was just as sensational as *Truth* could have hoped for. 'Happy end to girl's tragic plea,' read one line, and then, in bigger type and in capitals, 'WHOSE CHILD AM I? ASKS NOLA'.

Noel Jenkins read out the opening paragraphs to his wife:

WHOSE BABY?

'"Who am I?" a lonely, frightened 19-year-old girl asked Truth this week. The girl on the phone was Nola Jenkins. Near tears, she made an impassioned plea to *Truth* to help find Mr and Mrs W. H. Morrison — whom she still believes might be her real parents. Nola's plea dramatically revived one of the most poignant human dramas in Australia's history — the case of the mixed-up babies.'

The article then traced a brief history before continuing:

'Until nine months ago, Nola lived with her parents, the Jenkins, in Kyneton. "I love my parents," she said. "They are Mum and Dad to me — but I must find out who I am; who my mother and father really are. Please help me find the Morrisons."'

The *Truth* report said the newspaper tracked down the Morrison family in Bendigo and Nola had requested to be taken there to finally meet them. It explained:

'Nola asked *Truth* to help locate the Morrisons after doubts and fears that had built up in her mind since leaving school reached the point where they had to be answered.'

Again it quoted Nola:

'I have been worried sick about it. Every time I see my name I wonder if it is really Nola Jenkins, or isn't it. Lately it has been worrying me more and more. I've been going to the library a lot and reading about the court cases and looking at the photos. I don't look at all like my parents or my brothers. Yet I look just like the Morrison's son Blair.'

Truth said Nola told them she had been teased throughout her schooldays and she kept noticing how different she looked from her brothers.

'Whenever I tried to bring the subject up at home I could never seem to get a complete answer, one that would satisfy me.'

The story said her personal life, too, had been unhappy since she left school and she blamed the famous case for her misery.

> 'I'm sure much of it stemmed from this question I've always had in the back of my mind — who am I? I don't suppose I'll ever find out. In fact I don't suppose anyone really knows. But I can never be happy until I find Mrs Morrison or Johanne and talk to them.'

Reporter Francis rounded off his story with these three sentences:

> 'Nola has now talked to the Morrisons — and is a more content, happier girl for it. The revival of this poignant case has caused heartache for several people — but it seems that, in the long run it will be better for all. Nola thinks so.'

Arnold Jenkins saw the look on his mother's face and knew she was absolutely shattered. Rushing through her mind was: Had they gone through so much heartbreak over the years for nothing? Would Nola betray their love? Noel Jenkins kept his emotions better hidden but the paper was shaking in his hands, in anger and frustration. 'It was devastating, for Mum especially,' Arnold says. 'You never know with Dad. Things that hurt Dad he doesn't outwardly show. He can be very, very hurt but he doesn't show it. But I know that business was very hurtful to Mum and Dad at the time.'

When Noel and Jessie Jenkins recovered from the initial shock and their anger had subsided, they sat down together and tried to face up to this latest turn in their lives. Eventually, they came to grips with the situation. Arnold remembers his parents agreeing: 'If that's what she wants, then that's what she must do.'

Mrs Jenkins says the shock took some getting over, especially as they had to find out about it through *Truth*. But, they realized that Nola was an independent person and entitled to visit the Morrisons if she wished, no matter how they might feel about it. Says Jessie Jenkins:

'We realized, yes, OK, Nola was grown up and if she wanted to do it, that was her privilege. You've only got control of a child, I mean, they're in your keeping until they are sixteen or seventeen and after that they are individuals. If this was something she felt she had to do, well OK.'

While Noel Jenkins and his wife had come to terms with Nola's flirtation with the Morrisons, they were still anxious to talk to her and point out sternly that she owed it to her parents at least to have consulted with them, and that they did not think much of her association with *Truth* newspaper. Nola, however, had gone for cover after seeing the *Truth* article herself. When Jessie Jenkins called to her Melbourne address, there was no sign of her daughter. She was lying low with friends until her parents cooled down.

What they didn't know was that Nola was also making plans for another, secret visit to the Morrisons, the reunion she had promised Bill Morrison that night before she left the home in Bendigo. This time there were to be no newspapermen, she was to stay a night and there would be a real opportunity for them all to get to know each other.

Nola's departure from the Morrison home did nothing to assuage Lee's fears. Before anyone went to bed that night there were long and spirited discussions with first her mother, then her father and sister, all assuring her that her place in the Morrison family was secure. Lee tried hard to believe it but when she finally went to bed, all the trust and love she had for those three people was not sufficient to smooth out the inner turmoil. She felt it now, more keenly than ever. As she tried to sleep, her father's parting invitation to Nola kept ringing in her ears: 'Please come back and see us again — soon.'

Nola walked out of Bendigo station two weeks later and was met by the taxi driver who had been waiting eagerly for the arrival of the passenger train from Melbourne. Bill Morrison greeted her cheerily, but Nola was feeling depressed and unhappy, still wondering if she was doing the right thing, and more than a little ashamed to be betraying her parents yet again.

There was no drama about her arrival at the Morrison home this time, everyone was more at ease, although there was still underlying resentment from Lee and her newfound ally, Colleen.

Nola's boisterous personality grated on the two Morrison girls. They didn't really accept her in their parents' home and there was little she could do to retrieve the situation. Nola could sense that it would be an uphill battle to establish some real rapport with a family she had never known, and the harder she tried the worse it got. Even her clothes failed to meet with approval from the Morrison girls. They both remember her attire as being 'old motorcycle gear — leather jacket and pants'.

Whereas the first visit had been taken up with nervous small talk, Nola and the Morrisons were now able to discuss the past and what might lie ahead of them. Gwen and Bill Morrison were forthright when it came to Lee's position. They told Nola they accepted that Lee was a Jenkins, that Nola was the daughter born to them, but there was an important thing to be made perfectly clear. Nola has a clear recollection of what they said: 'They stated to me that they were perfectly happy with Lee, that they loved her. And nothing was going to alter that.' It was an awkward moment for the visitor, but Nola made her own position equally clear. 'I had no intention of altering that, or anything like that. As far as Lee was concerned, I would do nothing to hurt her.'

That night, Nola and Lee shared a bedroom, and there was a thaw in the relationship, a natural easing of tension as two teenagers gossiped before going to sleep. Lee remembers asking Nola when her birthday was, then realizing what a stupid question it was. They chatted amiably enough. Lee wanted to know what Nola's parents were like and Nola was equally curious about Lee's life with the Morrisons. In the intimate surroundings of the bedroom, Lee was once again able to closely examine her rival's facial features. No, there could be no mistake, this girl was like a teenage version of Gwen Morrison. 'You didn't have to stare or try to pick out characteristics,' says Lee, 'the resemblance was uncanny.'

After breakfast the next morning there was a long, frank discussion about where they should go from here. Nola poured out her troubles, her painful experiences of the past, and her anxiety about what the future held. She found a ready listener in Gwen Morrison and pledges of fatherly support from Bill. Later in the morning she was driven in the taxi down to Colleen's home for an hour's chat with the elder Morrison girl. It did nothing to establish friendship between them. Colleen's reaction to Nola's visits had been to draw closer to the sister she had always known.

She found Nola too 'rough and ready', a reaction perhaps caused by Nola being nervous and ill at ease? 'She was anything but nervous,' corrects Colleen. 'She came to my place and stayed with me for an hour or so before she caught the train. She didn't appear nervous to me.' That was to be the last time Colleen Morrison would see the girl who had pushed her way so abruptly into their lives and was to disappear almost as suddenly. There had been little chance of Nola ever being accepted by Colleen as a sister. She was utterly loyal to Lee. 'I regarded Lee as my sister then, and always will. I'd never swap her for a thousand Nola Jenkins.'

Bill Morrison drove Nola to the station and they waved goodbye, both promising to keep up the relationship. They were sincere about that wish but, as the train moved slowly out of the station, they were not to know that fate had something else in store and that their paths would never cross again.

Years later, Bill Morrison was to find himself asking to see Nola, but being turned away because he was not her father.

15 NOLA DECIDES

The train trip back to Melbourne took about three hours, plenty of time for Nola to review the events of the past few weeks and mull over the dilemma which had dogged her life. Morrison or Jenkins? Both families wanted her, she knew that. Even though she was yet to make peace with her parents in Kyneton, Nola was praying that forgiveness would come readily.

She did not know much about the Morrisons, yet she was positive they were willing to take her in as a member of their family. If they did, where would that leave Lee? And Colleen? Nola didn't feel much warmth there. To join the Morrisons outright would break her mother's heart. Then there was her father, she could not have wished for a better Dad. How could she hurt him? Her brothers and sister, Arthur, Arnold and Helen? They had always made her feel a Jenkins. Could she turn her back on them?

As the train pulled into Spencer Street station, Melbourne's country rail terminus, Nola had made up her mind. It was a relief. She felt as if a heavy burden had been lifted from her. Nola had left Melbourne a doubter, she had returned a Jenkins. 'I knew who I loved and who my parents are,' she declares. 'It wasn't a bad experience. I suppose it was a thing that shouldn't have happened, but actually it set me straight on a lot of things. There were no more questions as far as I was concerned. That finished it.'

It had been a gruelling time emotionally. For all that, Nola is grateful that she took the plunge and discovered the truth about herself and the other family. 'It was a very awkward situation. It must have been more awkward for them, I think. I suppose in lots of respects I was more settled afterwards.'

Bill and Gwen Morrison were convinced that Nola would be back to stay. As a precaution, they took Lee aside and had a heart-to-heart discussion with her. 'They told me that I was their daughter and I had first priority. They were very good.' Even so, Lee still has the impression that Bill and Gwen Morrison had reserved a special place in their hearts for Nola. 'I'd like to think they did. I don't think they were cold and callous people. They were very warm and loving. I think they believed that she was their daughter and had a special place for her.'

Bill Morrison was determined to assume a father's role in Nola's life so he drove to Melbourne a couple of days later to see his solicitor from the 'Whose Baby Case' days, Jack Galbally, now a leading Labor politician. Galbally was still a man crusading for causes, among them a lone campaign to have hanging abolished in the State of Victoria. No one is quite certain what was in Bill Morrison's mind that day, but he may have been hoping to legalize, in some way, his family's new link with Nola. He called at her address in the Melbourne suburb of Malvern but no one was home. He waited and waited in vain, then wrote her a note, slipped it under the door and left for home. There was never any reply. Colleen Morrison says her parents took it badly. They were hurt and bewildered. 'She just disappeared off the face of the earth,' says Colleen.

Nola had not disappeared, she had taken refuge with the people she knew best, her parents. After the second visit to Bendigo and the heartrending decision to break permanently her new ties with the Morrisons, Nola felt the need to restore the bond of trust with her mother and father. She did it the easy way, by writing a contrite letter. The Jenkins parents were quick to respond as she had hoped they would be. Jessie Jenkins telephoned her daughter, then took the train down to Melbourne for an emotional reconciliation in the city. They spent the day together, mother and daughter, going through the shops, having lunch, laughing and joking just like the good old days.

When Jessie returned home that night she was able to tell Noel they had their daughter back. They were both on top of the world

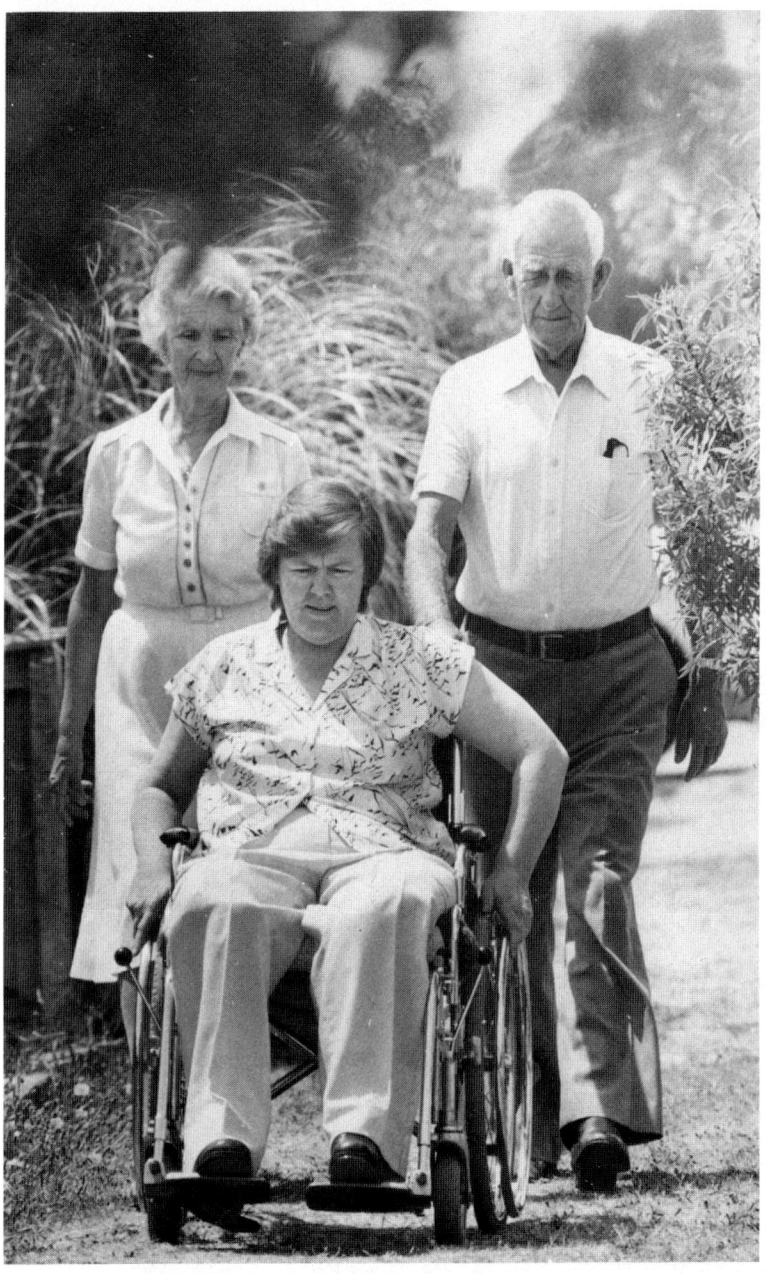

Noel and Jessie Jenkins with their daughter Nola today. She is making a great fist of life despite her handicap and tragic past.

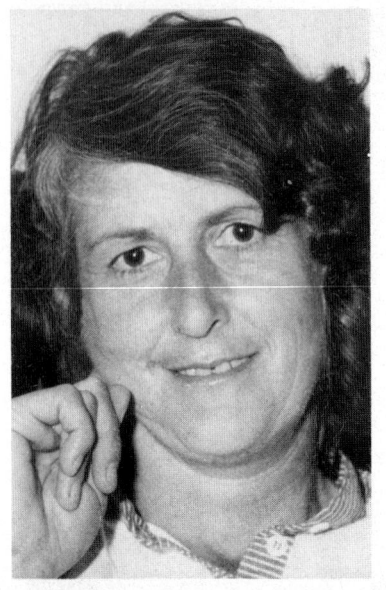

Left: Lee Morrison today. A mother of three children, she was brought up by the Morrisons always in the belief that she was the child of Noel and Jessie Jenkins. Except for that brief moment in court in 1948 she has never seen either of them, though they live just an hour's drive away.

Below: One of the last pictures taken of Gwen Morrison, with husband Bill. She was already suffering from cancer and was soon to die.

Above left: Lee Morrison at her Catholic high school in Bendigo. Few of her schoolmates had any inkling of her controversial background and Lee was able to enjoy a happy school-life.
Above right: As always, Nola Jenkins is smiling. The picture, taken with her mother during her high school days, shows no hint of the torment that is to come for Nola.
Below left: Still smiling. Nola Jenkins at the Austin Hospital learning to live with the fact that she is now a paraplegic and has lost both her legs. Her durable spirit could not be crushed.
Below right: Teenager Nola Jenkins with sister Helen. Is there any family likeness?

Above left: Amelia 'Ma' Williams at the entrance to her hotel. Inside, she ruled with an iron hand and, occasionally, the kitchen poker.
Above right: Stern, self-assured, a force to be reckoned with. Amelia Williams leans on the front gate. The matriarch of the family, she was the first person to declare that the babies had been mixed up.
Below left: Gwen Morrison's grave in Bendigo. Her husband Bill has since died and is buried in the same grave.
Below right: Amelia Williams is buried in this grave, only a few steps away from her favourite daughter Gwen.

again. They might not have been quite so jubilant if they had known the real truth. Nola had not mentioned the second, private, overnight visit to Bendigo. She had felt they were upset enough about the public visit, it was better to let sleeping dogs lie. It was almost twenty years later that Nola let it slip in a conversation, but Jessie Jenkins, ever loyal, dismissed it with a shrug and the comment, 'Water under the bridge.'

The peacemaking process had been a lot easier than Nola expected. 'I thought I was going to be on bended knees,' she says. 'They were very understanding. I hadn't thought they would be. I probably didn't realize until that time how much I loved my parents. You know, I thought that was the last I'd see of them. They were not going to have me in the house. I think that was when I realized I loved them and that was all there was to it.'

Nola eventually returned to Kyneton to live, thinking she had left the worst of her problems behind her. Life should have been plain sailing. She renewed an old friendship with Bernard McGuane, the young man in the builder's yard from her schooldays. Nola's outgoing personality made her a popular figure at social gatherings and there was a happy home always in the background. Still, Nola's penchant for attracting trouble had not deserted her.

From the age of twenty she began drinking heavily, to the extent that it was talked about around the small town. The police in Kyneton and a number of nearby towns soon learned well the name Nola Jenkins. It was all minor stuff, really, just carousing, driving after a few too many or, as bluff sergeant Jack Bourke, from nearby Trentham, puts it: 'She was just a bloody nuisance.'

He bumped into her on one occasion after her car had mysteriously left the road and ended up in a paddock late at night. There was another time when her car performed a cartwheel or two before coming to rest on its hood. Nola needed the wit and services of the family friend and solicitor, Graham Bolton, to extricate her from a drink-driving charge.

Noel and Jessie Jenkins were greatly relieved when Nola announced that she had decided to marry. Perhaps now she would settle down, they thought. Her husband-to-be was Bernard McGuane, now working in a new job as a ground crew member for a crop-dusting firm. Nola was twenty-two and Bernard twenty-four when they took their vows. It should have been a happy ending to a simple love story, but instead the marriage began to founder almost as soon as it began.

Jessie Jenkins puzzled as to why it did not turn out as well as they had hoped. 'It was one of those funny things,' she says. 'If they'd never got married they would probably have stayed friends for life.' The family believed Bernard McGuane's new job was partly to blame because it kept him away from home for long periods. Then there were money problems. They always seemed to be short. Lastly, Nola was not a good housewife, she couldn't settle into the monotony of that existence and spent more and more time out socializing. 'It was a rough marriage, really it was. We'd be lucky if we had three cents in the purse, you know, and he was away a lot. The wages were inconsistent. We both used to drink a lot. They were wild days,' she admits.

Arnold remembers Nola as a slipshod housewife who would drive any husband mad. One day she'd have the place looking like a dream home, the next it would be a complete mess. The same with meals. Sometimes she'd invite Arnold over for dinner and he'd turn up to an empty table. Then she'd make up for that by cooking a splendid meal the following night.

Nola and Bernard gradually drifted apart and the marriage ceased to exist in all but name. Neither did anything about it until years later when it was formally dissolved. 'Married unsuccessfully, divorced successfully,' is how Nola laconically dismisses that part of her life.

Although Nola and her husband split up and lost the friendship they had shared for so many years, the Jenkins family found it hard to accept. Jessie Jenkins says: 'It was strange. They were inseparable before they got married.' Arnold adds: 'He was a friend of the family. One of the family. He's a really nice guy. His mother always asks about Nola.'

Lee Morrison was making a better fist of her life. With Nola now just a bad memory, Lee was able to relax and enjoy a normal, everyday existence. Joe Chant was still the man in her life and they finally tied the knot when Lee was in her early twenties. It was a pleasant change to have a new name, one that was linked with no controversy. 'It was a relief, I suppose,' admits Lee. 'Not that I was trying to hide behind it or anything.' Joe was now a state school teacher and the young couple soon became used to the country school circuit and Joe was to learn quickly the peculiar skills needed to be both father and teacher to his own children, two boys and a girl.

Grief became a frequent visitor to the Chant home. Lee's second child, a girl, died when she was only two weeks old and the stricken mother had to pack away, out of sight, the small garments she had so carefully readied for the arrival. She longed for another girl and when one finally arrived she brought great consolation and joy. The girl they lost may have been only a fortnight old but she has always been a name and a real person to both parents.

In all the troubled times it has been Joe Chant who has stood behind Lee, a supportive, cool character, with a sense of humour and an ability to keep his head when others are losing theirs. The rare kind of bloke who could make a success of life with the problems that he and Lee have had to endure.

Lee, the girl who was not keen on sport, found herself trapped on a tennis court for endless hours of practise with her husband, egged on by his promise of a dollar for every game she won. It worked, too, because she went on to become her local club's singles champion three times, and doubles and mixed doubles titleholder on several occasions. She branched out into golf and the Chant home, beside a small country school, is a showcase of sporting trophies. There are Lee's golf and tennis awards, Joe's prizes for football and tennis, plus a mixture from three talented children.

Another death rocked not only Lee, but the whole Morrison clan. Gloria Bock, Gwen Morrison's sister, who had provided a shoulder to lean on during those troubled years in Woomelang at the height of the 'Whose Baby Case', was diagnosed as having breast cancer. Her last year of life was spent mostly in hospital and she suffered much. Not one day went by without her mother, the ebullient but now subdued and saddened Amelia Williams, sitting by her bedside. When Gloria Bock finally died on 8 June

1966, it was a great relief to all who had seen her struggle against the disease, but it left a deep emotional scar on her ageing mother.

There was to be no respite for the family, however. With the memory of her sister's funeral still fresh in her mind, Gwen Morrison detected a lump in her own breast. For a time she kept it to herself, dreading the thought of a visit to the doctor, hoping it would just go away. The lump did not disappear and she finally had to talk to someone. Blair Morrison's wife, Elaine, was called into the bathroom and shown the lump, now larger and more obvious. 'You must see a doctor,' she told her mother-in-law. Still Gwen Morrison put it off. Eventually, Blair made a special trip to the hospital with his mother to have the tests.

The same terrible disease that had killed her sister was present. So soon after Gloria's painful death, Gwen Morrison could have been excused for indulging in a welter of self-pity, but that was not her style. When she received the grim news she took her family members aside and swore them to secrecy. Nothing on earth would allow her to put her mother through that wretched ordeal again. So Gwen Morrison kept her secret, suffering in silence for five years before the cancer drove her unwillingly into a hospital bed.

Lee, the girl who had never completely belonged, was her mother's right hand in those five years. Lee left her own home for stretches at a time to nurse her mother. It was a terrible experience, something she will never forget, watching her mother slowly wasting away.

Colleen was also tormented by her mother's ordeal. Both girls learned a lot about Gwen Morrison's inner courage in those unpleasant circumstances. Colleen recalls how the drugs her mother was given caused her to break out into tiny, itchy sores, which she would compulsively scratch until the skin broke. Colleen rubbed the broken skin with methylated spirits and could only admire the sheer will of the woman who would not even flinch as the raw disinfectant bit in.

The cancer spread to her bones and by September 1970, Gwen Morrison was having great difficulty keeping the secret of her disease from her mother. Gwen's sister, Audrey Moffat, visited the family that month, something she did every year to celebrate the September birthdays of her mother, Amelia Williams, brother Johnny Logan and Gwen herself.

Audrey remembers the pained effort of her sister to disguise the real cause of her limp, the bone cancer that was eating into her limbs. Gwen Morrison struggled into the room one evening on a walking stick and when her mother asked what was the matter, she mumbled something about a fall and a sore hip. The excuse satisfied her mother on that occasion but the truth was soon to emerge.

Audrey Moffat went back again for Christmas and Lee told her Gwen's resistance was crumbling. 'Mum's in a very bad way, we can't keep it fron Nana any longer.' Audrey Moffat and her brother sat down at a table in their mother's home. It was up to Audrey now to break the news. 'Mum, I've got something to tell you.' Amelia Williams knew instinctively that she was not going to like what she was about to hear, but she wanted it straight. 'OK, Aud, what is it?'

'Gwen's got cancer Mum.' There was just a moment of silence, no hysterics, then the old lady shook her head in anguish. 'Gwen too. No, I can't believe it.' All her daughter could think to say was: 'Well Mum, that's how it is.' Audrey Moffat had always admired, even envied, her mother's strength of character. Now she was to find it equal again to this latest, appalling test. 'No tears, no nothing. No tears from Mum.'

When Amelia Williams visited her daughter's sick bed she realized that death was only days away. 'My mother bought Gwen a beautiful blue nightdress to be buried in,' Audrey remembers sadly, 'We went home, played cards, everything like that, waiting for the phone to ring.'

As she neared death, the family conspired to hide the mirror in Gwen Morrison's hospital room with flowers so she would not see her own ravaged face. They piled the bench with vase upon vase of blooms but their kind ruse was a failure. Gwen Morrison saw her face anyway. They need not have bothered. She had enough courage left to take that and more.

The family gathered around her bedside for the final hours. Blair arrived last, after a rushed drive from many miles away to be with his mother. He was just in time, she had only minutes left to live. In those last few, precious minutes, Bill Morrison took his place at the head of the bed, wanting to be close to the woman he had so idolized. He pressed a cool drink to her lips, then picked up her engagement and wedding rings and slipped them on her finger. Their hands felt for each other, clasped, and she died. Bill Morrison rushed out of the room.

It was 6 January 1971, and Gwen Morrison was dead at the age of 56. They buried her on a hillside in the old Bendigo cemetery, a grave that probably goes unnoticed with its simple inscription: 'In memory of Alberta Gwen Morrison. Loved wife of Bill. Dear mother of Blair, Colleen and Lee.' No mention of a girl called Nola.

The two daughters, Colleen and Lee, share a sense of deprivation, a feeling that they lost their mother far too soon. Colleen says bitterly: 'It killed her.' She means the case, of course. Then she goes on to explain that she realizes the case and its aftermath may not have actually caused her mother's cancer, but they certainly made much of her time on this earth unhappy. To Colleen, that was not only tragic but unfair.

Lee was bitter, too, but she had to take over part of her mother's role to help her father rebuild his life. He was shattered by his wife's death and it needed much consoling from his favourite daughter to restore his own will to live. Again she left her own home and family to stay with Bill Morrison and help him cope with his grief.

There is no doubt that the alleged mix-up of babies at the Kyneton Hospital in 1945 cast a giant shadow over the rest of Gwen Morrison's life. However, it would seem that she finally found peace in her own mind in the later years. There was no more wondering about her lost girl, Nola. Lee was the daughter at her side. Even as she knew she was about to die, Gwen Morrison did not seek a last meeting with Nola. Says Lee: 'I was with her and she never expressed a wish to see her.'

16 THE CRASH

Soon after her twenty-eighth birthday Nola Jenkins made what was for her a typically impetuous decision. This time, however, it was to be a decision she would regret for the rest of her life. Despite the freezing weather and her dubious record as a driver, she confounded her parents by buying a motorbike, not a run-of-the-mill model but a tiny, low-powered, step-through scooter called a Honda Chelly.

Noel and Jessie Jenkins were unhappy about her riding 'this cross between a mini-bike and a ladies scooter' but she was a mature woman and they had long since abandoned trying to dissuade their strong-willed daughter once she'd made up her mind. Nola argued that it was cheap to run, 100 miles to the gallon, and with a gentle 70 cc motor she was hardly likely to run into any further trouble with the law.

On Monday, 23 July 1973, Nola set out for a test ride on her new motorbike. She was pretty vague in explaining where she was going, merely saying she was off to visit a friend and 'expect me when you see me'. After the visit, she decided to take the bike for a spin along the scenic, twisting bush road which runs between Blackwood and Trentham, beautiful mountain country laced with towering gum trees, about 20 miles to the south of Kyneton.

Nola was hurrying, encouraging the most out of her new bike because it was bitterly cold: it was about three in the afternoon and Nola wanted to be home for tea. She remembers it vividly.

Whose Baby?

Swinging into the sharp bend, the throttle jamming, straining forward to switch off the petrol, skidding, plunging forward, sliding along the ground, a sudden jarring halt and then, finally, a terrible crashing pain across her back.

A few hundred metres away nurseryman Dennis Norgate was working among the plants, cursing the cold that made 1973 the worst winter he had endured in the Blackwood hills. The nursery, near the top of the 2250-foot range is within shouting distance of the bend where Nola lay, now unconscious, but Norgate didn't hear a thing. That night, though, there was plenty of racket. His dogs wouldn't stop barking. Drifting between semi-consciousness and oblivion, Nola heard them too, a sound that remains indelibly in her brain. A sound that was to haunt her night after night. Why, if she could hear those dogs so clearly, could no-one hear her own wounded cries for help?

Back home in the warm kitchen of the Jenkins household, Jessie Jenkins was pondering whether to put on a bit extra, in case Nola turned up for tea. 'Don't bother, Mum,' said her husband. 'She'll probably be staying with her friend.'

When Nola's mind finally cleared it was a bitterly cold, frosty morning. She had spent the night in the open and her body was covered in the white mountain frost. She could feel its painful touch on her face and her hands but, strangely, nothing at all on her legs or feet.

The answer, she eventually reasoned, must be that her legs had sunk into one of the many old, abandoned mineshafts in the area. A terrifying prospect. If she moved too abruptly she could plunge down into the mine and never be found.

It was daylight and the dogs had stopped barking. The only sounds were the creaking of the trees, occasionally a birdcall and the drip, drip, drip of moisture off the gum boughs above her. Then came the sound she had wanted desperately to hear, a car winding its way slowly around the mountain road towards her. In that still mountain air she could hear it coming, long before it reached the spot where her bike had left the road.

Nola struggled to rise, shouting as loudly as she could. But her body refused to respond. It was only then that she realized that the bike had landed across her back, pinning her to the ground.

The front wheel was within reach of her left hand and she seized it in a frenzy, using all her power to thrust the bike from her back. The wheel just spun, frustratingly, and the car drove on, its sound disappearing slowly into the hills.

Nola remembers:

> 'I got fighting mad with that flamin' little bike. I couldn't understand that this stupid little thing and me, I was a reasonably strong person, why I couldn't throw it off my back. I just couldn't understand it. It just didn't ring true to me. You see I didn't realize that my back was broken.'

That day Nola went through an endless succession of struggles with the bike and futile sobbing, shouting sessions as car after car drove past, their windows tightly closed against the cold. She was not to know that a family friend, her best possible chance of being rescued, pedalled past every day to and from his work. She could not hear the bike and he had no way of knowing she was down there. By nightfall Nola lay exhausted, hoarse, frightened and frustrated, and those dogs began to bark again. She had been trapped for twenty-seven hours.

In Melbourne, prospector Graham Ashworth had spent the day on the telephone, making arrangements with his partners to take a trip up to Blackwood to check some mining pegs. It was an exciting prospect they had in mind, to get the old Barry's Reef gold mine into production again. The team consisted of Ashworth, the leader and a bubbling enthusiast about gold mining, who was one of the first men in Australia to revive interest in gold in the 70s; Ken Evans, management consultant and part-time prospector, and the young man of the group, industrial chemist Dennis Renowden, aged twenty-six, who was fed up with his job and saw gold mining as the way out. Ashworth finalized the arrangements: they would drive up together to Blackwood where they would meet mines inspector Mick Laby in three days time, on the Friday, to inspect their mining pegs.

On Wednesday morning Noel Jenkins and his wife finally put

into words what both had been thinking secretly for the past couple of days: Could something have gone wrong on Nola's trip? Noel decided to do something positive. He got in the car and went out to look for her, driving along the roads she might have used. His son Arnold joined in the hunt, making separate patrols of the same area. They both returned home that night worried men, oblivious to the fact that they had been searching just a couple of miles from where Nola lay.

For Nola the day had been much like the one before. There was no escaping the cold but, for the first time, she had felt hungry and her thirst suddenly became overwhelming. There was an added torment: her crash helmet had landed just a few feet away and was slowly filling with the water that dripped constantly from the overhanging trees. She recalls: 'That brand spanking new helmet had landed upside down and it was collecting water all the time. And I kept on thinking, "If only I could reach it, if only I could reach it."'

She began to search about her for some means of easing her hunger and quenching the unbearable thirst. It was then that she remembered something that may well have saved her life. A packet of pastry, bought to make an apple pie for her Mum when she got home. Now it was to become her means of survival. She tore the packet out of her overcoat pocket, split the plastic packaging with her nails and began wolfing down chunks of the tasteless, uncooked lump. She was now becoming more aware of her senses and it hurt her just to suck this livesaving morsel. 'My face was very sore,' she recalls, 'my teeth had split all my lip. The top was sort of all lying open. That was painful.'

Her hands, too, were painful where the skin had been ripped away in the accident and by her later exertions to try to free herself. The cold never seemed to ease, even when the sun was out, because she was always wet.

'There was the constant drip of moisture from the trees. It was wet all the time. I was going to light a fire to keep myself warm. I had borrowed my brother's good gas lighter that he'd been given for his twenty-first birthday and somehow it wouldn't work. It had got a bit wet or something. So there was no hope. I probably wouldn't have been able to light a fire anyway, it was all wet out there.'

Nola's next effort was to try to collect some water. She unravelled the plastic cover from the pastry and some more plastic from her tobacco pouch and lay the two small sheets on the ground to gather moisture. As a few drops formed on each sheet she would greedily lick them off. The pastry, what was left of it, was also absorbing moisture and Nola found she could relieve both thirst and hunger by rolling up tiny balls of the damp pastry and placing them under her tongue.

'I was even looking for something to eat on the ground. I was going to be a real Aborigine and try the witchetty grubs and things like that. Only there wasn't much around, believe me.'

By Wednesday night she had been lying pinned under the motorbike for more than fifty hours and her spirits were sinking fast. For the first time she really began to doubt if anyone would ever find her alive.

'I think I was a bit panic-stricken. It was frightening. There was no one. There were cars going past and nobody could hear me. I was panicking because I wouldn't be able to get home and see Mum and Dad.

They were going to find some bones out there and that would be me. I thought this horrible thing. All they were going to find was a rotten motorbike with bones sitting under it. How could I warn Mum that this was going to happen? You think of all these ghastly things and you worry how it's going to affect other people.'

Nola wept. She was frustrated and hoarse from crying out when she finally fell asleep on the third night of her ordeal.

Thursday morning at Norgate's nursery was crisp and clear. It was also the worst frost that Dennis Norgate, the weathered outdoorsman, can ever remember. Worse even than those of the previous few days and they'd been bitter enough. 'It was a real beauty,' he says with understatement.

Everything was white, as if covered by a blanket of snow. 'I reckon the frost was six inches thick into the soil,' he says. Norgate walked up to a pile of dry sand and threw his fork into it. It bounced straight back at him. The ground was frozen solid. Dennis Norgate still shakes his head in disbelief when he things of that critically-injured girl surviving that terrible night.

Nola had a broken spine, broken ribs, serious lacerations to her face and hands and bruises all over her body. Because of the fractured spine her circulation was reduced and frostbite had set in on both her legs.

Her only protection from rain, frost and freezing temperatures had been a heavy, lined gabardine overcoat, winter slacks and desert boots. Her morale had been dented, nearly destroyed, by the frustration of shouting day after day for help to cars that just whizzed past her. It was now, on the fourth day of her terrible ordeal, that Nola Jenkins could so easily have cracked, given up and died. Instead, she drew on her reserves of courage and determined to stay alive.

About this time Nola recalls something strange happening. She is not quite sure exactly when, but she suddenly became aware of a presence, as if someone else was nearby.

> 'I just wasn't alone out there anymore. There was something or somebody out there with me. There was some comfort somewhere. That made me relax and gave me the strength to keep yelling and screaming and whatever I did. It was — it was peaceful. No, I wasn't alone.'

Nola turned to prayer.

> 'I was brought up in the Anglican Church and sent to Sunday school and all that but I suppose we all go through a phase of saying, "What the heck!" It's not until something happens to you that you think, "Oh, there might be something to that."'

Her prayers as she lay there chilled and helpless with exhaustion 'weren't like any normal old prayers'. They were pleas for help, from the heart.

The crash

The fourth night brought with it the realization that she must surely be found soon or die a lonely death in the mountains. Her ordeal had been going on for seventy-five hours and she was near the end of her physical resources. Like the past nights she tried again to keep calm and tell herself to save energy, but when headlights appeared on the road she could not restrain herself.

'Each night I would think, "Right, I have to get some sleep." I'd see headlights coming and I'd start yelling and doing my little act again. I was getting terribly hoarse.'

Friday 27 July was a bright sunny day after the morning frost. Graham Ashworth set out from his home in the Melbourne bayside suburb of Brighton looking forward to a day in the bush doing what he likes most: scrambling around old gold mines. He picked up his mates Ken Evans and Dennis Renowden and they headed for Blackwood where mines inspector Mick Laby was to be waiting for them.

Renowden recalls that Ashworth was his usual, enthusiastic self during the drive, hardly letting anyone else get a word in during his patter about this great new venture which was going to make them all a fortune. Ashworth is the grandson of miners and likes to recall how his great aunt had been a close friend of Kate Kelly, sister of Australia's most notorious bushranger, and that his great grandparents were the first settlers in the McIvor shire near Bendigo.

Everything went according to plan and, after picking up Mick Laby, by 2.30 that afternoon there was just one last peg to check on the Blackwood–Trentham road. Ashworth pulled the car to the side of the road and the four men climbed out. Nola heard Ashworth's car coming towards her, heard it stop, and knew her last chance had come. She heard the car doors slam and the crunch of the prospectors' boots on the gravel above her. She yelled and yelled. She couldn't stop shouting though her hoarse throat was raw from the effort. Ashworth thought he heard an odd noise as he stopped.

'As we got out, we heard someone call out, "Help!" The others thought it was someone down in the nursery because we could see several people working down there. We heard it two or three times. Mick Laby called out, "Where are you?" There seemed to be no reply and the others continued down the gully to look for the peg.'

Nola can never forget the moment: 'I thought I was yelling out to ghosts or something. Then one of them said, "There's someone down there."' After hearing the strange cries, Graham Ashworth walked in the opposite direction from the mining peg. He looked over an embankment and saw an astounding sight.

As his eyes took in the scene beneath him he was reminded of an animal left to die in a trap. The ground around her was beaten flat from her struggles.

'I've seen foxes caught in traps or wallabies caught in a fence and the ground all around them is flattened. It is almost sickening to know something, or some person, has been trapped and can't free itself. And that was what it was like. The ground all around her was flattened as if she'd been caught in a trap and had been thrashing about trying to free herself.'

He goes on:

'She was lying downhill with the bike across her. The first thing I did was jump down the bank and throw the bike off her. She said, "How did you find me? How did you know where to look?" I said we weren't looking for her, we'd come to inspect the mining peg. She said she'd been there for two days or three nights. At first I didn't believe her but then I noticed she had brown corduroy slacks on and the grooves in the corduroy were all full of dew and I knew she had been there at least overnight.'

In fact, Nola had been pinned beneath that motorbike for ninety-six hours, much of that time in temperatures well below freezing. She had survived four days and four nights of hell.

The prospectors gathered round within seconds, each trying to help. Ashworth raced down to the nursery to raise the alarm. Dennis Renowden grabbed the upturned motorbike helmet and ran down to the nearby creek to get her some fresh drinking water. But Nola's main benefactor was the only smoker in the group, Ken Evans, who was able to place a cigarette between her battered lips and light it.

Evans remembers particularly how fatigued and blue with cold Nola looked. He and the others took off their jackets and made them into blankets for her. 'She could move her hands but not her legs,' he recalls.

Iris Norgate didn't waste a second when Ashworth battered on her front door. The nurseryman's wife rushed to her phone and called, in turn, Doctor Andrew Shipley, who was working in his surgery in nearby Trentham, the ambulance station at Kyneton and the police station in Trentham. Then she put the kettle on, as so many country folk are quick to do in times of crisis, and made a good strong billy of tea, heavily dosed with sugar. She rushed it down to the accident scene, handing it to one of the men, but not venturing down the steep embankment where Nola lay. She could see there were plenty of people around the prone figure and she didn't want to intrude.

Ambulanceman Ron Callaway turned on the flashing light as he steered his vehicle out of the garage and headed at high speed for the Blackwood road. He didn't bother with the siren because 'there was no traffic to worry about, not on that track.'

Just a few miles around the winding bush road young police constable Greg Falkiner, a city boy, was having the usual quiet day waiting for something to happen in the little farming hamlet of Trentham. When he heard the roar of a speeding car rushing through Trentham, he muttered: 'I'll book that bastard!' He was somewhat disappointed when he spun to the window and saw the old brown Holden of Andrew Shipley. Falkiner had often thought that the young Doctor Shipley was inclined to overdo the medico's unwritten licence to speed on special occasions, but he knew that this time the doctor meant business. 'I saw him fairly hoofing it out of town,' he recalls. 'I thought "I'll bet I get a call in 10 minutes."' In fact, it wasn't even that long before he heard the voice of Dennis Norgate's wife on the phone from the nursery.

She sounded a little confused and upset but Falkiner got the message. As he joined the rush to the accident scene he knew that the smash involved a young woman and she was in a pretty bad way.

There were about a dozen people standing around as the young constable jumped out of his car. He remembers vividly the shock of seeing Nola. 'She looked bloody awful. I didn't think she'd pull through.' He scarcely believed the others when they told him Nola had been lying there for days on end.

> 'I remember there had been some really bad frosts. It was amazing a person could lie outside for so long and survive. Amazing! She wasn't even unconscious. She had a tremendous will to survive, obviously. A lot of others would have thrown in the towel.'

To all the men Nola seemed lucid and calm, answering their questions and making it hard for them to believe she had been there for so long. Only when ambulanceman Callaway removed her slacks did they fully comprehend the horror of her ordeal.
Says Ashworth:

> 'I could see her legs were terribly bruised and blue. They looked lifeless. Her legs and her hips looked terrible. They were blue, black, yellow and green. I had no idea until then she had been there so long. She looked good before that. That's what frostbite must look like. I realized then she must have been there for days.'

To Renowden, the legs seemed 'white and pasty'. 'There didn't seem to be any blood flow. When you touched them, the mark would remain.' He also remembers the ants — 'they were crawling all over her.'

Callaway recognized Nola as the young woman he'd seen often enough around Kyneton. 'I wasn't sure of her name but I remembered her face. She had no feeling in her legs. You get them to wriggle their toes. Her feet were black from frostbite.'

Doctor Shipley knew within moments that Nola had a broken

spine and he remembers telling Callaway that he'd have to drive her immediately to the Austin Hospital, fifty odd miles away in Melbourne, where they specialize in spinal injuries. By now, Nola was fed up with what to her seemed to be interminable 'fiddle faddle'. She knew Dr Shipley as a 'boyish creature' — he was a fresh-faced twenty-nine-year-old at the time — and when he suggested that she'd have to go to hospital, she butted in belligerently. 'Take me straight home,' she demanded, a rather ridiculous request from a woman whose chances of survival were soon to be rated as very, very poor.

Callaway took a blanket from the ambulance and together they rolled her gently on to her side. Holding the blanket taut between them, they eased her on to it, then ever so gingerly, again everyone helping, they lifted her on to an emergency stretcher. Callaway strapped the stretcher into the ambulance and headed south for Melbourne with his reluctant passenger.

An almost farcical situation then took place inside the speeding vehicle, with Callaway trying to radio ahead for police help while being shouted down by a distraught Nola. 'You're going the wrong bloody way,' she was babbling. As far as she was concerned she wanted to go back home to Kyneton, in the opposite direction. Next came what can only be described as a Keystone Cops routine. Police blocked off intersections for the ambulance's last ten miles through the suburbs of Melbourne. Just one intersection short of the police 'protection', Callaway, siren now blaring, passed a truck, then saw — too late — a car 'come right across in front of me'.

Nola heard the screech of brakes, then the rending of metal and felt the stretcher shoot forward abruptly. The thought flashed through her mind: Had she survived all that time out in the bush only to die wrapped in blankets in the back of an ambulance? Nola needn't have worried. It was only a minor smash and another ambulance quickly turned up to complete her journey.

At 5.30 on the afternoon of 27 July 1973, Nola was wheeled through the doors of the Austin Hospital.

Journalist Stephen Foley knew he was on to a good story when the details started to filter through to his newspaper's office in Melbourne. A girl surviving in freezing conditions for four nights

...found by chance by gold prospectors...hospital battle to save her life...

Foley knew that it was the kind of story his paper, the *Sun*, Australia's biggest-selling daily, would find hard to keep off the front page. He needed no prompting to chase down every fact he could. He was soon chatting to Renowden and Ashworth, piecing together the report that was to appear the next morning under the heading 'Miracle' girl cheats death. Foley, the eager young reporter, didn't miss much.

However, there was just no way that he, or the prospectors, could have known that the girl now making the headlines had been in the news before — more than twenty years earlier, as a little blonde girl in a celebrated court case.

It was not until the next day that the *Sun*'s sister paper, the *Herald*, made the link. Nola Jenkins, said the *Herald*, was 'one of the two girls in the "Whose Baby" case — one of the most famous cases in Australian legal history.' Nola was back on page one.

One man who read Stephen Foley's article with more than passing interest, and took particular delight in viewing Dennis Renowden's picture, was his boss. He was one of the first to congratulate Renowden when he turned up for work the following Monday. And he was quick to remind the young chemist that he'd taken Friday off because he was supposed to be sick. 'Sorry about this Dennis,' he said, 'but I'll have to dock you a day's pay.'

Of the prospectors who found Nola, only one, Ken Evans, a pipe-smoking rugby fanatic, was to come across her again. Their meeting was to be less than a year later, in incredible circumstances.

17 FIGHT FOR LIFE

For five days Jessie Jenkins had waited with one ear always tuned for the phone to ring. She was anxious about her daughter. Even though Nola had had some escapades in the past, she always called her family to apologize and make up. When the phone finally rang late that Friday afternoon, Jessie Jenkins reached it in a stride. The voice on the other end was not one she could recognize. It was a young man and he introduced himself as 'Andrew Shipley, Dr Andrew Shipley'. The conversation that followed is still a painful memory to her.

'Nola's been found. She's had an accident,' he explained. Shipley broke the news as gently as possible, without trying to raise false hopes. He did not mention Nola's back injury but he did spell out the concern he had over her legs. 'Her legs are badly frostbitten,' Mrs Jenkins remembers him telling her.

'I said, "That sounds as if it might be amputation?" He said, "Oh well, yes." He didn't commit himself, of course.'

Within twenty minutes Noel and Jessie Jenkins were in their car heading for Melbourne and the Austin Hospital. Inside the casualty ward, Nola was near to death.

She was, in medical terms, 'grossly hypothermic'. In other words, her body temperature was critically low, to the point where survival was almost impossible. The thermometer recorded only 30.5° celsius (86.9° fahrenheit), almost seven degrees below normal. Her blood pressure could not be recorded. She had a broken back with complete paralysis below the mid-chest area. Her legs were both savagely frostbitten. She was in severe shock, there were complications with her chest and she was having trouble breathing. There were also minor injuries — cuts, abrasions, bruising and bleeding over the white of her left eye.

A team of specialists had been brought on duty to deal with the case. Dr David Burke, who was to lead the fight to save Nola's life, was taken aback when he examined her.

'She was barely alive,' he noted. 'Her body temperature was terribly cold, at a level not consistent with life. She was freezing. She was that cold you had to have special thermometers to record her temperature. Normal ones don't go that low. She was cold, cold, cold.'

As Dr Burke took in the situation, Nola was given the first of what was to be a series of blood transfusions. Her blood pressure was a big worry to the doctors. Says Burke: 'She had no blood pressure that was recordable, which meant she was in severe shock. She was barely alive really.'

The specialists hovering around her bed included John Royle, a vascular surgeon who was to take care of the frostbitten legs, the director of anaesthesia, to supervise the campaign to resuscitate her, a renal physician to monitor her kidneys which were failing due to the shock, and an orthopaedic surgeon for the spinal injury. For the orthopaedic surgeon there was little to be done at that stage. The damage to her spine was irreversible.

Dr Burke and his team began their attempt to save Nola's life with the most basic of treatments. Put simply, they had to try to take the chill from her body. 'The first job was to gradually warm her up,' he says. 'You mustn't do it too quickly. It's very important to slowly warm people up. The concentration was on resuscitation, that is saving her life.'

Surgeon John Royle confided to the other specialists his grave concern over the frostbite and gave explicit instructions to the nursing staff that Nola's legs were to be warmed very slowly and with infinite care. He explains why frostbite victims need such slow, careful warming up:

'Ice crystals form in the cells with frostbite and when the crystals melt it disrupts the cells. You get less swelling around the injured cells if they are warmed up slowly and the fluid can be conducted away. You tend to warm up the legs by warming the rest of the patient. You don't put a hot water bottle on their legs or anything like that.'

Dr Burke, a cheerful, optimistic character, was pessimistic about this particular case. He recalls having given Nola, in his own mind, a 'very poor' chance of surviving. In fact, he looked at it from the other way and reckoned there was an eighty per cent chance of her dying. Nola's body chemistry was 'grossly deranged' as the medical team began their lifesaving procedures. One immediate treatment was to have a catheter inserted into the bladder to drain it. The bladder was swollen with urine because it was paralyzed and unable to perform its usual function. Another tube was inserted through her nose down into her stomach to suck out any food which might have remained there. In cases of paraplegia the victims face an extremely dangerous period of a week to a fortnight when anything in the stomach can accumulate because the organs are functioning slowly. This can lead to vomiting and, because the victim cannot cough properly, they can easily choke to death.

Nola was given intravenous fluids to build up her strength, antibiotics to fight infection and numerous other drugs to support her circulation. Although most of her body was being warmed with blankets, her legs were kept cool, exposed to the air of the air-conditioned hospital room, as John Royle had instructed. X-rays revealed that Nola had a severe compression fracture of her spine at the ninth thoracic segment, about two-thirds of the way up her back. They also showed a broken eighth right rib and some marks on the right lung which could have been bruising or small patches of pneumonia. To further complicate matters she had developed an irregular heartbeat.

About seven o'clock that night her parents reached the hospital. They remember wandering through what seemed like miles of sterile corridors, trying to find the intensive care ward and the daughter whose troubled life had dominated their own lives. They had been told to hurry but when they finally found the right ward the door was firmly closed to them. An anonymous man in a white coat told them of the battle going on inside and asked them to be patient. The waiting was painful. They had time to worry about what was going on behind the closed door, and imagine the worst. Finally, the door opened and they were ushered inside.

It was a terrible shock. Nola lay motionless in the bed, stiff and grey. Her appearance was so much like a corpse that her parents were stunned. 'There she was with all those tubes sticking out of her and heart machines and heavens-knows-what, surrounded by doctors and nurses,' Jessie Jenkins recalls. Then, to their amazement, the 'corpse' opened her lips and greeted them with: 'Where the devil have you been!' They were the only words Nola was able to muster and once her parents had established for themselves that she was, indeed, still clinging on to life, they allowed themselves to be shown out again.

In a room close by the intensive care ward, a young doctor listed to them the extent of the damage to Nola's body, suffered both in the accident, and in the five days that followed. It was almost impossible for them to digest what he was saying. Nola was crippled. She would never walk again. Her spinal cord was damaged beyond repair.

That wasn't the end of the bad news. He went on to describe the shocking frostbite in both her legs. The parents must understand, he warned them, that Nola faced a desperate fight to save her legs.

Finally, came the grimmest news of all. Nola had expended almost all of her strength just staying alive after the crash. Now, in her weakened state, she could die at any time. Having told them all that, he tried to offer a ray of encouragement. 'Never give up hope, we'll do everything we can,' he said as he left the room.

The night of 27 June 1973, was the closest that Nola Jenkins came to death. The Austin specialists were astounded by her survival. Dr Burke, the director of the spinal injuries unit, regards the Nola Jenkins case as being 'extraordinary'. 'That a person could be pinned under a motorcycle and still survive in that cold ... remarkable that anyone could survive that long with a severe spinal cord injury as well.'

Oddly however, Dr Burke attributes her feat in remaining alive to the extreme cold. The same cold that caused her shocking pain and discomfort and ate into her legs, played a part in her cheating the odds. He explains: 'That she was sort of frozen helped a little

FIGHT FOR LIFE

bit because that reduced the body metabolism to a very great degree. At that time she was almost in a state of suspended animation.' He goes even further: 'If she had done the same thing in the middle of summer she would not have survived five days. No way.'

On the Saturday morning, the day after she was found, Noel and Jessie Jenkins returned to the hospital to be greeted by good news. Nola was still alive, still fighting. But when they reached her bedside they were to see something that is etched into their minds like a horrible nightmare. Nola's legs. Ten years later Jessie Jenkins is still almost sickened by the thought. 'If you've never seen frostbite, I hope you never do. It's the most shocking looking sight. Terrible. There were these huge blisters. I've never seen anything like it. Black. They were terrible.' Nola could recognize them, but that was about all. Parents and daughter looked at each other in silence.

There was more good news the following morning. Nola's temperature had stabilized and, best of all, the doctors were feeling reasonably confident about her pulling through. She had become the star patient at the Austin as her name and link with the famous 'Whose Baby Case' spread like wildfire. Nurses were often seen making obvious little detours past her bed so they could tell their friends they had seen 'that Nola Jenkins'. Doctors, too, visited her bedside in increasing numbers, but they were taking the opportunity to examine a condition which is rare in Australia's climate: severe frostbite.

Bill Morrison's breakfast on the Saturday morning had been brought to a sudden halt by the news story in the *Sun*. He instantly recognized the Nola Jenkins of Mitchell Street, Kyneton, as the girl he regarded as his own daughter. Even though she had turned her back on his family, he knew where his obligations lay. He knew he had to be at her side if she was fighting for her life. The following day he drove to Melbourne and presented himself at the reception desk at the Austin Hospital. 'I'm here to see Nola — the girl in the Kyneton accident,' he announced. 'I'm sorry, sir,' he was told firmly, 'only parents allowed.' His protests went unheeded and Bill Morrison walked away from the hospital a lonely figure, head bowed in the rain which had begun teeming down outside. He consoled himself with the thought: 'At least Gwen would have expected me to try.'

Monday and Tuesday were two more cheerful days for the Jenkins family. The doctors were enthusiastic now that she had won her fight for life. Nola, herself, was beginning to feel her body slowly regain its strength and she was able to tell her parents a few details of her ordeal in the Blackwood Mountains. Some natural colour had begun to return to her legs, her parents were told, and there was reason to think they might be saved, despite the fact that her paralysis had affected the circulation in her legs and hampered the body's natural defences against the frostbite.

Wednesday saw an ominous sign when the nurses took her temperature. For a couple of days it had edged up, just slightly above normal. Now it was 38° celsius (100.4° fahrenheit), which was alarming. Still, the doctors decided it was too soon to take any drastic action. They knew that the temperature was beginning to rise because muscle tissue was dying in her feet. For the first time, amputation was being considered seriously but they chose, of course, to wait until that was the only course left to them. Dr Burke explains:

> 'One delays amputation for as long as possible. Nobody likes amputating legs. I'm aware from past experience that a paraplegic person has enough problems to cope with psychologically after being paralyzed, that to remove their leg or legs as well, on top of that, is a very big psychological burden to add to it. I'm sure that amputation is a much worse disability to cope with psychologically than a spinal cord injury. At least as a paraplegic you don't look different, you're a whole person. If you are missing a part you don't look normal. So we were very reluctant to amputate and I think if we can err here, we err on delaying too long, because we don't want to do it.'

So delay they did, but the doctors closest to the case knew that day that the tough decision was rapidly closing in on them.

Surgeon John Royle was the man who had to ultimately make that irretrievable decision. He had been bracing himself for it from the moment he saw the blackened mess that was Nola's lower legs. Like Dr Burke, Royle dreaded the operation, even though he had performed scores of amputations. 'You have to be absolutely right. Once it's off it's in the bucket,' says Royle in the blunt terminology of his profession.

> 'You tend to be quite conservative. You do anything you can to save the limb, particularly in a young person. Often we wait a bit too long. You take the limb off and the next day, or the day after, the patient is so much better in health. You say: "Gee, we should have taken the limb off a day or two earlier."'

On this day, sticking exactly to the pattern of delay until all hope is lost, John Royle examined Nola and again put amputation to the back of his mind.

When Noel and Jessie Jenkins visited Nola the following day, Thursday 2 August, they could not help but notice how well she was looking. Their daughter was cheerful and the colour had returned to her cheeks. With each day in hospital they had noticed a big improvement. Nola's cheerfulness reflected on the couple as they drove home to Kyneton around midday. As far as they were concerned the worst was over.

They had lunch and a cup of tea in front of a blazing wood fire. Noel was thinking about going back to work — he'd lost a lot of time since Nola's accident — but a ringing telephone put a stop to all that.

Noel answered the call. His wife knew from his manner that something was terribly amiss. He put the phone down and walked over to her, placing his hands on her shoulders. 'Mum, we have to go back to the hospital,' he said gently. 'The doctors say they have to take Nola's feet off.' It was the most shattering news they had been given since that day almost twenty-five years before when Judge Barry ruled that Nola was not their child and they must part with her.

What the team of doctors had feared from the beginning had happened. Gangrene had set in — the tissue in her legs had died.

Nola's temperature had risen to 39° celsius (102.2° fahrenheit) an extraordinary jump of 8.5° celsius, or 15.3° fahrenheit, in the six days since she was brought in nearly frozen to death.

There was no longer any hope of saving her feet, they had to come off. Dr Burke says: 'We had all this dead tissue in the legs and it became infected.' And he explains, in simple terms, what that means: 'You get pus in there and you've got a very severe problem on your hands. The pus would eventually overwhelm the patient, who would die of infection.'

When the doctors broke the news to Nola they found her, naturally, obstinate about amputation. It may have been a matter-of-fact decision for them but, after all, she was the one who faced the surgery and hadn't she been getting better all the time? Couldn't they put it off for at least another day? Give her more time. There was no more time they warned her, using blunt language to persuade her to consent to the operation. It was her feet or her life. Still Nola held out: 'I want to see Mum and Dad,' she told them.

The doctors tried another tack. She was already paralyzed, they pointed out, she would never walk again and, although it was a harsh way to put it, her legs were useless and now an actual threat to her very existence. 'It doesn't matter, you'll never walk again anyway,' one of the speakers told her. Nola believes this was the first clear indication she had of her paralysis, of the fact that she would be a cripple for life. 'Get me Mum and Dad,' she ordered them.

Nola's parents agreed with the doctors that the operation should go ahead, but they were not about to sign any consent form themselves. 'I'm not signing any papers,' Mrs Jenkins told them. 'She's got to do it herself.' What went through her mind was that if she did sign, her daughter might come to regard it later as the wrong decision and never forgive her. They decided that Nola just had to be persuaded to sign the papers herself. When they walked into her room, Nola greeted them with: 'I'm sorry to have brought you down.' Noel, close to tears, replied: 'That's OK, that's OK. If you want us we're here.'

The presence of her parents and their comforting persuasion gave Nola the strength she needed to accept the inevitability of the operation. She signed the consent and even managed a throwaway line before they wheeled her off: 'OK, but I want both legs even, thanks.' Her father remembers on a more serious note that Nola insisted that the operation be completed in one go. 'She didn't want to have her feet off first, then higher and higher again as the gangrene crept up,' he explains.

A nurse pushed her off to the operating theatre just before 5.30 that evening. Her parents still recall her last words on the way into the theatre, a whispered plea: 'You will be here when I come back, won't you?' David Burke, the kindly doctor the Jenkinses had come to know quite well over the past few days, reassured them. He explained that there certainly was a risk involved in such an operation but Nola was again strong and obviously had a powerful will to live. Burke, the man who had given her only a one-in-five chance of surviving when she first came into the hospital, now believed she was ninety per cent sure of pulling through. Without the operation, the position would be reversed to a ninety per cent chance of dying.

John Royle realized that this was to be no simple amputation. Both legs would have to come off below the knee and the patient, although her condition had improved, was still seriously ill and must be spared as much trauma and shock as possible. He called in Brian Buxton, another honorary surgeon at the Austin Hospital, and they decided to operate in tandem.

Royle explains: 'She was fairly ill so we thought it better if the two of us operated simultaneously. Then you spend less time under the anaesthetic. He did one leg and I did the other.'

Working swiftly and neatly under the brilliant lights of the operating theatre, each surgeon used his scalpel to make incisions just below the knee. They looked at each other across the operating table and shook their heads. 'The muscle was dead, a pinky colour. It doesn't bleed when you cut it,' Royle recalls. Both surgeons moved further up the legs, making new incisions at the lower end of each femur (thigh bone). Here they found healthy tissue, so at least part of the legs could be saved. They were both concerned to retain as much of Nola's lifeless legs as possible because, as Royle explains: 'Even though they are paralyzed they have got to balance and sit in a chair and that little bit of extra length makes that balancing easier.'

The new incisions were made a short distance below where the bone was to be cut. This allowed the two surgeons to fold back the skin and muscle which they later used to cover the stump of the bone and form a resting point for an artificial limb. John Royle and his partner agreed on the points where the two thigh bones should be severed and each reached across and picked up the small handsaws used in the grisly task. In seven seconds it was all over. Nola had lost her legs.

'Amputating a limb is just a bloody disaster,' Royle says passionately. 'You never like doing it. It's an awful operation. Mostly it means it's a failure. You haven't been able to salvage the situation. The nurses don't like it in the theatre either. If you haven't seen it done before it's likely to turn the young nurse's stomach over seeing it, particularly when the leg comes off and it's dumped into a bucket.'

The surgeons left Nola's wounds unsutured, left open so that they could be checked later to ensure that the infection had spread no further. If that happened, she could be forced to endure another, higher operation. Normally in cases of gangrene there is little bleeding but this wasn't the case with Nola. She lost large quantities of blood during the operation and had to be given several transfusions.

Royle was pretty pleased with the way the operation had gone.

'I wasn't really in doubt she'd survive, but it's a fairly major procedure. It's a shock mentally to the patient. The psychological trauma of it is pretty marked, but in fact at the time of the operation the patient is so sick and doesn't realize it so much. Later, the realization hits them.'

The surgery was all over at 6.45, just seventy-five minutes after it had begun.

At 7 p.m. Noel and Jessie Jenkins saw their daughter emerge from the theatre, unconscious, on a trolley. The wait had been harrowing. They will never forget it. The feeling of being alone in that vast hospital, knowing no one, not knowing where to go or who to talk to. When they left the hospital that night they had one last straw to which they could cling. If nothing else, at least Nola was alive.

Nola spent the following day in a dream world of hazy hallucinations. 'I was being shifted from tent to tent. I was daydreaming, hallucinating...' But she was still losing blood and needed a further series of transfusions. Her parents spent hours at her bedside but there could be no real communication between them.

Several days were to pass before her mind finally cleared and her memory returned. There is one day that stands out above all others. 'I remember one sister came in and said: "It's about time you had a look at your legs." I was still under the impression I had lost my feet. And with that, the sheets came back and up pops this little leg.'

The shock was stunning but Nola fought back the tears and tried desperately to control her emotions. First a paraplegic, then a paraplegic without legs. It was almost impossible to bear this latest burden. However, it was not until some time later that the full trauma of the situation overcame her and threatened to shake her sanity.

Two days after the operation, Nola was wheeled back into the theatre and the surgeons partly closed the wounds. They were confident the gangrene had been stemmed. She was progressing well, although she had a minor infection in the stumps, and needed further blood transfusions on 10 August, eight days after the operation. By 14 August, they decided she was well enough to have the leg wounds fully closed.

There was to be a further crisis, however, this time involving the right lung; the same lung that had shown up as injured in her X-rays on the first day in hospital. Fluid accumulated rapidly in the lung cavity. On 16 August she was back in the operating theatre. This time almost a litre of fluid was drained from her chest.

As their daughter fought again for her life, against this bout of pneumonia, Noel and Jessie Jenkins continued what had become a daily vigil. Their routine was always the same, day in and out, for those first six weeks after she was rushed to hospital. Noel would work all day, leaving early to pick up his wife for the hour-plus trip to Melbourne in the late afternoon. They would sit at her side for four hours every evening before tackling the drive back to Kyneton. Seldom did they make it to bed before midnight.

Nola, whose health they were concerned about, found herself worrying about them.

'They were really looking wrecks. Sometimes, really, they shouldn't have come... I didn't know what was going on. They had put up with a lot from me. They struggled to get down there and I'd go crook when they got there. You know, it couldn't have been very pleasant really.'

Jessie didn't mind her daughter's bad moods and biting tongue, nor did they mind the fact that some days she was hardly coherent. 'No, you were alright love,' she tells her daughter. 'You mightn't have talked much but we knew. We were there and that was the main thing when you needed something.'

After the battle with pneumonia had been won, Nola grew stronger by the day. At times she was depressed, though the worst was to come later, but generally she was fighting back despite all the odds. Dr Burke had got to know his star patient well and was one of her admirers. 'She must have been a pretty tough lady. Tough physically and psychologically. Tougher, perhaps, than she was given credit for.'

That toughness of spirit was to be tested sorely just when Nola appeared to be getting back on top of it all. She remembers the mail arriving at her bedside one morning. She always got a stack of mail from wellwishers around the country, people who had followed the fortunes of the Jenkins family during the 'Whose Baby Case'.

This day there was one letter which, for some reason, caught her eye, so she opened it first. There were two pages and the handwriting was large, Nola noticed at once.

It began simply.

'Dear Nola,
  I am sorry to tell you, your mother has died.'

18 THE LONG ROAD BACK

It took a few seconds for the words to sink home. 'I am sorry to tell you, your mother has died.' Nola dropped the letter from her shaking hands. Tears ran down her face and she screamed at the top of her lungs for the nurse. 'Who the hell is this? Why wouldn't my father let me know my mother has died?' The thoughts rushed through her mind in the brief moment it took for the nurse to answer her urgent summons.

Nola picked the letter up again, but the only words she could see were: 'Your mother has died.' She couldn't bring herself to read past that first brief sentence. 'It was just those words I saw.'

Nola called for the social worker, a buxom, no-nonsense woman who had helped her before when she had been feeling low. Together they digested the contents of the letter. 'We sort of read it through slowly, together. We worked out what it was all about,' Nola recalls.

At the bottom of the second page was the signature — Audrey Moffat. The address was somewhere in NSW. Nola had never met Audrey Moffat, nor had she ever heard the name, but the letter made it clear that Audrey Moffat knew Nola's name very well. The letter explained that Audrey Moffat was Gwen Morrison's sister. And the 'mother' who had died was Gwen Morrison. Actually Gwen Morrison died two years earlier but Nola had lost contact with the Morrisons almost a decade before.

Nola's emotions were already stripped bare by the trauma of her accident, the fight for survival, the loss of her legs, and the painful realization that she faced the rest of her life as a wheelchair cripple. To say that the letter was close to being the last straw was no exaggeration.

Her feelings were torn between relief and sorrow. There was enormous relief that the mother she had known from her earliest childhood was still alive. But there was sadness, too, for Gwen Morrison was the woman she had sought out in her confused teens and the same woman who had welcomed her into the Morrison home as one of their own. She could be glad that Jessie Jenkins was not the 'mother' referred to in Audrey Moffat's letter, but there was no cause to celebrate when another woman, so closely linked to her own life, was dead. Nola cried a lot that day and she was still crying when Jessie Jenkins, cheerful and encouraging as ever, walked into the ward that afternoon for her daily visit.

Mrs Jenkins remembers the scene at her daughter's bedside.

> 'She was still weeping when she told me about it. It didn't take much those days to send Nola into a state of shock. She'd had enough. She was battling to find her own stability and something like that was very upsetting.'

Nola is harsher with her correspondent. 'I think I went into a bluey of some description. Well, you see, I thought my mother had died and I was really sort of knocked out about it. What a damn thing to do.'

The social worker, an English woman, told Nola: 'Don't you worry about this. I'll fix this in no time flat.' She tucked the letter into her pocket and that was the last Nola ever saw of it. Nola took care, though, to write the name Audrey Moffat in her address book, thinking to herself: 'Right, if I get another letter from her I'll know who she is and I just won't bother to open it.' To this day, she has never seen or heard again of the woman who would have her believe she is her aunt. Although Nola understandably regards that ill-fated letter as an unwanted intrusion into her life, her mother is more sympathetic. She points out that Mrs Moffat had offered 'to come down from Sydney to be with you'.

Audrey Moffat, living in Sydney at the time, was never to know the upset that her letter had evoked. Of the three daughters of Amelia Williams, Audrey is the one who appears to have inherited the blunt nature of 'Ma' Williams. She speaks her mind, if necessary, to the point of impoliteness. This was one case where her methods, however good her intentions, had proved to be monumentally ill-advised.

Amelia Williams had written to Audrey informing her of Nola's accident and enclosing a newspaper clipping which told of the double amputation. Audrey Moffat remembers thinking of the heartbreak her sister Gwen had endured over the loss of Nola and then thinking: 'Thank God she died before this!' She decided to try to take her dead sister's place as Nola's 'mother'.

> 'I wrote to Nola... telling her that Gwen was dead because I thought she might have thought her mother had neglected her. So I wrote and told her her mother was dead, and asked her to write to me but she never, ever did. She'd never known her mother. I would have liked to take the place of her mother.'

The Audrey Moffat letter was the only sour note among hundreds that poured into Nola's hospital ward. 'I was getting mail from everywhere. I just opened them and read them and answered most of them.' There were several encouraging entreaties from would-be suitors, who saw themselves as Galahads rescuing the stricken damsel from her lonely hospital bed. One in particular, sticks in her mind. It came from a man in New Zealand and he was very keen to marry her. 'He was quite an athletic sort of chap for his age. I think he was in his early sixties,' Nola laughs. Then, more seriously, 'I think he was probably a very lonely man who had decided he was willing to take on someone like this. He seemed very sincere and everything like that.' Nola put it with the small pile of other proposals, the ones she didn't bother to answer.

These funny times she recalls willingly, preferring to gloss over the dark, deep days of depression, when life didn't seem worth the trouble of living. The man in charge of her rehabilitation, Dr David Burke, who is the first to express admiration for her fighting qualities and courage, sums up the situation Nola faced just a couple of weeks after her arrival at the Austin Hospital:

'You must remember she had three problems to deal with — three disadvantages. She had paraplegia, which is hard enough for anyone to adapt to, she had problems with being without feet, and she had a long standing problem with alcohol and that's not so easy to recover from either.'

Dr Burke does not mention two other obstacles in Nola's struggle to resume what she could of a normal life. Her marriage was over in all but the formal legalities and there was, and always will be, an inner conflict over her own true identity.

Nola recalls her own struggle as a series of ups and downs, her own flagging spirits bolstered by a small, intimate group of people.

'There's the bitter stage, the confused stage, the what-the-hell stage. There's all these growing things that you go through. I think everybody goes through them, we all go through them in different ways. My parents were fantastic, they saw a future for me. They wanted me to know there was a future for me. But, that doesn't help when you've got it in your head you'll never walk again. You'll never do this again. They tried to help but you've got to get yourself through it yourself. It's one of those fights you've just got to take on and do your damndest. If you succeed that's fine, if you don't you'll end in a bad way.'

Apart from depression and a sense of futility, there was also another emotion to conquer — the urge to feel sorry for herself.

'I used to think, "Why should this have happened to me?" But then I turned that around and thought, "Why shouldn't it happen to me. What was so special about me that it shouldn't happen to me?" I was very savage on the world there for a while. It didn't last terribly long because I was fortunate I had good friends around me. I was very lost...'

For a long time, like most paraplegics, Nola rejected the cold fact that she would never walk again. She was convinced that she could manage it, with artificial limbs.

'I'd feel sorry for myself and wonder what was in the future. I wanted artificial legs that would help me to walk. No one was going to stop me walking. It took a lot of getting through to the brain that because of the back injury I wasn't going to walk again.'

Eventually, after seeing other people in wheelchairs, the truth came home to her and she finally admitted to herself that she was, indeed, a paraplegic. 'How can I cope with a wheelchair,' she worried. 'I don't think I've got the ability to live in a wheelchair.'

If Nola needed someone to inspire her to pull herself together she did not have far to look. The doctors offered all sorts of advice, well meaning and sincere enough, but they were walking around on two good legs and it was all very well for them to talk. But, across the ward, in a bed just opposite her lay Sheila Dykes, a fighter from way back. Mrs Dykes was another road accident victim but her injury was even more terrible than Nola's. Her spine had been broken near her neck, leaving her a quadriplegic, unable to use her hands or arms, having just slight movement in her shoulders.

The accident happened when she was the mother of three children, all aged under six, and living with her husband in the country. Somehow, despite the bleakness of her situation, Sheila Dykes managed to inspire all those around her. When Nola came into the ward, Mrs Dykes was 'in for repairs' at the Austin. She usually lived in a private hospital, unable ever to return to any normal life with her growing family. That decision was her own; she had no wish to burden them.

Told that the cheerful woman across the room had been a quadriplegic for seventeen years, Nola found it impossible to believe. How could she face life with such spirit and good cheer when all she appeared capable of doing was turning the pages of a book or typing letters with a stick in her mouth? Their first conversations were shouted across the ward, both of them being confined to their beds.

One daily routine Nola always dreaded was the arrival of breakfast. Her doctors were determined to rebuild her strength with hearty servings of food at every opportunity, but Nola found it near-impossible to face up to bacon and eggs in the morning. She found a willing accomplice in Sheila Dykes to assist in avoiding this 'punishment'. Every morning, Nola would slip the bacon and eggs to a friendly nurse who, in turn, would pass them on to Sheila, whose appetite was unaffected by her rigid life in bed. Nola preferred to begin her day with a couple of cups of coffee and a cigarette.

Her addiction to cigarettes had never waned, despite the many days she spent without them while in intensive care. One thing she had to learn all over again, especially because she was a smoker, was how to cough. To the rest of us, it's a natural habit but people who are paralyzed have problems. 'You think coughing is easy. It's not,' explains Nola. 'The physiotherapist would have to come in and say, "One, two!" and she'd bounce on me. And I'd have to cough. You more or less learn to breathe again.'

Nola continued to surprise the staff with her remarkable progress, and by 11 September, just five weeks after having her legs amputated, and only three weeks after her bout with pneumonia, she was rolling around in bed doing exercises.

A week later came a real landmark day. She was told she would be allowed out of bed for her first attempt at sitting in a wheelchair. For Nola, it was to be harder than most because she had no lower legs to act as a counterbalance. She had been looking forward to the experience for days, but when it arrived she was wishing it hadn't.

'They sat me up in this wheelchair, you see. The nurses sit you up and say, "Now you're likely to be sick, you're likely to pass out." I sat in the wheelchair, no problems. I felt fine sitting on nothing because you can't feel a thing. I thought, "Blimey, I'll have a cigarette." Was I sick! Urgh! I thought I'd never smoke again in all my life. While I was lying down I could smoke alright, it was just when I was sitting up.'

Nola soon mastered the art of smoking in the wheelchair and she was also quick to learn to manoeuvre her chair across the ward to sit at the bedside of her new-found friend 'that gorgeous woman' Sheila Dykes. Sheila saw her young friend go through all the phases of the typical spinal trauma victim. She knew from her long experience in and out of hospitals that even the chirpiest of characters, and Nola certainly belonged in that group, suddenly plunge into periods of blackest depression. Nola was no exception. 'She didn't know where she was heading,' Mrs Dykes recalls, 'And I don't think she even knew where she had been.'

Nola found in Sheila Dykes a willing listener, a shoulder to lean on, a person to whom she could talk openly about her life. She even confided her deepest conflict: the never-ending doubts that she may really be a Morrison and not a Jenkins. 'She never tried to hide anything,' Mrs Dykes remembers. 'She hadn't had a normal childhood, or anything else in fact. She was definitely unhappy.'

Mrs Dykes quickly came to the conclusion that the accident was the turning point in Nola's life. 'Certainly she lost both legs but it seemed to make her all the more determined to fight life. She was still very bitter, but she just didn't want to lie down and die.'

When Nola was down in the dumps, Sheila tried to ram home her own philosophy on survival as a paralyzed person. 'Well, OK, I'm not that badly off. My brain's alright. I can't walk, I can't use my hands, but life's pretty good. And away you go.' Nola appeared to adapt that to her own terrible experience in the Blackwood mountains. In Sheila Dyke's words, Nola was thinking: 'Alright, I didn't die of cold. I didn't die of shock. I didn't die through the accident. I'm here. Well, let's get on with it.'

Their friendship was no one-way street. Nola repaid Sheila's kindness and encouragement by becoming, almost, her beside servant. 'I was still confined to bed,' Sheila recalls.

'Nola has two good hands and was a real friend to me. She used to do loads of things. I used to enjoy a cigarette. She'd come over and light my cigarette for me and make sure I had cups of tea. She needed somebody to help which, in turn, helped her. Yes, she was very good to me.'

Along with that old habit of smoking, Nola was now slowly but surely slipping back into another old practice, one which would pose the greatest threat to her recovery. It began simply enough with a couple of drinks when friends visited. That was allowed, if not encouraged, at the Austin Hospital because it was designed to be more of a rehabilitation centre than formal hospital.

But, while some patients knew when to stop, Nola did not. It began to slow her recovery to the extent that her doctors were forced to intervene. Even Sheila became alarmed at Nola's growing use of alcohol to hide her problems.

> 'She knew that I knew what was going on but I didn't say anything. I thought, "No, I'll just see if she's going to be honest with me and tell me." She knew what I'd say, not that I could do anything about it, physically, but without sounding presumptuous, she did take a bit of notice of what I said.'

The other patients watched bemused as Nola used her considerable talents of persuasion to get friends, acquaintances, in fact, anybody, to bring her in a drink.

Dr Burke knew what Nola was going through and he provided some of the vital support she needed if she was to win the fight against her compulsion to drink. Nola recognized that she had a problem, but as Dr Burke puts it, 'At first, like a lot of people, she didn't want to do anything about it.' Slowly, but surely, Nola began to curb her downhill slide, but it was to be some time before she could finally put the temptation behind her. As far as Noel and Jessie were concerned, Nola was making splendid progress back to health and late in the year they were given their happiest news for many a day; they could take Nola out for a day.

They made a real outing of it, Jessie Jenkins packing a picnic lunch of all the things her daughter loved. They were all nervous, but excited, to have Nola back as one of the family again, and there was incessant chatter as they enjoyed their picnic in the bright sunshine of an early summer's day in Melbourne's beautiful Fitzroy Gardens. It wasn't long before the family got another welcome surprise; they could have Nola home for Christmas, although she would need to return later for therapy. Those Christmas days were full of joy, of course, but now the whole family, Nola included, began to experience some of the problems they would face in the years ahead as she adjusted to her new life.

On 22 January 1974, Nola Jenkins, paraplegic, rolled her wheelchair out of the Austin Hospital. Her final, formal discharge from the hospital which had saved her life had come 180 days after that chance discovery and rescue by the gold prospectors on the lonely Blackwood road.

Nola had been lucky to survive the accident, lucky to be found and extremely lucky that such a hospital existed at all. Until the early 1940s, patients with spinal fractures such as Nola's usually died. It wasn't until a crop, or really an epidemic, of spinal injuries occured among servicemen during the Second World War that medical science really tackled the problem of keeping these people alive.

Dr Burke, using techniques developed by the pioneer of the treatment of spinal injuries, Professor Sir Ludwig Guttmann, at Stoke-Mandeville Hospital, in Aylesbury, England, had helped to make the Austin the foremost spinal treatment unit in Australia. It was Nola's good fortune that such specialist care was so close at hand after she was found.

Just before she left the hospital to rebuild her life back home in Kyneton, Nola got a rude reminder of her accident and the interrupted ambulance ride to Melbourne. It was a solicitor's letter, demanding money and claiming that she, the hapless patient in the back on a stretcher, was responsible for the damage incurred by his client's car in its brush with the ambulance on the outskirts of the city. Nola gave this letter, too, to the social worker and heard nothing more of it. 'I suppose anything is worth a try,' she laughs.

Noel Jenkins spent a lot of time preparing for his daughter's return home. There were many building jobs, small alterations here and there to make life simpler for the girl in a wheelchair; like removing the old washbasin and replacing it with a new unit which would allow her chair to fit under it. A trifling thing, perhaps, but important to a young woman who wanted independence, to do things for herself, such as washing her own hair.

One thing he neglected to do, because he had forgotten all

about it, was to put out of sight the Honda Chelly motor scooter that was leaning against the garage wall. It wasn't long after her return home that Nola spotted the machine. Her eyes were drawn like a magnet to the little bike. There was a hushed embarrassed silence, then Nola wheeled slowly across to it, taking note that the only visible damage was a tear on the seat. Her eyes also took in the reading on the speedometer. The new bike had travelled precisely seventy-six kilometres before they parted company. She turned to her father and said bluntly: 'Get rid of it.'

The Jenkins family, now reunited, began to cope with Nola's new body. There was much to learn. Nola had been given several warnings by the hospital staff. She had to take good care to avoid getting constant pressure on parts of her body that were paralyzed. A normal person shifts weight when part of the body becomes tired in a certain position, but the paraplegic, feeling nothing, risks getting painful sores in the dead parts if areas are left too long with pressure upon them. Some paraplegics and quadriplegics have to rely on friends or relations to turn or move their bodies. Some set alarm clocks to wake them up at night when it is time to be turned, something that just occurs naturally in the sleep of the unhandicapped.

Infections, too, are a real worry to the paralyzed because their circulation is diminished and less able to rush blood to any affected area. Nola and her parents soon learned to steer her clear of anything hot, like boiling kettles, which could burn her without her even realizing it and then take much longer than normal to heal. Before leaving the home, even today, Mrs Jenkins brews a pot of coffee and leaves it in a vacuum flask for her daughter. Anything to make sure that Nola doesn't have to boil water while she is away.

Another thing Nola soon learned to avoid was any car seat that had been exposed to the blazing sun. She once had a row of ugly blisters across her bottom, a legacy of one careless mistake. During those first few days at home there were times of pain, deep physical pain, which Nola tried her best to hide from her mother. There was mental anguish, too, as she tried to cope with her whole new way of living.

But always Nola's tough effervescent spirit carried her

through, to endure and, ultimately, to see the funny side of life. Like the day the wheel toppled off her wheelchair outside a Kyneton pub. Nola was sitting there scarcely daring to breathe lest she fall head first into the gutter. Her predicament had not gone unnoticed however, and a man tripped unsteadily through the bar-room door to come to her rescue.

'Could you put the wheel back on,' she pleaded. 'Certainly love,' he responded. 'Just climb out and I'll bung the bugger back on for you.' She still giggles at the memory of that hilarious encounter which ended when more sober aid arrived.

Those first few months of 1974 were spent overcoming one small problem after another. Her major problem, alcohol, was still very much with her. Her time was divided between Kyneton, the Austin, and a hostel for paraplegics in Kew, a Melbourne suburb. It was in this hostel that Nola began to slip back into her old drinking habits.

The John Newman Morris Hostel for Paraplegics provided Nola with the opportunity to fend for herself, a halfway house between home and hospital. Supervision was minimal and inmates were encouraged to develop some independence by carrying out simple, basic tasks for themselves. Most of them went off to work each day, leaving Nola with free time on her hands because she had no job. That free time became a drawback for Nola, leading her more and more into the practice of having a few drinks to fight the loneliness and apparent hopelessness of her situation.

Sheila Dykes was still in the Austin and she could see what was happening, when Nola came to visit her. 'It all began again because she was out on her own,' she says. 'Nola was bored stiff, so what would she do? Get a taxi, then down to the pub. Come over and visit me, absolutely rolling. It made me feel dreadul to have a good friend sitting in her wheelchair a little glazed.'

Dr Burke, too, was still keeping a watchful eye on his patient.

> 'I remember having long talks with her in outpatients, and on many occasions, going over this problem and how she was going to overcome it. What she was going to do about it. It was something we talked about a lot together.'

To be fair to Nola, she had been thrust into the independent hostel life a little too soon. No other resident there had the dual handicaps that she was attempting to conquer, paraplegia and the loss of both her legs. She found the hostel totally unsuited to her needs and Noel Jenkins agrees vehemently; 'For the condition she was in at the time, it was totally wrong and put her under a great deal of pressure.'

Nola recoils at the thought of those early days in the hostel:

> 'All of a sudden I was thrown out into the cold. I had had nurses to handle personal hygiene, catheters and the like. Now I suddenly had to do it all myself, and I couldn't cope. I couldn't even go to the toilet on my own.'

The pressures built up. Noel and Jessie began to worry. They could see their daughter's morale slipping, her jaunty determination slowly turning to despair. Then one day, without warning Nola decided she'd had enough. Her mother puts it simply, 'The inevitable happened. There was an incident involving drink and an overdose.' An ambulance arrived just in time and Nola was rushed to hospital. Once again she had had a close call with death. 'The hostel was just too much,' she explains. 'It just built up. I just couldn't take it any longer.' Says Jessie Jenkins. 'That was the end of the brave experiment. It was back to the Austin.'

To her credit, despite the traumatic events of her early life and of her accident, and her great dependence on alcohol as a crutch, Nola Jenkins was now able to face the toughest decision of her life. She decided the booze had to be beaten.

> 'I had been knocking the booze around a bit. It was getting worse. It did a lot of damage to me. Mentally, I think. Everyone would say, "Here's an alcoholic." They classed me as a problem drinker. When I had problems I'd get drunk. The accident changed everything. I mean, OK, I've been tempted. Just after my accident I was sorely tempted to try the old way out. There was no old way out at all. And I knew it.'

Dr Burke had long admired Nola for the manner in which she had fought back against her devastating physical injuries. Now he was to find himself respecting her mental toughness. Nola told him she could do it. And she did.

Early in April 1974, the Melbourne *Herald* published a story about a character who was being billed as the oldest man playing competition rugby union in Australia, fifty-six-year-old Ken Evans. Evans, the sturdy son of a Welshman, was an addict of the game. The following Saturday his age was proving no handicap as he scored a dashing try to give his team, Moorabbin, the lead in a match on a ground in suburban Elsternwick. Moments later, hooker Evans was involved in an incident which changed his life.

> 'I went down in the scrum, the top of my head hit a shoulder. When the two packs came together my back was sandwiched. There was a blinding flash down my spine, or rather, in my brain. I just slumped to the ground. I couldn't move my hands or feet.'

The tough old hooker had never been so frightened but he managed to look up at his mates and gasp: 'Jeez, my back's gone!'

Evans soon found himself in the Austin Hospital where the doctors broke the bad news: 'You'll never walk again.' They were wrong. Two weeks later he started to feel some movement in his feet and a week after that he astounded everyone by walking unaided out of the intensive care ward. His miraculous recovery was the talk of the hospital, until one day in physiotherapy he suddenly collapsed.

Doctors found that further dislocation of the vertebra had occurred and he was rushed into the operating theatre for a laminectomy to fuse three vertebra. 'Then, for a fortnight, I was away with the fairies. I had three cardiac arrests.' When he finally returned to the land of reality, the hard-as-nails rugby veteran found himself wearing a jacket which stretched from the head to the waist and prevented the slightest movement. 'Again they said I wouldn't walk, but eventually I started to get a bit of movement in my legs and arms. Finally, after about three months, I got up out of bed and walked.'

WHOSE BABY?

Like the way he lived his life and played his rugby, Ken Evans set about his rehabilitation with gusto. Hours and hours of his time were spent in the physiotherapy unit, doing far more than the doctors had ordered. He was puffing away, a mass of sweat, when his attention was drawn to a young woman who wheeled into the ward and began cracking jokes with the staff and other patients.

Something about her was familiar, so Evans decided to take a closer look. Suddenly he remembered exactly where he had last seen her. A frail, half-frozen figure pinned beneath a motorbike. 'You look a lot better than the last time I saw you,' he shouted out. 'Who the hell are you?' was the reply. Nola Jenkins and Ken Evans, two of the toughest individuals to have been given a new grip on life by the Austin Hospital, had much to talk about that eventful afternoon. Each took inspiration from the other.

When Evans left hospital he refused steadfastly to become an ex-sportsman. He might have been forced to make a premature retirement from his beloved rugby, but he still managed to take up jogging — 'more of a shuffle really' — and turn his hand to bowls and golf. Sport had never played much of a role in Nola's life but she also turned to it for therapy and relaxation. Table tennis was a game she found she could play and after a time a friend, who played in the local competition, asked her, 'Why don't you come up for a hit?'

Nola was reluctant at first, fearing she might make a spectacle of herself but eventually she took the plunge. 'I felt a bit stupid but, with encouragement, I found I could win the odd game.' The odd game turned into a lot of games as she found herself a regular member of a team playing in the competition. They had mixed fortunes, winning one premiership but also qualifying for the wooden spoon for finishing last in another. During her matches, one of Nola's teammates would stand behind her to retrieve the ball and the only shot she found difficult to return was the little drop shot just over the net, and out of reach from her wheelchair. Nola even invented her own unique style, whipping the bat from right hand to left to cover forehand and backhand. As she puts it, in the heat of the match 'the chair would get quite a rock up at times.'

She also tried rifle shooting, resting her weapon on a mobile hospital tray her family had managed to scrounge from somewhere or other. Nola found that, despite her paralysis, she could still enjoy a swim even if it was a lot more complicated than before. The paralyzed section of her body floats and tries to take over from the rest of her. She has to paddle like mad to keep her head above water. All the family agree, it's quite a sight to see Nola thrashing about in the water.

Her toughest physical ordeal came about as the result of a whim — a sudden impulse decision to enter a canoe race down the Murray River.

'I had a chap with me and what was supposed to happen was that I was to paddle until I got tired. And then they were to get me out and put someone else in. Now that was all very fine. We were going the wrong way when the gun went off, so we had a lot of trouble. We had to turn around. We'd never paddled together, or even practised, or anything like that. So we got going and by the time I got tired, you know what the banks of the Murray are like. Steep! There was no way they were going to get Nola Jenkins out of the canoe and put someone else in. So it was paddle on.

I think we ended up about eighth in our section, which wasn't bad. I was so tired. When we got to the end of it, there was this great big river bank. Poor old brother Arnold had to lift me up and carry me up the bank. I was so tired driving home, I was thinking, "I'll never be able to get up in the morning." But that driving back wasn't going to beat me.'

Jessie Jenkins could hardly believe her eyes when Nola arrived home that night. 'I've never seen anyone so tired.'

Driving her own specially-modified car had been another of Nola's achievements and she was outraged when some young fellows took her vehicle for a joyride when it was parked outside the Austin Hospital one day. The car was recovered, badly damaged, and Nola had to pay $120 out of her pension money to an insurance company. That incident reinforced Nola's opinion of Melbourne, or big cities in general, as places with little heart. 'I don't think I could survive in Melbourne in a wheelchair,' she says, 'but the people here in Kyneton are fantastic. They treat you like a person, not a blob sitting in a wheelchair.'

Unfortunately, not all the citizens of Kyneton have been so understanding. Nola's mother remembers the early days when Nola first came home from hospital in her wheelchair, and some thoughtless people stopped and stared at her in the street. It must have reminded her of the time twenty-five years earlier when the little blonde girl at her side was the key figure in the famous court case. People then, too, could not resist staring.

'When Nola first came home from hospital she didn't have the artificial legs,' Mrs Jenkins recalls. 'From an appearance point of view, it wasn't easy for her to take because people used to stare. People who should know better, too, as a rule. I've seen people walk right around the chair to have another look. That took a lot of getting over.'

Nola accepts her fate with the good cheer that is often the case with people who have had to overcome a tragic affliction. She still suffers frequent pain. Jessie Jenkins says: 'She has spasms. Sometimes they nearly throw her out of the chair. They say it is nerve ends looking for somewhere to go.' Nola talks of the phantom pains in her missing limbs. 'Apparently when nerve ends get smashed they don't grow back or they grow back the wrong way in the wrong places. Sometimes I get pains in the feet and at night-time I often get my feet all crinkled up.'

The accident has left Nola with physical, as well as mental pain, which she attempts to hide behind an air of excessive good cheer. But her mother recognizes the symptoms:

'She has her days when she's not as happy as she might be. But then again I think those are the days when she has her pain. I have a terrible job finding out what's troubling her. She never lets on to us. I know something is wrong but she never tells me until I think finally, "It's such and such," and she'll admit it. She won't tell you. She just goes off to her room and works away at something and works it off.'

During the day Nola may be able to maintain her cheerful

exterior but at night the accident often comes back to haunt her. 'It's a rotten dream I have,' she says, explaining the recurrent nightmare. 'Something is gnawing away at my feet. It's shocking. It's like I have rats. They're eating at my feet. I suddenly wake up and I've got the pain there and everything.'

The dream became so vivid, so real, that she tried to exorcize it by asking the medical staff at the Austin about the condition her feet were in before the operation. Had anything been eating them when she was paralyzed in the bush?

'This dream still gets me time and time again. There must be a reason for it, but apparently my feet were alright. They hadn't been eaten by anything. I still get the dreams. I'm still sitting out there in the bush, waiting to be pulled out. And those rats, they still keep coming, keep nibbling...'

19 WHO WAS RIGHT?

Gwen Morrison never forgot that winter's night in the labour ward at Kyneton Hospital. Just before each of her daughters went into hospital to have their own babies, she took them aside and gave them some very specific advice, advice that they didn't really need. The message was simple: Make sure you have tags on all the baby's clothes.

Colleen Morrison was already the mother of two girls, so she had got the message twice before. Nonetheless, Gwen warned her as she was about to leave for her third confinement to take good care that the clothes were properly marked. 'Mum was very cautious,' Colleen recalls. 'She made me get the name tags. Everything was tagged.'

The third child, another daughter, duly arrived and everything went according to pattern for the first couple of days. Then one morning, the nurses carried in all the babies to their mothers to be fed and Colleen Morrison's was not among them. She called the nurse and was assured that her child would be along any minute. Time ticked by and Colleen became agitated. Was something wrong with the baby? She climbed out of bed, determined to go to the nursery to find out for herself, but a nurse cut her off in the ward and ushered her sternly back to bed, still reassuring her nothing was amiss and that the youngster would be at her side in just a few moments.

At last the tiny bundle arrived, the nurse handing it gingerly over to the anxious mother. Colleen bent to feed the baby, but as soon as she caught a glimpse of the features she knew something was terribly wrong. She began to weep, calling to the nurse. It wasn't her child!

'Sister, sister, this isn't my baby,' she cried. The nurse's smile froze. 'No, it's not. Why, it's a little boy!'

Colleen had been the worst possible victim of what was a traditional joke by the nurses in the hospital. 'I was really upset. I told her the story of my mother, and the poor girl couldn't apologize enough.'

For three other nurses, there was never anything at all amusing about babies being mixed up. Elizabeth Lockhart, Olive Cass and Tessie Atkinson were all victims of the 'Whose Baby Case', regardless of what really happened in the early hours of the morning of 22 June 1945. They were all forced to endure lengthy cross-examination in court, caustic admonishment from the judge and the harsher, more lasting penance inflicted by their friends and workmates, and even by the public. Today, none of them likes to talk about the incident that blighted their lives. Tessie Atkinson is the one least reluctant to discuss her role. Even thirty or more years after the case, she still bumps into people who remember her name for its notoriety back in 1948. She wonders if the judge was right, that she carried out the two babies under her arms, that she might have made an innocent but unforgivable error. Her memory won't provide the answer to that question, but she feels sure that she would never have been allowed to carry out the two babies when there were two qualified midwifery sisters and the doctor present in the ward. She is happy in her own mind that she told the truth, to the best of her memory, to the court.

If the babies were mixed up on the morning they were born, it may be that none of the nurses was aware that any mistake had been made. But there is also the possibility that one of them found herself in a hopeless, terrifying quandary. Two baby girls in her charge and unsure which was which. Put yourself in such a desperate situation. Do you reveal what has happened? Or, do you examine the children, strain your memory, and, ultimately, make your own decision? If that is what did, indeed, happen, then some person has had to live with the most terrible secret for many years.

The one person who could have helped to solve the mystery was Dr Gerald Loughran, but he chose instead to remain silent, thousands of miles distant in Singapore. Loughran had been given the opportunity to settle the matter when the Jenkinses came to him for advice after the Morrisons had told him of their blood test results. He elected to carry out his own, basic blood tests, then assured them that they 'could' have the right child. The 'Whose Baby Case' might never have evolved if he had opted to seek the sophisticated tests that were available from specialists in Melbourne. Positive, or negative, they may have set everyone's minds at rest.

Gerald Loughran was a witness that Mr Justice Barry badly wanted to hear. He knew which nurse carried the babies out. Did he depart for Singapore to avoid embarrassing and unpleasant experiences in the box? Both his sister and his wife are eager to rush to his defence. Says Patricia Loughran: 'Leaving Australia had nothing at all to do with the case. My husband was an honest, sincere and dedicated doctor — very sincere, very honest, and very dedicated. Our leaving Australia had nothing to do with it.'

Mrs Loughran says her husband rarely spoke of the Jenkins–Morrison affair.

'All I know is that when it happened my husband said to the nurse: "Please don't mix those children up." I believe the nurse later said in court she thought he was joking. My husband was very strict in his beliefs about medicine. Anything that happened to his patients was never discussed in the house. I never discussed any of his cases with him, including this one.'

Loughran's sister, Eileen Rhoden, agrees that he kept the case out of family discussions and the only reference she can remember was 'that it had nothing to do with him, that we knew it was not his mistake'.

The backwash from the case did not reach Singapore and Gerald Loughran and his wife enjoyed the life of the successful professional man, travelling widely in Europe and Asia. During their tours they discovered the delights of a beautiful Italian seaside town called Positano. It became a favourite.

Ignoring the oft repeated warnings of his own profession, the doctor persisted with his lifelong habit of smoking heavily until his lungs were badly affected by emphysema, the crippling, creeping affliction that makes breathing more and more a struggle.

Forced to seek a less humid climate than Singapore's, Gerald Loughran and his wife decided to retire to the Italian seaside in the late 60s. They bought a villa on a headland, above Positano, with lovely views out across the ocean. In his bedroom there were cylinders of oxygen to assist his breathing. Even in retirement Gerald Loughran remained a member of the Australian Medical Association. Then one year, in the mid-70s, his subscription was not renewed. The doctor had died. They buried him in the cemetery in nearby Sorrento and his widow moved to London, where she lives today.

Patricia Loughran says that her husband's strict adherence to the principle of keeping his professional work away from the family meant that his own two children, a son and daughter, were unaware of their father's link with the famous Australian court case until many years after his death. She, too, knew little about it. 'I believe the two young girls had tragic lives. But we didn't follow the court case or what happened afterwards. We had left Australia...'

The lawyers involved in the case found it difficult to put it behind them. Jack Galbally and his barristers had their detractors, men who argued that they had taken on the case because it would generate such widespread interest and publicity. The critics reasoned that even if there had been a mix-up, it was better left alone. Their criticism seems unjust. All the lawyers involved on the Morrison side were successful long before the case began and Galbally himself could ill afford the time which he was giving for nothing. Long after his retirement from the law and politics, Galbally had no hesitation in defending his decision to take Gwen Morrison's case to any court that would give her a hearing. He felt it a duty. 'I think that they had less of this world's goods than the other people.' Frank Galbally recognizes the emotional bind it had on his brother, and on the barristers, Robert Monahan and Charles Sweeney. 'The nature of the case was such that it did get to the depth of one's emotions.' He says Jack Galbally took the defeat very badly. 'He believed very much that the children should be put back with their real parents and I think there's a great deal of force in that argument. No matter how loving and caring foster parents are, they are not always an adequate substitute for real parents.'

But wasn't it too late for exchanges when the children were three or more years old? Frank Galbally: 'I feel in my own mind that I'd have loved to have got my child back.' At the cost of giving back the one you had? 'If necessary, yes, but always showing that willingness to keep the child if it wasn't wanted by the other. Believing on the strongest grounds possible that it was my child, I think I would set out to get that child into my custody.'

Even though he was on the side of the Morrisons, Frank Galbally realizes that the Jenkinses had much reason to fight.

'I've no doubt that they believed they were right in the stand they took and I don't think anyone could argue convincingly that they were wrong. I think that all concerned were very loving, very good people, on both sides. They certainly had their differences in relation to what should be done as regards the children, but, nonetheless, I've got no doubt they were very caring people and very loving people. It was one of those tragic situations, unique in our legal history, where people had to make a judgement one way or another and no one in my view could argue that they were wrong.'

Robert Monahan also took defeat as a personal loss. He never, ever forgave Mr Justice Webb for casting his vital vote against the Morrisons on the 'red herring' theory of the extra two babies. He often complained in later years that the Chief Justice, Sir John Latham, had assured him that the theory was irrelevant and he was furious that it could be used to destroy Gwen Morrison's case.

Barry, too, had a long memory and was slow to forgive. His associate, Jim Edwards, says: 'Until his dying day he believed he was correct. He always believed that, finally, an injustice was done to the Morrisons.'

Barry must have wondered what might have happened had he

ordered blood tests from the Jenkinses. He claimed he had the power to do so, but would Noel and Jessie Jenkins have meekly submitted? And if the tests showed Nola was not a Jenkins, would that have solved anything? Would Jessie have ever been satisfied? And what of Lee, the bystander? Would any court have formally ordered a swap of children more than three years old, no matter who the parents?

Amelia Williams, the woman who set the Morrison and Jenkins families on their tragic road with the words, 'Gwen, this is not the baby I saw in the hospital,' remained steadfast to the last. While others in the family, notably Bill Morrison, preferred to forget the past, Amelia Williams saw no reason to disguise her feelings. She would tell anyone who showed the slightest interest that her daughter had been cheated by the courts.

Amelia herself was never given a chance to vent her feelings from the witness box. It would have been interesting to have seen her in action with the great legal minds. She had provided a tantalizing twist to the whole case by claiming that she was shown a fair child as Gwen Morrison's baby in the hospital the day the two girls were born. She further claimed that she raised the alarm two weeks later when Gwen brought a dark child home. Amelia appeared to be suggesting that a mix-up happened several hours after the births, a theory that is dispelled by her own daughter's testimony.

The likelihood is that when Amelia Williams visited her daughter in hospital she was told of the turmoil in the labour ward at the time of the double birth and of the doctor's warning to the unknown nurse not to mix the two girls up. She then saw a baby in the nursery. No one will ever know if, in fact, she was shown Lee or Nola, or if the glimpse she was given was too brief to form a distinct impression.

There is no doubt that she was the person who raised the alarm later, but was it because Gwen's story had preyed on her mind or had she really been shown Nola instead of Lee in the nursery? With so much confusion surrounding Amelia's story — and the fact that it was not consistent with Gwen Morrison's version that she got the dark baby shortly after the births — is it any wonder that neither side called her as a witness?

Bill Morrison and his mother-in-law, two outspoken, obdurate personalities, clashed frequently in their lifetimes. When Gwen Morrison died there was no one to act as peacemaker and they saw less and less of each other.

If Amelia's attitude to the courts did not waver, nor did her free and easy lifestyle. Hers was a spirit that was not dampened for too long by heartbreak and she had had more than her fair share of that. Two husbands dead, two daughters dead, and a lot of suffering in between. Typically, she made some radical decisions late in her years. Firstly she decided to shed the hated name Williams, after bearing it for four decades, and had her name changed by deed poll to Logan, the surname of the husband she had loved. Secondly, she decided to embrace religion and had herself baptized a Catholic at the unlikely age of seventy.

When the family gathered, Ma would remain the jolly matriarch, pumping away on the piano, a glass of beer at hand and a cigarette between her lips. Lee Morrison's husband Joe remembers joining the redoubtable Amelia and a group of others for a game of euchre. She was in her late seventies and they were all comparative youngsters. The beer flowed and the hours passed until it was very late in the night and Joe 'could hardly stand up'. And Amelia? 'She was still going strong.'

Her spell as a publican had not been an outstanding success, so she turned her hand to real estate and became a shrewd and canny investor. Grandson Blair Morrison admired her acumen. 'She bought and sold and bought and sold.' Even into her eighties, she could be found peering through the newspaper classifieds, scouring them for a bargain. By now, her constitution was beginning to let her down. The brain was still alert, the memory impeccable, and the tongue had not lost its lash. Living each day, though, was a struggle against heart problems, high blood pressure and chronic breathing difficulties.

On 16 February 1981, Amelia Williams died in her home in Neale Street, Bendigo, and was later buried just a stride or two away from her daughters Gwen and Gloria. She was only a few months short of her eighty-sixth birthday.

No one was more distraught than the bachelor son who had

lived with her for his entire life. Johnny Logan, known to the family by his nickname Reg, doted on his mother, and the others could almost forsee what was about to happeen. 'I tried hard to help him,' neice Colleen Morrison says, 'but he just gave up.' She took meals around to his home, spent hours chatting with him, trying to cheer him. It was no use. Johnny Logan died just five weeks after signing his own mother's death certificate. He was only fifty-two and his family believe he 'just pined away'. Colleen Morrison finds it hard to understand. 'I could accept the death of my grandmother, she was an elderly woman, but my uncle... there was just no reason for it.'

Bill Morrison had not spoken to Amelia, his mother-in-law, for months before she died. They were having one of their regular tiffs. He was not a well man himself, with heart trouble and generally failing health.

Morrison had used the press, *Truth* newspaper, as the springboard to launch the campaign to win Nola but he became disenchanted and extremely acrimonious towards newspapers as time wore on. After the final decision had gone against him, his antipathy towards reporters hardened into outright aggression. One who contacted him many years later was taken aback by the vitriolic dismissal he received. 'I've had the brush-off before,' he told colleagues, 'but never one like that.'

Just months before he died, Bill Morrison agreed, grudgingly, to talk about the case. He was still bitter in defeat but the anger had given way to sadness and regret that it had ever happened. He was living in retirement in a modest brick home in Bendigo. With his favourite daughter Lee sitting opposite him, herself visibly affected by the emotions that this affair always disturbed in the Morrison household, he talked about his regrets and what might have been. There was no suggestion, however, that they might have made a mistake, that Lee was really their daughter. He looked squarely at her as he pronounced: 'I believed then and I still believe that we did the right thing. It ruined me but I still think we did the right thing.' There were tears in his eyes and Lee, too, was close to crying.

That was the end of the interview for that day. A few weeks later, again with Lee and her husband Joe present, Bill Morrison went on an emotional, rambling trip back into the past. 'Jack Galbally was a good man. Frank was alright. Frank was very young at the time.' How did he view the way things had ended up? 'I'm just as pleased the way it is, for the simple reason that after they got to a certain age I couldn't see that there was any value in carrying on with it.' How did they live with their loss? 'When you are defeated in these things and you know there's no comeback, there's only one thing to do, to the best of your ability, forget all about it. And that's exactly what I've done.'

Regrets? 'Did I ever regret it? Well, after it's all over you do regret it a bit don't you.' Then he added, 'I do regret it ever happened. I'm just an ordinary human being.'

Did Gwen Morrison ever accept the result? 'She had no option but to. Well, we thought we were right but apparently we weren't. I myself, personally, was satisfied to forget all about it. But the mother, I don't know...' Bill Morrison did not spell it out fully, but the message was there. Gwen Morrison did not, ever, accept the verdict and the loss of Nola.

Could he have parted with Lee? 'There would never have been a changeover. Somebody asked me, didn't we want the one we had. I said, "Yes, we want the two of them." We knew that was stupid but we would have accepted that.' You must have wondered about Nola? 'Yes. We couldn't do anything about that.'

Just a few months later Bill Morrison's health faltered and again it was the loving Lee who left her own home and donned the role of nurse. On 16 February 1983, Bill Morrison's coffin was lowered to rest with that of his wife in Bendigo cemetery. They are all there now, a tight little family group. Amelia, Gloria, and Bill and Gwen.

The last of the Logan sisters, Audrey Moffat, says:

'Bill and Gwen, there was quite a bond between the two of them. They stuck together through thick and thin. They had a lot of downs. They had a few ups. But they stuck together. Bill idolized Gwen and she, in her own way, idolized him too.'

Audrey carries on her mother's tradition of firing straight from the hip.

'While my sister was alive and while my mother was alive, they both went through hell over this. My sister, really, she was a very brave girl to have weathered the storm she did. My family were not wealthy people but well educated, honest, and very, very brave. And that's not emotional, that's bloody fact.'

Blair Morrison is the only member of his family never to have met Nola. When he first saw her picture he was rendered speechless by the apparent likeness. 'She's got a lot of features like I've got,' he said at last, 'That's fairly obvious. My father had a lot to do with me, so he must have had a lot to do with Nola. That's all I can say.' He expresses no wish to meet her in person. 'Not now. I don't think there's much reason for meeting her really. I mean, she's gone one way and I've gone the other.' Blair's two boys, Bill Morrison's grandsons, know nothing of the case, nothing of the controversy surrounding Auntie Lee.

Noel and Jessie Jenkins still maintain that they got the right child. Even today she is the centre of the family, smothered with affection from her mother, adored by brother Arnold and father Noel. The four of them still live in the house in Mitchell Street, Kyneton, the same house that Noel was building when Bill Morrison approached him back in 1946 and all the trouble began. They are a closely knit family — the women shop together, they all play bingo together, and they share a perky sense of humour, usually sparked off by Nola herself.

Noel Jenkins retired several years ago from the building game and keeps himself busy growing prize-winning dahlias in the garden and running a few sheep on a small property outside Kyneton. At the age of seventy-three, he is still working off a lifetime debt of gratitude. The debt is to Victoria's volunteer country firemen who passed around the hat to aid their colleague Noel when the court costs threatened to overwhelm him. Noel speaks with sincerity of his mates, most of them unknown personally.

'If it wasn't for the support of the fire brigade and the townspeople, I don't know where I would have got the money from.

It sent me broke anyhow. The fire brigade contributed throughout Victoria, that's why I'm still indebted to them. I'm still in the fire brigade and working because I feel I owe them.'

In his younger days, Noel Jenkins would be in the thick of the action when bushfires blazed. When the disastrous Ash Wednesday fires raged through the nearby township of Macedon in 1983, he was at his usual post helping to keep communications open.

Nola has made a remarkable success of life from a wheelchair. She is independent enough to drive wherever she feels like, wending her way through the traffic in Melbourne to visit friends and have regular checkups at the Austin Hospital. Alcohol no longer plays any part in her life. 'I seldom have a drink now — Christmas or something,' she says. 'There's no way I could go back to that. I've sort of got a bit of respect around this town now, whereas I'd lost it there for a while. And I want to keep it.'

Nola works part-time at a centre for handicapped children, gaining self-esteem by giving her time to them. 'I get enjoyment seeing what they achieve,' she explains.

> 'I think I've got more in common. Any disability is a disability and I believe everybody's got some sort of disability. I find enjoyment now in things I took no notice of before. Like a young kid trying to ride a horse. I see what that kid's trying to do and I hope that he or she will master it. I enjoy seeing that.'

Talking of the intellectually handicapped children she works with, Nola says:

> 'Most of those kids have a lot of love to give and who cares about the brain? If they've got the love to give and you want to accept it, it can be a fantastic sort of experience. After all, their brain works well for them. My brain works well for me. I mean, there are all sorts of variations.'

It must be with a twinge of envy that Nola reads of other accident victims being awarded hundreds of thousands of dollars in compensation for their injuries. Because she was the motorcycle rider and no one else was involved, there was no insurance payout for Nola. She could easily have bent the truth and claimed that an anonymous car ran her off the road. That way she would have been entitled to a damages claim against the unknown driver. Nola preferred the truth — to her cost. All she has is her invalid pension, but she does not complain, except to protest about the fact that a paraplegic is given her first wheelchair and from then on it is up to the person concerned to provide replacement. Of course, that is not easy on the money a pension provides.

Noel and Jessie Jenkins do not find the case too unpalatable to talk about. The hurt and the fears are behind them and, after all, they did end up with the child they loved. Both insist they never, ever, considered they could lose the case and Nola. But what if? Jessie Jenkins replies:

'We would have grieved for her if we had had to part with her. We definitely would have grieved for her, but we'd have recovered far quicker than she would have. That was always my idea of the thing. I could never quite understand what they [the Morrisons] would do if it came to the showdown. Would they part with that child?'

Would she have accepted Lee if the court had ordered them to be exchanged?

'You see, the same thing applies. You take that child from the surroundings she knows. I would have thought that would have been cruel too. If she had come to us, yes, we would have grown to love her probably and everything would have been alright. But, then again, it would have taken a lot for that child to have got over that, wouldn't it? I think so. I think the child's wellbeing had to be the first consideration. If they were really fond of her and loved her deeply, it would have hurt them, too. It would have hurt everybody. I really don't know what the solution would have been. I can't really envisage a satisfactory conclusion.'

Whose Baby?

Although there was bitterness towards the Morrisons at the time, Jessie Jenkins is willing to make one concession to Gwen Morrison. 'I don't think either of us wanted to hurt either of the children. We definitely didn't. You had to put them first. You can't take a child, just willy nilly, and turn them from one thing to another.'

Did you ever think you were going to lose?

'It's one of those things, if you don't think it's going to come out alright then you're a defeatist, aren't you? You can't let these sort of things get you down, you've got a life to live. You don't just up and die because of these things happening. I think it made us a closer family.'

There were many stories told against both families during the heat of the contest. One which went the rounds in Woomelang had a particularly unpleasant scene occurring in the Jenkins home. According to this scenario, Gwen Morrison went down on her knees and begged Jessie Jenkins to have blood tests but was brushed aside. Jessie says it was a figment of someone's imagination. 'She never came to see me.' Knowing both women, it is a scene that could never have happened.

Today, Lee Morrison and Nola Jenkins are just a few years older than the mothers who fought for their custody in the 'Whose Baby Case'. Only a handful of people have seen both girls, both mothers and both fathers in their adult years. Resemblances are often misleading or imagined, but there are striking similarities in each case. Nola Jenkins and Gwen Morrison provided perhaps the most persuasive of the likenesses. Nola could also be said to resemble Blair, and to a lesser extent, Bill Morrison. On the other hand, any resemblance between her and Colleen Morrison would be hard to detect.

Lee is dark like Jessie Jenkins before the years softened the colour of her hair to the gray it is today. There are moments when she can look a lot like Noel Jenkins, in expression as well as features.

Well, was there a mix-up? The Morrisons saw the teenage Nola Jenkins in their home for a considerable time, giving them ample opportunity to make their own comparisons. They had needed little convincing, but Nola's visits were conclusive as far as they were concerned. She was a Morrison.

Noel and Jessie Jenkins have never seen Lee since their brush with the other family in the court in Melbourne when she was a mere three-year-old. They still insist that they were right all along, that they got the right child. To reinforce their own intuition, they say they have had private blood tests which have 'proved positive'. Questioned about these tests, Noel and Jessie are vague. Jessie Jenkins explains: 'We only did that for Nola's peace of mind. We thought it might help her if she needed it. Don't ask me when we had it. I have no idea.'

'We just happened to have an old friend of Noel's who did all the groundwork and did it for us. I don't think Nola's ever asked, really. But it was alright, no problems.' Arnold Jenkins says: 'I'm not interested in whether she is a Jenkins or not. It never enters my mind. To me she is my sister and that's all about it. If you live somewhere for the greater part of your life, then surely you are there, whether you are born there or not.'

Sitting in her wheelchair at home in Mitchell Street, Kyneton, Nola says she shook off her doubts back in the 1960s after her visits to the Morrisons. 'I decided at that time it was best left alone. I had to make a choice, so the sooner I made it the better. I've been brought up here and I belong here.'

Do you regard yourself now as a Jenkins?

'Yes.'

Where does that leave Lee? She has not the slightest doubt that she is a Jenkins. She answers the question with her own challenge: 'If I'm not a Jenkins, then who am I?' She still storms inside at the people she regards as her real parents, Noel and Jessie. 'They must know they were wrong,' she insists angrily. 'I still believe, and I always will, that they are my parents.'

Lee blames the Jenkinses for the whole unhappy affair and feels that if they had acted reasonably it would never have happened. She just wishes that someone in Kyneton had taken the initiative and somehow brought the two families together for a peaceful and personal solution. Once it had gone into the courts it was much too late to switch the children. 'We were too old. I think the way it is now is probably right. It's just the way it is now, that's it, you can't change it.'

Lee Chant, the mother, has a tradition which she observes with each of her children. When they are about to start secondary school, she takes them aside and explains the facts of life. At the same time, she relates the strange story of her past. The children are surprised and intrigued.

Was she pleased to shed the name Morrison, with all its controversial past, and become Lee Chant, housewife? 'Yes, I suppose so. Not to hide behind, or anything. That's gone, that's past. It's done. Right. I'm Lee Chant, I'm a married woman, I'm a mother, I'm a different person, perhaps. I mean, I still know I'm a "Whose Baby Case" child and I've never been ashamed of it. At times I haven't liked it, I wanted just to forget all about it and leave it alone and just be me. So, perhaps having another name does help. I don't know.'

Colleen Morrison accepts that Nola Jenkins is her blood sister, not Lee, but there is no doubt where her affections lie. 'I regard Lee as my sister and always will. We came out on the best side eventually. I'd never swap her for a thousand Nola Jenkins.'

There is a hunger, a curiosity, in the back of Lee Chant's mind. Like an adopted child, she longs to meet the two people, the two strangers in Kyneton, whom she regards as responsible for bringing her into this world. It is not something she brings up frequently, but it is always there.

Both the Morrison parents are dead, Noel and Jessie Jenkins are in their 70s — is it not time to make peace? Lee turns it over in her mind, even to the stage where she has a beautifully prepared speech to deliver on arrival. 'In my dreams I'd be knocking on doors and I'd fantasize.'

In reality, she has gone a lot further than merely dreaming of meeting Noel and Jessie Jenkins. On many occasions, she and sister Colleen, or husband Joe Chant, have actually sat down and planned the trip into the unknown at Kyneton, wondering what sort of reception awaited them at the other end. Lee usually makes the suggestion: 'Let's get in the car and go down to see them tomorrow.' Everyone is enthusiastic until the morning arrives and they never go ahead with it.

There are too many doubts and fears — they may be unwelcome, feelings may be rubbed raw once again. 'It's something I've put off and put off,' says Lee, 'and perhaps something I'll never do.'

One day, though, they may go through the whole charade again.

One day, they may start the car and set out for Kyneton.

One day, Lee may not turn back.

APPENDIX

Statement made by Dr Lucy Meredith Bryce to the Supreme Court on blood tests she carried out on the Morrisons:

In accordance with accepted present day knowledge, practice and available facilities, tests were carried out to determine the blood group (A B O factors), Rh type and M N type of each of the three persons.

The results of the two series of tests were in agreement and showed that: the blood of William Henry Morrison belongs to group A, sub-group A1, type Rh1 and contains the factor N. The blood of Alberta Gwen Morrison belongs to group O, type Rh1 and contains the factor M. The blood of the child Johanne Lee belongs to group B, type Rh1 Rh2 and contains the factors M and N.

In accordance with the laws governing the inheritance of the blood groups and types, the factor B cannot appear in the blood of a child unless present in the blood of one or both parents; the factor Rh2 cannot appear in the blood of a child unless it or both its component antigens (RhO and Rh") are present in the blood of one or both parents. Moreover, the inheritance of the blood group and blood type factors cited above occur independently of each other.

The possibility that the child Johanne Lee (who belongs to group B, type Rh1, Rh2, type M N) is the daughter of William Henry Morrison (group A, type Rh1, type N) and Alberta Gwen Morrison (group O, type Rh1, type M) is therefore excluded by the findings in respect of either the A B O factors or the Rh factors.

During the course of the investigations on the blood groups and types of these three persons, consideration has also been given: (1) to the further information concerning the genetic composition of the Rh types which may be obtained if one or more of certain rare sera known as anti-Hr sera are available. (2) to the problem of the identification of the rare sub-type N2.

The investigations in relation to A B O, Rh and M N factors show, however, that neither tests with anti-Hr sera, nor identification of the N2 factor, add information relevant to the exclusion of parentage of the child Johanne Lee by William Henry Morrison and Alberta Gwen Morrison, this having been established as a result of the tests in respect of the A B O and Rh factors as cited above.